MW00462426

Available at www amazon . com

# Where Do We belong?

© Mandy Bjordal -Louis

For my lovely niece Lucy Amina in memory of a wonderful mother you did not get to know and for my children Helen Sharon, Jacqueline Brigette and Harald Matthew to know your roots.

# ACKNOWLEDGEMENTS

I wish to thank my late brother-in-law, Prince Henry Kimera, for the original impetus to write this book and much help in organizing the material.

I also thank the many friends and family members who provided the material from their records and recollections.

Other friends- especially Linda Ayoki, the late Nancy Bwuzu and my daughters Helen Sharon, Jacqueline Brigitte and my niece Alexandria Epaminondas -deserve thanks for typing and re-typing the material.

My warm thanks to my son Harald Mathew for the art pieces.

My gratitude to my sister Helene Epaminondas for the scenic book cover photograph.

My sincere thanks to Mr. Stanley Irura for choosing and arranging the photo graphs.

Above all, my gratitude goes out to those whose care and support helped Sylvia and her family through her last days. In particular, the Director and staff of St. Joseph's Hospices, Southgate Catholic Chapel, friends and colleagues too numerous to mention individually.

I wish to thank Marjorie Oludhe Macgoye who has been helpful and supportive far beyond the duty of call.

# DEDICATION

In loving memory of:

Josephine Martin, Valerie Peters, Jane Henriette, Maria Koriac, Sister Mary de Lorette, Morote, Mr. Parson, Georgina Zamamu, Mrs Ella Hart, Sir Edward Mutesa II, Dr. Billington, Priscilla Hughes, Kapere, Sister Aristide Landry, Princess Kajja-Obunaku, Lorna Cook, Prince Badru, Prince Henry Kimera, Prince Walugembe, Mr. Lawrence Brown, Peter Brown, Rosy Pereira, Nancy Bwuzu, Rebbecca Nava, Sister Miriam, Miss Sonia together with all the nuns and friends departed whom I've not mentioned.

**May God Grant Them Peace.**

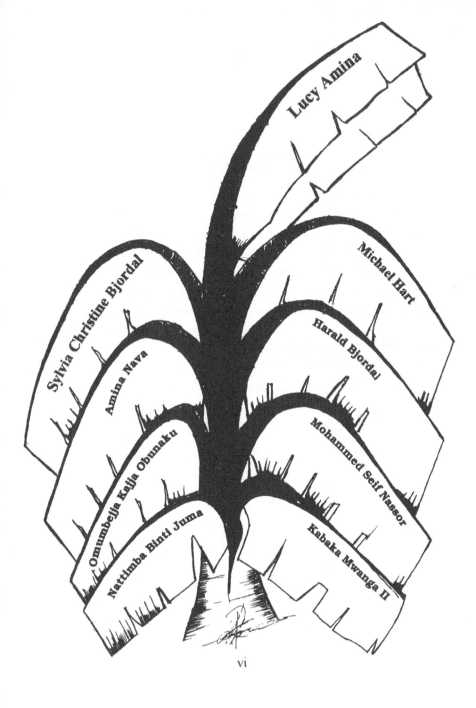

Seif Nassor, Kabaka Mwanga II, Our Dad and Sylvia
*Art by Harald Louis*

# TABLE OF CONTENTS

# TO SYLVIA LET US SING

Who is Sylvia? What is she?
That all our swains commend her?
Holy, fair and wise is she
The Heaven such grace did lend her
That she might admired be.

Is she kind as she is fair?
For beauty lives with kindness
Love doth to her eyes repair
To help him of his blindness
And, being helped, inhabits there.

Then to Sylvia let us sing
That Sylvia is excelling;
She excels each mortal thing
Upon the dull earth dwelling;
To her, let us garlands bring.

William Shakespeare.

*(The Two Gentlemen of Verona, Act IV, Scene II)*

# INTRODUCTION:SYLVIA

Mother was nearly due to have another baby, a fourth one. As there were no hospitals available up – country at Rubugure in Western Uganda where we lived, we had to come to Kampala. It was a tiring, seemingly endless four hundred and fifty miles. The roads were murram, dusty, rough, lonely - nothing but wilderness, as far as we could see, with hundreds of wild animals in the distance. This was no trip for young children and a pregnant woman, but mother felt more secure leaving us in the care of Aunt Nuru, or with Grandma Kajja-Obunaku, when she went into hospital, rather than leaving us with a maid in the bush. Although our father loved us dearly, he could be called down to the mine at any moment, so he did not accompany us.

Arriving in Kampala was always a big ceremony. Water was poured on the roof, letting it drip down on us as we entered the house. This was believed to wash away any mishaps we might have carried with us on our journey (not astonishing after all the dust we had collected). Prayers were said to Allah in thanksgiving for our safe arrival. A goat was slaughtered as an offering whilst all the neighbours rejoiced. What a welcome we got! There was an exceptionally big crowd on our arrival, more out of curiosity than anything else. People who had for a long time been friends of my mother and grandmother still wanted to see what children of a black African and a white European looked like. We were an unusual sight during the colonial era.

Our exhausted mother began having severe pains, probably due to travelling in a taxi for almost a week. It was not what a town-dweller might think of as a taxi, but more dependable than making the slow stages by country bus. Mother was rushed to the Protestant Missionary Hospital at Mengo Hill, one of the cluster of villages which make up Kampala. I screamed and kicked as Mother was being carried into the taxi. Severe labour pains caused the bleeding to increase and Mother was almost unconscious on arrival at the hospital. Dr. Billington, who had delivered me only nineteen months before, saw the emergency involved and worked so deligently that he saved the lives of both mother and baby. Sylvia was born on the 31$^{st}$ March 1947 at 1.30 p.m.

"I saw darkness for days," Mother told us years later. On receiving the new, Dad immediately came down to Kampala to see his new baby daughter.

"What a beautiful baby!" exclaimed Dad, as he lovingly held the little wriggling infant. "Sylvia ..... We shall call you Shakespeare's Sylvia," he said as he smiled proudly.

Sylvia was considered beautiful according to our Arab relatives. She had a sharp nose, a spotless, clear skin as well as hair on the head. I, however, was the exact opposite. At nine and a half pounds I had been Mother's biggest girl - baby and she had quite a time looking after me. She had to make sure all my double chins, including folds, were washed and powdered. Mother was forever feeding me as I screeched for food with my wide mouth.

Sylvia was born, with lovely big eyes of a greyish blue colour. "Oh Amina, you must have stared at your husband for your baby to get these 'transparent' eyes" they would say. Little as I was, I kept wondering about this adorable creature.

"Who is Sylvia and where did she come from?" I wondered..............

"Mum has gone to heaven, hasn't she?" little three and a half year old Lucy asked me thirty-four years later, her beautiful hazel eyes giving me a questioning stare.

" She is coming back when God makes her better, isn't she?" she asked us again with determination, tentatively shaking her little finger. A cloud went over my face as I was buried deep in thought. I decided not to lie to her as many had done.

"Lucy, Mum has gone to heaven - She's not coming back. God and the angels will look after her," I responded, forcing a smile. She shot me another quick glance and kept quiet.

There and then I decided to reconstruct my sister, Sylvia's life for her daughter lucy.

The whole family, helped by friends, teachers and church members contributed, piece by piece, the information out of which this book is built. Inevitably it is the story of our family as well as of Sylvia herself, what we know of ourselves with certainty starts from the marriage of our great-grandmother to the Kabaka of Buganda at the end of the nineteenth century.

# CHAPTER ONE:
# ADVENTURES OF GREAT-
# GRANDMOTHER

In 1898 an attractive brown Muhima girl called Nattimba Binti Juma came with her family to Kampala, which is now the capital city of Uganda. She was named after the Ntimba River in her home area. Nattimba always travelled with her family from Mbarara, a town in Ankole, about a hundred miles southwest of Kampala, for short visits or to buy in the stores. Although the settlements may not have looked much like what we call towns today, life in Uganda was much more centralised and sophisticated than in other inland parts of East Africa at that time. Nattimba's family was well-to-do and respected by their people. They belonged to the, e'fumbe, or civet cat clan, although they followed the Muslim religion introduced by early Arab settlers. They were also well known to the outstanding Protestant leader, Hamu Mukasa.

The Bahima are much lighter in complexion than most Ugandan communities. It was believed that they originated in Abyssinia, now called Ethiopia. They were traditionally herdsmen and had great affection for their animals. They did not slaughter their cattle for food but drank their milk. This cult of the cow is extremely ancient. The Egyptians followed it as far back as pre-dynastic times. The Bahima lived in kraals at the foot of mountains, cultivating the mountain sides. The men smoked a pipe, engungu, and believed in a creator called Ruhanga. Their diet was mostly vegetables together with sweet pota-toes. The Bahima had their own King known as the Omugabe.

(Overseas readers will get used to our Bantu system of naming. A place-name commonly starts with Bu- as in Buganda, the land of the

1

Ganda people. The language, in this case, will be Luganda, a single individual is Muganda and people in the plural Baganda. Buganda and Ankole are only two of the ancient kingdoms making up the modern nation of Uganda.)

One day during the visit, Kabaka Mwanga II, the King of Buganda set his eyes on the young Nattimba. Although just thirteen years old, she seemed quite mature and well developed for her age. The King ordered his guards to persuade Nattimba's family to bring their daughter for an audience at his palace. She was taken aback when approached, but dared not refuse the King's request. On arrival at the palace, she knelt before Mwanga, as was the Buganda custom.

He requested her parents to let their daughter stay at his palace. This was a great honour to her parents and they were given land in Buganda. Thereafter Nattimba Binti Juma became one of the Kabaka's youngest wives. Not long after, Nattimba was expecting her first baby. Every care and respect was given to her by the *Abazana*, ladies in waiting, whilst she lived at the palace Lubiiri.

It is hard to imagine how she related with our great-grandfather. Kabaka Daniel Basammula Mwanga II was then thirty years old. He was the thirty-first King to rule Buganda and had been on the throne for twelve years, succeeding his father, Kabaka Mutesa I. Unlike his tactful, wise father the new ruler was a temperamental, nervous, young man. In his youth he had been surrounded by the trappings and traditions of the absolute power granted to him by virtue of his position as King. He was like a god to his people. He shunned old traditional ways as much as he dreaded Christianity and foreigners.

Before his ascension to the throne, Islam, Catholicism and Protestantism had begun to find their way into Uganda. Kabaka Mwanga II became fearful and very suspicious of these influences. In February 1885 an alleged plot to kill him was unearthed. Mwanga suspected that the white men were behind the plot. It seemed to him that his kingdom was being threatened from all sides.

Mwanga became very confused by these influences, yet sided with whichever religious group seemed likely to prevail at that time. He had not forgotten the ancient Baganda prophecy foretelling the time that strangers would enter from Busoga (the back door) to conquer his kingdom. In October 1885 the prophecy came true. An Anglican Bishop, James Hannington, entered Uganda through Busoga, after travelling from Kilimanjaro with a party of Christians. They were immediately arrested and held by Luba, the Musoga Chief. After five days detention, the Bishop together with his immediate party were dragged from prison and speared to death. Survivors in another camp were led back to the coast by an African clergyman, the Rev. William Jones. During 1885 and 1886 many young Christian boys were martyred as well. At the end of 1886 Mwanga was deposed and fled the country, taking up residence at Kukumbi, at the south end of Lake Victoria.

When Mwanga's brothers, Kiweewa and Kalema, vied for the throne, the country was thrown into complete chaos. In October 1888, Mwanga drove his brother Kalema out of Buganda, only to be himself driven out again a couple of weeks later. Mwanga then heard of the coming of Sir Frederick Jackson of the British Imperial East Africa Company and asked for his aid. Although Jackson was told not to assist Mwanga in protecting his kingdom, he defied his orders and endeavoured to help Mwanga, who, however, recaptured the capital without Jackson's help.

In 1890, a Roman Catholic party attacked a Protestant group at Mengo. Mwanga gave his support to the Roman Catholics, but an armed force led by Captain Lugard (later Lord Lugard) entered Uganda and sided with the Protestants. This force was victorious, On 30th March, 1892 Mwanga placed himself at the disposal of Captain Lugard. Several treaties were drawn up and in 1894 Uganda became a British Protectorate. This was the direct result of the treaty concluded by H. M Consul-General Raymond Portal and Kabaka Mwanga II.

For the next two years Uganda enjoyed peace. Although Mwanga retained his throne, he was not happy with the way things were proceeding. Uganda had run peacefully for hundreds of years with its own well-established governments. Unlike many African chiefs, Mwanga was not going to accept foreign rule and so he put up a resistance. Because of this, history which was written from the point of view of white civilisation, characterised him as an uncivilised mad tyrant. East African children up to the present day were to learn about this horrible African leader.

In 1896 the Kabaka had a son who would later become the next Kabaka, Daudi Chwa II. In 1899 Mwanga II and the Kabarega, the ruler of Bunyoro, were sent by the British government into exile, first to Kismayu then to the Seychelles Islands, in the Indian Ocean about a thousand miles east of Mombasa. Mwanga left his family, wives and children in Uganda without saying goodbye to them, as the British were afraid of what his people's reaction might be if they heard of their king's captivity. James Bunkeddeko, one of Mwanga's right-hand men, and a few others went with their King to share his exile.

Near the end of 1899, our grandmother was born and named Kajja-Obunako, meaning "born in difficulty" or "born in misery." Her mother, Nattimba, was determined, after recuperating from the difficult birth, to show Mwanga his baby daughter, come what may. Being a bold and brave girl, she persuaded her eldest brother to pretend to be her husband and to act as her guide.

"It is not quite right for a young Muslim girl to travel alone with a baby unaccompanied by her husband," she explained.

He agreed to help her. They boarded the *William Mackinnon*, the first steamer to sail on Lake Victoria, up to Port Florence, Kisumu. From Kisumu an English couple gave them help with their travels to the land of the Maasai, Nyarobi (Nairobi). The next day they boarded a train going to Mombasa. People whispered as they watched this fascinating couple. The young girl stood just four feet eight inches tall, while the man, appearing much older, was a towering six feet six inches. They could not have known that this majestic looking Muhima man dressed in a *kanzu* long tunic, holding a Hima pipe to his mouth, was the girl's brother!

They stayed in Mombasa for a couple of days whilst arrangements were made to board a ship to the Seychelles via Zanzibar, about six hundred miles away. However, when they reached Zanzibar, Nattimba decided to settle there. She loved Zanzibar. Anyway she believed there was nothing to go back to in Uganda. Her brother stayed with her until she was well settled, before returning to Uganda to join his family.

The government of Zanzibar assisted Nattimba in every possible way when they heard she was Mwanga's wife. During this period the Arabs were friendly with the Baganda people. They traded in slaves, guns and ivory. Some had even intermarried with them.

With the money she came with, Nattimba was able to buy a small clove plantation, *karafu shamba*, at Mutendeni. So great was her determination that she learned Arabic and *Kiunguja*, a local dialect of Kiswahili, dressed in a *bui-bui*, a local Arab black satin outfit, and lived like any Zanzibari woman. There must have been something infused into her by those few months of royal status as the Kabaka's consort to enable her, at such an early age, to live alone and control her wealth without being molested. But before long her position was eased when the Sultan of Zanzibar recognised who she was.

During his exile the Kabaka had another daughter Mere Mazi: Mere, meaning "mother" in Cre`ole, Mazi, meaning "water" in Luganda, born in the Seychelles. She was later brought to Uganda and was given her due respect as a *Mumbejja*, meaning "Princess." She was the step-sister to our grandmother. She was light brown in colouring with black straight hair.

In 1903 the deposed King died in the Seychelles Islands. His infant son, Kabaka Daudi Chwa II, had three regents, Apollo Kaggwa, the (Anglican) *Katikiiro*, Prime Minister, was the head. Zakaria Kizito, known as *Kisingiri*, second in charge and Stanislus Mugwanya, a Catholic, the third in charge, helped him rule until he was eighteen years old, when he took complete power.

Meanwhile in Zanzibar, Nattimba's little girl grew into a lovely, strong, healthy, intelligent child. The *Omubeija*, Princess, Kajja-Obunaku, was given the Muslim names Mboni Mariamu. By now she was speaking fluent Kiswahili and Arabic, as well as a smattering of Luganda. Sultan Hamoud, King of Zanzibar, had not met Mwanga's daughter until one day, while taking his customary ride on horseback, he caught sight of a young, plump and very pretty little African girl. He stopped his horse and tenderly bade the five year old to come to him. This was in the year 1904. He gently asked her name, where she came from and who her parents were.

"My name is Mariam. My father was Kabaka Mwanga, but he's dead and I live with my mother Nattimba," she answered boldly.

She told him everything about her father, mother and home. Sultan Hamoud was greatly impressed. He immediately asked for an audience with Nattimba. Nineteen year old Nattimba was, now a well cultured young woman, dressed modestly in her black satin *bui-bui*. She adorned her little girl charmingly, and then nervously set out for the palace, accompanied by a female escort. When she arrived, the Sultan spoke to her in Arabic.

"My main reason for inviting you here is that I would love to adopt your little girl. I will take care of her just as my own child. I have a daughter who is about the same age as Mariam. They will be good company for each other."

Nattimba agreed, provided she saw her daughter every day. The Sultan did not object to this arrangement.

Kajja-Obunaku soon went to live at the palace. She enjoyed her new companion, the exotic cuisine, outings, the way of life at the palace and felt very much at home. The Sultan requested St. Monica's, an exclusive Zanzibari school that catered mainly for the children of the royal families and diplomats, to have Mariam.

There Kajja-Obunaku learned many things, including three more languages English, German and French. Life was beautiful. After learning the new languages, peoples and places, Kajja-Obunaku developed a burning desire to travel, maybe visit some of the countries she learnt about. She could hardly wait to grow up.

In 1910 the government of Uganda wrote on behalf of the thirteen year old Kabaka Daudi Chwa to the Seychelles government to have his father's body exhumed and brought back to Uganda for a royal burial at Mutesa's tomb at Kasubi which was known as *Nabulagala*. Here to this day one finds a huge dome-shaped thatched roof with deep brown bark material draped over poles. The floor is covered with soft hay. At the entrance stand a stuffed leopard and a chair. The tombs were in the "inner hut" where the Kings' remains were actually buried. This is where relatives go and pour out their problems to the, *lubaale*, spirits of their dead Kings.

On 2nd August 1910, nearly seven years after Mwanga had died, his remains were exhumed and returned to Uganda where he was given an honourable royal funeral. After the funeral ceremony Bunkeddeko was made the *Katikiiro* or chief in charge of the tombs at Kasubi on his return to Uganda from Seychelles.

Time passed swiftly for it seemed like only yesterday that Kajja-Obunaku was preparing to live in the palace. In the year 1910, when the Kabaka's body was taken to Uganda for burial, Nattimba and Kajja-Obunaku planned to leave Zanzibar for good and return home to Uganda, but Nattimba was taken ill. A year later, in 1911, Sultan Hamoud died. This was a blow for the little twelve-year old girl.

Sultan Hamoud was succeeded by Seyyid Khalifa IV. He accepted Mariam as a member of the family. Kajja-Obunaku was now already twenty-one years old and was a copyright of her father in looks. Undaunted by past events, she made a reality of her desires and dreams to go abroad. She travelled throughout Europe. She enjoyed her travels extensively. Perhaps we were not old enough, when she told us these stories years later, to ask questions in detail. Where did she go? Where did she stay, on her visits to non-Muslim countries? Who acted as chaperone? Would not her mother have accompanied her? Did not her beauty and strength of character attract offers of marriage? Did it not occur to her to visit Uganda, which she had left as a baby?

Grandmother told us that she contemplated buying a cargo ship and entering the Spice trade. After all cloves, though plentiful in Zanzibar were a rare commodity in many parts of Europe. Exciting business ventures lay ahead for the adventurous young Princess and nothing would stop her now. Why couldn't she sell her gold bangles,

6

rings and necklaces if finances were slow in coming? Her fantasies and search for adventure were at their height when suddenly she met Seif Nassor. All her other dreams and desires dwindled away, for the love for this strikingly handsome Arab man seemed to flood her soul. Kajja-Obunaku was twenty-four years old now, a most extraordinary age for a Muslim girl to not have been married. Seif Nassor stood six feet two inches tall. He was slim, with a medium brown complexion, and thick straight, jet-black hair. Whenever he walked into town shopping or visiting a friend, young Arab girls would peer at him behind their half hidden faces, wishing that one day he would be their chosen husband.

Nassor, like-wise, fell in love with this extrovert young Princess and took her to meet his family. They announced their engagement and coming wedding. It was not like a traditional Muslim wedding as it was not arranged but a marriage founded on love. The happy couple moved into a double-storey mansion.

The family owned houses which they let out for monthly rent. They also sold cloves, *karafu*, from their plantation on the neighbouring island of Pemba. Unlike most Arab families, the newly-weds lived alone in their own home. Their son, Shabaan, was born ten months after their marriage, a month before Ramadhan, the fasting month. To have a son was great honour to an Arab family and Shabaan's birth ceremonies were impressive. A month after his birth, *Maulidi*, prayers were held with hymn singing and drums and tambourines played by young boys. Two goats were slaughtered, prayers were said by the men while the women prepared a big dinner. Shabaan was then circumcised as was the Muslim custom, and hundreds of gifts were brought.

Kajja-Obunaku was an esteemed, dignified and austere lady, well known by people of rank. She lived an idyllic life filled with big functions held at the palace by the invitation of the Sultan. She met diplomats from all over the world and joined in their discussions. That was what she was and did not change even after marriage, absolutely refusing to become a submissive wife or stay at home as the other Arab women did. She made sure she had a cook, servants and an elderly woman to take care of the baby.

Two years after Seif's and Kajja-Obunaku's marriage, a pretty daughter was born to them. An elder full of wisdom, and religiously committed, prayed the *Adhani*, a special prayer said after the safe delivery of a child, most earnestly as he touched the new infant, putting

7

a little honey on the baby's tongue to purify it.

Amina, our mother, was born beautiful, with a delicate nose, lovely big eyes, dimples on her cheeks, straight, thick jet-black hair and a rich chocolate brown complexion.

Seif looked at his daughter and said, "Thanks be to God."

After seven days of confinement at the hospital, the mother and child were taken home. Nattimba was honoured and proud to be a grandmother of two grandchildren though she was not yet forty.

A month later an elder, *Mwalimu*, came again to pray the *Azim*, a special prayer said over babies. The baby's unclean birth hair was shaved off. The priest touched and prayed over the baby's head, ears and eyes to protect her against mishaps. She was given the name Amina after the prophet Muhammed's mother. A goat was slaughtered and offered as a *sadaka*, sacrifice. Then there was a huge dinner for all the relatives and friends. Each member brought a gift for the baby - clothes, food, oil, toys, some even had gold bangles and earrings made. The baby was given an *Irizi*, prayer relic, by the priest; this could be worn around the neck or the wrist. *Wanja*, a black eye-liner, was put on the baby's eyes by the *shangazi*, aunt, to keep away the evil eye or ill wishes.

As Kajja-Obunaku sat breast-feeding her baby one day, she told the old woman, in her soft majestic voice, "There is always something wrong when a baby cries, so mind you check the children at all times."

Three months later, she became pregnant again. She weaned her infant and her *ayah*, nurse, took complete care of baby Amina. Kajja-Obunaku was sick for almost two months. She became moody and irritable. Her friends predicted that her symptoms presaged a male child. Nine months passed quickly, eventually Kajja-Obunaku was rushed to the hospital with severe labour pains.

"These signs are sure to bring a son!", the *bui-bui* clad Arab women said to one another.

But, much to their disappointment, Kajja-Obunaku gave birth to a healthy nine-pound baby girl whom they named Nuru, which means "luminous" or "bright light." Celebrations, like those marking the birth of Amina, were held for two days.

Seif had grown up knowing that man was the head in the home and in society, at all times. Men definitely considered themselves superior beings. He saw his mother and sisters doing practically everything for his father and brothers. Therefore he had hoped he would meet a woman who was like-wise-minded. Women are there primarily to satisfy man and it was believed that any man who does not

8

beat his wife from time to time is less than a man. At that time most Muslim women had very little formal education as they were married off when very young. They only had to know the basic things a woman ought to know: to recite the *Quran*, pray, keep house, cook all kinds of delicious meals, sew, and take care of the children and most important, mother-in-law.

However, Seif's love for Kajja-Obunaku seemed to overlook the fact that Kajja-Obunaku was well educated, and mixed with people of both sexes freely, even to the point of joining in political discussions with men! She was rich, a property owner, and very independent.

As time went by Seif became over-possessive of his wife and became the typical man he was supposed to be. When the beatings, threats and orders to stay at home started, life became unbearably difficult for Kajja-Obunaku. This behaviour towards a Princess was unheard of in Uganda where she would be addressed as *sebbo*, meaning "sir"; even men knelt before her when greeting her. The love bond between the two dwindled away.

One day, however, Kajja-Obunaku went to do her daily shopping. She asked Nassor to keep an eye on the children while she was away. We do not know all the circumstances. Perhaps he had dismissed the servants in order to keep her confined at home. When she returned, her two little girls ran to welcome their mother.

"Where is Shabaan?" she asked her daughters casually.

"He is asleep!" they answered simultaneously.

"Asleep at this time of day?" she asked, almost in a whisper.

She put her shopping in the kitchen and went to check on her baby. He lay in his cot motionless! She felt his chest, he wasn't breathing.

"Shabaan, Shaaban, this is Mama, Shabaan," shaking him she screamed hysterically.

"Nassor! What have you done to my son, he is dead!" she cried out.

The neighbours soon came to hold down the grief-stricken woman. Shabaan was dead! Nobody knew how or why but he was dead. Kajja-Obunaku believed that he was murdered. She was furious with her husband and told him that she was going to leave him because of his irresponsibility and negligence. For two months she practically lived at the little grave and mourned for Shabaan. Soon after this she asked for *talak*, divorce, and it was granted.

About this time Kabaka Daudi Chwa heard of his sister who had settled in Zanzibar. He was determined to find her and if possible bring

9

her back to Uganda. He sent Serwano Kulubya, his English language interpreter and advisor Sam Mukasa and Spire his private secretary, to Zanzibar to find Nattimba and Kajja-Obunaku.

"Tell them I send my personal greetings and that I would be delighted if they would consider coming back to Uganda to settle, they are family and Buganda is their home."

Nattimba and Kajja-Obunaku were overjoyed with the good news. After some time, Kabaka Chwa sent Kulubya and Spire back to the Island to bring his long lost family. They were going back to their homeland after nearly twenty-eight years! Kajja-Obunaku sold nearly all her property and left her furnished house all locked up. She couldn't wait to leave Zanzibar!

"My father's spirit would not desert me, I suppose we may come back one day," she said as she was packing.

Nattimba, Kajja-Obunaku and the girls went to the palace and bade farewell to the Sultan. A banquet awaited them. The Sultan offered them all the assistance they might need.

"You will be welcome back, Mariam," he said, his eyes full of sincerity and love.

"Thank you, your Majesty, *Inshallah*, God willing, we'll come back and visit you," they replied.

# CHAPTER TWO:
# RETURN TO UGANDA

The journey on the ship was quite fascinating for the excited little girls. Their grandma, Nattimba, kept a watchful eye on them. Every day they gazed at the limitless blue ocean with many Arab dhows on the horizon. After several days of sailing they reached Mombasa, a typically Arabic Muslim island. Here they spent a couple of days with their Arab relatives before they boarded the train for Nairobi. The climate was cooler than on the Island of Zanzibar.

"Mother, this is a beautiful country, we should get a house here," remarked Kajja-Obunaku.

"We should, but let us see what awaits us in Uganda!" replied Nattimba thoughtfully. From Nairobi, they boarded a train to Kampala. On the way the African men, women with long decorated earlobes, some bare chested, Maasai men practically naked and children brought whatever they could sell to travellers. Life was exceptionally exciting for the girls.

At long last Nattimba, Kajja-Obunaku and her daughters were in their homeland. What a welcome they received on their arrival! The Baganda populace flocked to see new members of Kabaka Chwa's family. They were curious about how Arab/Muganda *Navas*, daughters of princesses, looked. Kabaka Chwa gave them a warm welcome at the *Lubiiri*, palace, until they could move to Nabweru, a town in the Buganda region. The Kabaka also gave his family land at Jinja, Nabweru and Kawala. These areas were all in the care of Aziz Bulwadda one of the members of the Queen Mother's clan, *e`mamba*, lung fish, which was one of the largest and most important in the kingdom. Bulwadda was also one of the leading Muslim chiefs.

What progress Nattimba found in her homeland, Uganda, after twenty-eight years she had spent in far-away Zanzibar. She listened to

11

stories of the great Englishman, Winston Churchill who had visited Uganda in 1907 and 1908. He was so impressed with the country that he had it called "The Pearl of Africa." He promised aid from the British Government and King George to help Uganda.

Nattimba found that a few cars had been introduced into Uganda and they could be hired on certain days of the week for a few shillings. Otherwise, rickshaws and donkeys were still in use. Kajja-Obunaku's brother, Kabaka Chwa, had a grand black car, presented to him by the British Government. Many people owned motor cycles which had first come into the country in 1912. Kajja-Obunaku bought herself a bicycle. Some privileged people played cricket, a white man's game. This was introduced in 1907.

In 1902, Alidina Visram, was given the contract of building Bulange. This was the centre of administration in Buganda.

In 1911, the first national bank in Uganda had been opened. Nattimba and Kajja-Obunaku soon opened their accounts too. The former had to use a thumb print for her signature, whereas her daughter signed her name beautifully in the Marion-Richardson writing style she had learned at St. Monica's School in Zanzibar. Nattimba and Kajja-Obunaku found many whites and Asians in Buganda. The Asians were the builders, contractors and businessmen. The white missionaries ran clinics, hospitals, schools and churches.

They visited Mulago hospital, which had been opened in 1910. Kajja-Obunaku also learned that her brother Daudi Chwa had celebrated a Christian marriage on 19th September, 1914.

Our grandmother vowed never to marry again but follow her mother's footsteps and bring up her children single-handed. She soon learned Luganda and changed her way of life including her way of dressing. She began to wear the *Busuuti* or *Bodingi*, bodice, a long Ugandan costume. She still kept her head covered with a *leso*, a brightly coloured coastal cloth used by Muslim women, and deep inside, she was very much an Arab. She kept to her rich Arab food, all the Arab delicacies and remained a devoted Muslim. A part of her would always be Mariam, brought up in the Sultan's palace rather than at the Lubiiri.

It took Amina and Nuru some time to feel at home with their Baganda relatives, due to the language barrier. The girls spoke Kiswahili and Arabic, two languages which were never used to any great extent in Buganda. Their little Baganda friends would sing *"Abazungu, Abazungu,"* (the whites, the whites) every time they saw Amina and Nuru.

12

In Uganda, Kajja-Obunaku and her two daughters found the people, habits, food and customs, very different from Zanzibar, except that the Baganda women, like the Arab women, took great pride in their looks. They had a glossy skin which was always oiled and kept very clean. Their idea of beauty was to have a plump, rolling body. Little Amina and Nuru would watch their Baganda relatives as they dressed - it was quite a ceremony! The women wore about six or seven *Ebikoyi*, colourful rectangular two and a half yard pieces of cloth, under their main garment. These made up about eighteen yards in all! When they were securely tied and folded neatly over the hips, a gorgeous *Busuuti*, a Baganda outfit, was worn over the top. This dress is usually seven yards of material, cut wide with a square neck, two big buttons on the side and big puffed short sleeves. The *Busuuti* formed a unique pattern wrapped round and round the hips and a thick belt starched at the centre was tied in a neat knot in the front. Thus, the outfit portrayed a graceful woman with unusually large hips and tiny waist. The Muganda woman was trained to hold her chin high. Her shopping was placed on her head on a *nkata*, a small banana mat. The woman would then gracefully sway her lovely big hips. Amina and Nuru would playfully imitate the Baganda way of walking.

The girls had to watch their manners, young as they were. They learned that greeting people was of the utmost importance, especially in the mornings. If they came across anyone older than they were, the girls had to greet them! *"Wasuze otyanno, Nyabo,"* "Good Morning Madam," or *"Wasuze otyanno Ssebo,"* "Good Morning Sir."

Amina and Nuru noted that very intimate friends and relatives would embrace one another when they met. Children would sit on the laps of their elders or mothers when greeting them. So, little Amina and Nuru were always on every relative's lap! Even the Kabaka would sit on his mother's lap when greeting her. Shopkeepers, farmers or even shoemakers would expect a greeting before a request was made of them. The only time the greetings were omitted was when there was a death in the home or when one came to give a death announcement.

In the presence of an adult, a child was not to speak unless spoken to. If she had something to say, she asked permission to speak and ended her sentence with *Nyabo*, Madam, or *Ssebo*, Sir. Discipline of children among the Arabs was, in contrast, not very strict, until the age of twelve or thirteen, when the children were considered mature.

Grandma did not have to kneel before anyone, except the Kabaka, because she was a *Mumbejja*, Princess. Men knelt before her and called her *Ssebo*, Sir. The *Banava*, daughters of a Princess, would kneel before the Kabaka, *Balangira*, Princes, or the *Bambejja*, Princesses, but anyone else was expected to kneel before them. The *Sabaganzi*, maternal uncle of the Kabaka, was allowed to greet the King standing. Respect for the elders, teachers and people in good positions was taught to children at a very early age. A neighbour was expected to correct any child who was rude, or misbehaved. Amina and Nuru quickly learned the authority of grown-ups and where they stood.

When a friend or neighbour fell ill or had any kind of misfortune, neighbours and friends were expected to visit. If anyone gave warning that they were in any sort of danger, neighbours would raise the alarm *"Ulu, lulu, lu"* or beat certain drum rhythms. The victims had the support of the whole neighbourhood. If a neighbour did not give assistance, he would be reported to the village chief who would deal with him severely. This custom has been kept up to the present times.

At funerals, the digging of the grave and provision of, *Lubugo*, bark cloth material, in which the body was wrapped was done by relatives, friends and neighbours. The body was carried, feet first, to the grave . . . After the burial the people danced, sang and ate. They joyfully sent their loved one to the spirit world. If a neighbour did not turn up for the funeral he would be considered an enemy!

As the girls grew older, they had to learn the Kiganda dances, which were alternately quick and slow waist-and-hip gyrations matched to the fast beat of drums, *Doom - doom - doom* in staccato short beats. The dancers swayed and shuffled their feet in perfect rhythm to the drum beat. Amina and Nuru soon learned to dance with verve, grace, and stamina . . . They did not have problems with the movement of the stomach muscles as they had had a little Arabic training in *kiuno*, belly dancing, although this dancing was a little slower and less vigorous and the music was quite different.

Amina and Nuru kept to their Muslim culture, observing Fridays and fasting during the month of Ramadhan, besides praying five times a day. Nattimba and Kajja-Obunaku wore their *bui-bui* and the little girls wore long dresses and covered their heads with a *chuni*, a long head cover. They said their prayers and read from the Koran, all in Arabic.

As the years went by, Amina's straight hair changed into thick curly hair, but was kept long. Her complexion became a much darker shade, more like her mother's, yet her features remained very much like her father's. Her sister had a lovely tan complexion, her hair was more kinky and she looked exactly like her mother. Being Muslims, the girls grew up under their mother's constant watchful eye. Kajja-Obunaku, although very well educated herself, was determined to teach her daughters just the basic things a woman ought to know and to get them married off to a Sheikh or Sharrif, Muslim leaders, as soon as possible. After ten years passed, Amina grew up into such an exquisitely pretty fifteen year old girl that, her mother was afraid to let her out of her sight.

Kajja-Obunaku was now very busy constructing and building houses to let, on the land Sir Daudi Chwa II had given her. Her brother, Daudi, had not been in good health for about two years. His people were confused as no-one had been able to diagnose his illness. One day, he made a special visit to see his mother, Namasole, at Lukuli. Two days after his arrival, he collapsed and died of heart failure in the presence of his mother and relatives. This sad event occurred on the 22nd November, 1939. This was a shock for the whole family. Grandma was dumb-founded. Sir Daudi Chwa's death was soon widely reported. The entire populace of Buganda was in shock.

Sir Daudi Chwa's body was wrapped in white cloth and carried to Mengo where it was placed in the Council room of Twekobe, the "Kabaka's house." Two chiefs, the Kangawo and the Mugerere, guarded the corpse. The sacred fire called *Gombolola*, which burned constantly at the entrance of the palace, was extinguished, not to be ignited again until a new King had been chosen.

On the 24th November, Sir Daudi Chwa II's body was washed and prepared for interment, then placed in a lined coffin. The following day, the remains were taken to Namirembe Cathedral for a service. Sir Daudi Chwa II had been a great believer in the Christian faith. The service was conducted by the Bishop of Uganda. Sir Albert Cook, a great English pioneer, gave an address. He had known the late King since he was a baby.

Great-grandma Nattimba, Grandma Kajja-Obunaku and her daughters, Amina and Nuru, attended the service. It was only ten years previously, when Grandma returned to Uganda, that her brother had been a young, strong man and now he was gone.

"My son went and now my brother," she thought sadly.

His Highness Mutesa II, a young lad of fifteen years, was at boarding school at Budo when he was told of his father's death. He was at once brought home and attended the service at Namirembe. After prayers his father's body was taken to Kasubi and lowered into the grave; it was not filled for three days. People from all over Uganda came and mourned.

15

The 25th November, 1939, the day after Kabaka Daudi Chwa II's burial at Kasubi, was a great day for the whole of Buganda. Sir Edward Mutesa II was the chosen new King and the ascension ceremonies took place. These were conducted in the traditional Buganda manner, with much pomp and symbolic style. The royal carpet, *ekiwu*, was produced. New bark cloth was spread on the ground. On it several layers of different skins were placed; first a cow skin, then a lion skin, then a leopard skin and finally a hyena skin. The *Katikiiro*, Prime Minister, gave Mutesa two new spears and a shield. He was then placed, standing on *Namulondo*, a special stool. Here Mutesa was dressed in a bark cloth called *Luyira*. He now stood before all his people. The smoke of the royal fire, *Gombolola*, soon rose again to proclaim to all that a new king reigned. *Ntamivu*, one of the chief Royal drums, was played and the singing started, people danced and rejoiced. There were the main workers for the King in attendance;

*Omuwanika* - the minister of finance and treasurer

*Omulamuzi* - the minister of justice

There were different chiefs:

*Saza* chiefs in the twenty counties in Buganda followed by the *Gomboloza*, *Muluka* and *Mutongole*.

*Seruti* - the Kings head brewer

*Namusa* - keeper of the Royal latrines and always of the Musu clan          *Nkuluze* - was the King's treasury store.

Everyone greeted the Kabaka kneeling, except the *Sabaganzi*, his maternal uncle. Grandma Kajja-Obunaku was overwhelmed to see her young nephew now become the new King of Buganda.

But Grandma had seen the world and grown up in the palace of another monarch. She must have known that a new World War was beginning to turn things upside down. She could not have forgotten that both she and her mother had made prestigious marriages outside the community they were born into. Although she had not passed on her own formal education to her daughters, did she really believe that in the multi-cultural city of Kampala only Sheikhs and Sharrifs would take a second look at her lovely daughters? If she did, she was underestimating them.

My Father, Harald Bjordal, was born in Bergen in Norway on 4th June 1915, the third child in a family of five. He was a typical Norwegian, blond and blue-eyed, a healthy and extremely intelligent child. Excelling in his school work, he received top marks without any difficulty. Unfortunately while still very young he was struck with rheumatic fever which left him with a heart defect as well as a deformed ankle. Being determined to overcome these problems, he became an outstanding athlete, participating in every school sporting activity. Medals he had won in the swimming competitions and skating championships were displayed in the lounge. As a means of relaxation, Harald took music and art lessons. During the holidays, he worked tirelessly to save enough money to buy an accordion, the instrument that intrigued him the most. Eventually his father helped out, on condition that he was not to play the instrument on Sundays.

The Bjordals were religious conservatives; they spent practically the whole of Sunday in church praying and meditating. The Sunday meals usually consisted of cold meat, salad and sandwiches, as no food was cooked on that day. Silence, no playing and Bible reading was the order of the day. With such strictness, Harald decided at a young age that, when he grew up, he would never go near a church.

Unfortunately Harald's mother died of tuberculosis while he was still at school. Her stay in the sanatorium had been expensive. Life became more difficult. The boys had to take on odd jobs to help out. Delivering newspapers was one of those Harald enjoyed doing most, though it was pretty hard during the long, cold, gloomy winter months.

He finished secondary school at the age of seventeen, and longed to enroll in the University, but this was beyond his father's means. He therefore joined the Navy and worked hard. Travelling gave him the opportunity to visit countries all over Europe and invest the money he earned. Having saved for about three years. Harald left the navy and fulfilled his dream of higher education; he proceeded to University in London where he obtained degrees in Mathematics and Science. He then re-entisted in the Navy, sailing down to South Africa. Whilst in Durban he heard of the plentiful existence of gold, diamonds and phosphate in Kimberley and Johannesburg.

He was quite fascinated when he heard of the money made in the mining industry; it was a lot more than the income earned by a sailor. What dreams he had! "That is it, I shall become a miner!" He made up his mind and there and then resigned from the navy.

On his next trip to South Africa, the ship anchored at Cape Town. Harald decided it was time to investigate the mining industry. From there he travelled to Beaufort West, Richmond, De Aar and finally reached Kimberley. Here he visited the mines. He then thought he had better have a second opinion from another mine. He decided to go further up to Johannesburg. Here he met many important men in the industry who interviewed him, finally he was accepted as an apprentice. He worked tirelessly with great interest, persevering through long hours of hard work until he mastered every step in the mining profession. He was soon made one of the supervisors.

Whenever he was off-duty he relaxed with his accordion. One day he saw an advertisement "Musical Competition . . . Anyone with any musical talent is welcomed!" He seized the opportunity and played a tune, "The Laughing Policeman". It was a hit which won him first prize of a hundred pounds. He also appeared in a South African newspaper.

He then told his bosses of his decision to start his own business in Uganda. I do not know how he came to hear of the mineral possibilities of that distant country, but his instinct was right. Deep inside himself he was not happy with the socio-political situation that existed in South Africa. Two of his colleagues asked if they could join him on his mysterious journey. He was pleased to have company.

They travelled with Harald part of his journey but were not brave enough to continue in the face of the dangers that lay ahead of them and so they turned back to Johannesburg. Photographs of part of the journey with Harald and his guides in a boat on the rough Limpopo River appeared in a South African newspaper. The paper reported that Bjordal was exceptionally brave and wished him all the luck and success he might need.

He hitch-hiked his way to Western Uganda which took months; sometimes he accepted lifts from an occasional missionary car. He walked miles on end, even paddling canoes across rivers. Every now and again he hired new guides, when passing from one country to another. Malaria and other fevers, blisters, colds, coughs, and sunstrokes did not spare him. Fortunately, he had carried all sorts of medicines to fight any tropical diseases. Obviously he spoke Afrikaans fluently; but if he could not be understood he used gestures to get a message across to his guides.

Finally he reached the Belgian Congo, now Zaire. He passed through dense forests, rough rivers, marshes infested with mosquitoes and dusty roads. He was almost attacked by lions, leopards and hyenas but his gun saved him on several occasions. Occasionally he met Congolese who spoke French, a language he understood and spoke a little. After getting over his exhaustion and regaining his health, he finally reached Western Uganda.

Here he met two European men who wanted to be partners with him, but they became dispirited, sold their shares and returned to

England. He employed Ruzindaro who was to be his comrade for years to come. Harald called him over after watching him frantically scratching his head. He cleansed him with every disinfectant possible to remove the lice. Ruzindaro, a strong Christian, begged Harald to stay, convinced that God would help him. And sure enough He did. There was a torrent of rain which swept tin and wolfram, a black ore yielding tungsten, right to their doorstep. At Nyamolilo wolfram is found in the rocks in great quantity, and this became his headquarters.

After the rainstorm Ruzindaro was frenzied:

"Look, Bwana, what God has done!"

Harald was overwhelmed. Being an ambitious man he also prospected the lands of Rubugure. He discovered a little gold in the river there and tin at Itama. Work was progressing. Harald built himself comfortable huts at each mine. So great was his joy that he gave his old car to Ruzindaro as a reward.

He then hitch-hiked 350 miles to Kampala to see what the Buganda Kingdom was like. He continued playing his accordion for entertainment, earning extra money. So it came about that in 1940, some months after the installation of the new Kabaka, Kajja-Obunaku's two teenage girls heard rumours of a certain European young man who was to perform at the Speke Hotel. This was one of Kampala's most famous and well known hotels, catering mainly for the elite, diplomats, Europeans and the royal family. The girls gathered courage and timidly knelt before their mother and told her about the musical show.

"No! No! You are not to go to public places exposing yourself!" she said.

"Please, Please Mum, just this once," begged the girls.

"All right, I'll take you, myself, but remember, you are not to wander off away from me. You are to sit right next to me. Is that clear?"

"Yes, Mum," they answered.

When the show started, a young Scandinavian man began to play his accordion; the girls fell into a trance just listening to the melodious music. At the interval while a band played, the young man approached the three African ladies and asked Amina for a dance. Amina asked her mother's permission and Kajja-Obunaku gave her approval only because she didn't want to cause a scene in public.

Harald and Amina met several times after that. Then one day he asked her for her hand in marriage! Amina was all excited and could not wait to tell her mother.

"How dare you see this foreigner?" demanded Amina's mother.

"I specifically told you never to mix with immigrants; he is a *Mkafiri*, a non-Muslim believer. He will make you his slave. If it is marriage that you want, I'll be honoured to marry you off to a Sheikh or a Sharrif."

She spoke at the top of her voice, shaking her fore-finger. She was very angry! Amina met Harald again and explained the situation.

"Why don't you go and talk to my mother yourself?" She persuaded Harald.

Harald went several times to see Kajja-Obunaku but to no avail. Nattimba, in the meantime, took a great liking to Harald.

"Why don't you let Amina marry the young man, Kajja-Obunaku, and give them your blessing," she pleaded with her daughter.

Finally, Kajja-Obunaku agreed and the young couple were married in the traditional African custom. Harald gave the only hundred shillings he had as a dowry. They went to Rubugure and lived in the dense forest, where they started raising their family. About this time Norway fell under German occupation, so Harald would not have been able to communicate with his family from a British territory.

Meanwhile Great-grandma Nattimba, had fulfilled her dream of buying a house at Pangani, in Nairobi, and becoming a *Mwananchi*, citizen, of Kenya though it was not yet independent. Here she learned the Kikuyu, Luo, and Kikamba languages, in addition to speaking perfect Arabic, Kiswahili, Luganda and of course her mother tongue Hima. Nattimba would leave Kenya now and then, to take short holidays in Uganda.

# CHAPTER THREE:
# A HOME IN THE FOREST

In the flourishing forest of Rubugure, we lived in an unlimited green world. Even the sky looked blue-green as our little heads followed the length of the over-grown trees which seemed to stretch out towards the sun. The tree trunks were always green due to the soft velvet moss, entangled with hundreds of creepers. Beneath our feet, was soft moist grass, everywhere was green except for the clearing near our huts. Flowers, plants, insects, butterflies and birds filled our little world. The air was clear and fresh. We lived in absolute bliss, wrapped in mother nature.

During the day, there was a dim cool light as the tall trees never let the sun penetrate through them. The nights were not only cool but freezing cold! Mother always dressed us in trousers, thick coats, woollen socks which she crocheted and boots. A fire was kept going the whole night to keep us warm. It always seemed grey in the late evenings and early mornings due to the heavy mist. Was this really equatorial Africa?          During Mutesa's reign, between the years 1940 and 1945, Amina gave birth to three daughters. Mboni, her first born was named after Grandma. Helene was the second born, Dad named her after the Greek legend of Helen of Troy and I was named Mandy after Dad's favourite childhood teacher.

Life was admirable . . . untouched, unspoiled with much tranquillity, it was a haven. We went down the emerald stream, felt the cool rippling water, watched the wild ducks swimming. We took the wet clay-like soil, put it into our pockets, boots, hair, face, even had a taste of it. We really messed ourselves up; laughing away as we ran and skipped. Back home mum and our maid would dump all three of us in a big tin tub and scrub us clean. Exhaustion had overtaken father that day and he decided to take an afternoon nap.

21

So, mother took us for a little walk. On coming back, she went into the hut to check on Dad. "Good Lord!" A huge python was on the bed, its head up in a striking position, tongue flicking in and out at Dad.

"Harald," whispered mother "just roll slowly to your left and fall to the ground."

No questions were asked. Dad did as he was told, picked up his gun and shot the snake.

"Amina you saved my life," he said, thanking her.

Dad was always going on safari, journeys, on foot with lots of enthusiastic men to carry his equipment, food and medicine which he really needed in case of danger. His gun was his life guard. He killed wild animals, especially man-eaters, and brought home their skins.

An alsatian German-Shepherd dog was bought to protect us in his absence. Every night we heard the terrible roaring of wild animals, chiefly lions, leopards and hyenas, cackling like witches. Mother, who was rather timid by nature, would huddle us all into our bed, and sit up practically the whole night praying, "Allah, protect us." The dog's terrifying barks usually kept the wild animals from prowling near our huts.

One evening, however, mother forgot to unchain our brave dog. A leopard came and attacked him. The barking and growling were terrifying. Poor Rover, how he fought to survive, but was torn limb from limb. Mother, who saw it all, cried and cursed herself for being negligent.

Every time Dad went prospecting, Mother was never sure she would see him again. But . . . he always did come back.

One day towards evening, mother saw a creature that looked like a brown gorilla walking towards the hut. Dad had vanished for almost two months; anyway she ran screaming, frantically ordering us to get inside the hut. Then she heard a gentle voice saying,

"*Nava, Nava*, it's me."

Even within the family, *Nava* was the correct form of address for the daughter of a Princess.

"Oh, thank God it's you. I thought you were a monster," she said in relief.

Father had come back very tanned. His beard reached down to his bare stomach, his hair was over-grown covering his back. He looked like a pre-historic man! Years later Dad showed us a photo of what he looked like that day.

His journey had been successful. Dad had found gold, but only in an inconsiderable quantity, at Rubugure. He employed Bachiga labourers at Kigezi, who were very happy to earn something for a living. Father was not happy with the way he and his young family were living and was determined to give us the best he could. After searching, days on end and doing months of tedious work, he finally found large quantities of wolfram in Nyamolilo at Kigezi, this was his dream. Father brought his brother Svaren, who lived in Norway, to join him as there was a fortune to be made. His brother came with his family - a wife and two daughters. The two young men were indistinguishable; everyone thought them to be identical twins.

The Bjordals decided to build stone houses. Dad drew the plans, got the stones cut and after some zealous work, they had their comparatively beautiful mansions. Down to Kampala they went to buy all the household furniture.

So great was father's determination that before long he built a water reservoir, a small petrol station and a power station for electricity using a generator. Nature had provided a waterfall. They lived in total comfort, out there in the bush. Subsequently, he had a Chevrolet, a gramophone, a comfortable home with a store full of all kinds of food. In those days we could buy ten eggs for a shilling, a whole sheep for just fifteen shillings.

When we first moved into this lovely house, mum was always busy with baby Sylvia, and I felt insecure. I therefore clung to father. He always welcomed me in his arms and covered me with kisses. Dad decided to employ an ayah, a house servant, a cook and a gardener. Hopefully our parents would have time to give us all the love and attention we needed. I remember mum being very patient, loving and always smiling. When Dad came home from hard work, he was not too tired to occasionally give us baths, teaching us to wade or swim in the bath. He dressed us, combed our hair, then read us fairy tales, while he gently rubbed our foreheads until we fell asleep. One tale I particularly loved was a Norwegian folkstory, The Three Billy Goats Gruff.

Mother normally had us around her when she tended the baby, therefore, as time went by, we came to know and accept Sylvia as our new member of the family. The baby would stretch out her arms toward me, bubbling, gurgling, cooing, every time she saw me. I began to change my attitude towards her. One evening however, when the ayah had dressed us in our warm clothes, as Kisoro got very cold in the evenings due to the mountains and high altitude, ready for our evening walk, I was my usual grumpy self, seeking for attention just because the ayah was holding Sylvia and laughing with Helene.

We went walking in the valley surrounded by high green hills. They seemed gigantic; they touched the sky! We walked along a narrow path which meandered in and out of the hills, rows of huts cascading down the side of the mountains. The whole atmosphere was very quiet and lonely. I listened to the birds softly twittering in the nearby trees. As usual there were lots of butterflies and I was chasing a few. Then I heard the crickets chirping, *crick, crick,* the croaking of frogs, *croak, croak,* had just begun, the gentle stream was rippling away. This captured my curiosity. Instantaneously, I decided to put my foot, shoes and all into the cool clear water. Water . . . the great temptation to children.

Unfortunately, the mud at the bank of the rivulet was clayey and slippery. Into it I slipped, screaming for all I was worth I gasped as the water was icy cold against my warm skin. The ayah put baby Sylvia down screaming, shouting just as any panicky mother would, she rushed to my rescue. I was smacked, scolded sternly, she warned that the Bwana would tell her off, probably even sack her for letting me wet my clothes. I had been lucky enough not to be swallowed up by quicksand!

Much to my surprise when we went home all was well. After a change of clothes, as I was fussy about my appearance, I went into father's loving arms and soon all was forgotten. All the unpleasant experience completely vanished from my memory.

After living in the forest this long, mother, who had grown up in a big family commune, began to feel terribly lonely and home-sick. She had practically no-one with mutual interests to talk to when Dad was at work.

Although she had us around her, mother felt she needed the comfort of her extended family. Mum often wondered why Dad showed no concern for his people or his country. He seemed content living in the wild. Mother would often leave Dad, telling him she would be away for a week or so, but would stay away during the month of Ramadhan, sometimes two months. This went on for a couple of years until Dad could take it no more. Dad wanted to be in the bosom of his family, eat, talk, laugh, exchange views. Instead he came home day after day, month after month to complete loneliness. What was the point of having a family?

Father was fed up. So great were the religious conflicts, cultural and social differences, that Dad thought it better that mother should return to her own environment. A separation was arranged. We left Dad thereafter and went to live in Buganda. This dramatic change brought me and Sylvia even closer. I was absolutely disrupted by the separation. I wanted to stay with father. I loved the wildlife, the little rodents, animals, plants, fruits, flowers, the peace and quiet in the bush.

Dad knew how I felt and therefore he sent his English secretary and his brother Svaren to collect me. Mum agreed and I left with my uncle. I had hidden in the car anyway. Dad was very glad to have me back. I was a friend to him and he to me. We went down to the mine to work, up the hills and down the valley, swimming on his back in the streams. We often went hunting, chiefly for wild ducks or rabbits. We ate, talked and played together. I was by now nearly four years old.

As time went by, I became quite independent in this boundless world. The Bachiga herdsmen in the valley below were my best friends. I sat with them, watched them smoke their pipes near a burning fire. They smelt of smoke and wore very little clothing, just a blanket thrown around them and they always held a strong sturdy stick. The herdsmen began teaching me their mother tongue Luchiga. In no time at all I was speaking the local language. Every time I would speak in Luchiga the men would laugh in short staccato bursts. I found it very amusing and I imitated them, "Hah, hah . . . hah."

I helped them mind their sheep and their long-horned cattle with birds perched on their back picking bunches of blue ticks like ripe grapes. I felt sorry for the cattle because they carried such sad faces. How I enjoyed the sticky cooked millet bread the folks offered me.

When I got bored with the herdsmen, I would go to the miners, lifting little stones alongside the big, tall miners, not that the Bachigas are tall people, on the contrary they are small. Dad was very proud of me.

"Look at your little muscles, Mandy, if you were a boy, you'd have been very tough like your Dad!" he would proudly say.

My cousin Svanhilde and I became very close friends. She now had a baby sister- but I wasn't terribly interested in babies. Meanwhile mother was being advised by the women-folk:

"My child Amina, how could you leave your baby with a man? Who ever heard of a man taking care of a child? What if he forgets about her and some wild animal kills her . . . God forbid!" they speculated.

This last remark made Mummy leave the next day to get me. I cried, kicked and screamed but nothing I did could make Mum change her mind. Dad was sad, he too cried when I left. The arguments, trauma and sudden departure made me have a total memory blackout. I do not remember a thing about my journey, what was said at the time, or being re-united with my sisters. Absolutely nothing.

# CHAPTER FOUR:
# LIFE IN KAMPALA

We lived at Nabweru, a small town in the Buganda region, until arrangements were made for us to move to Namirembe. Our family rented a house from a Muganda lady who had quite a large undeveloped piece of land in Mengo. Grandma owned quite a number of properties and estates at Mengo which had been given to her by the Kabaka Chwa and it was inevitable that we would move there while our house was being built. We had a comparatively large area for playing. In a short time we became the centre of attraction. We were nick-named *Ba-Nowe*, the Norwegians. As we only spoke Luchiga, the native language spoken in Kigezi, Kiswahili from our relatives, and a smattering of English from our Dad, we had no friends because we didn't know Luganda and the others did not speak any of the languages we spoke.

Although Dad and Mum separated, that was not the end of everything. Dad still visited us and took care of us in every necessary way. Dad and Mum always hugged each other when they met, and we never saw them ever raise their voices at each other. Maybe this was because they were both very gentle, happy and sensible people. Every time Dad came home, I felt this closeness which I hoped would last but he was never able to stay.

We had warmth, love, endless hugs and cuddles from our short, fat roly-poly Grandma. She always had us on her lap with our heads resting on her big warm bosom. Nana often told us stories and sang a few lullabies as I sucked my thumb for comfort. She would tell us the story of the sleeping princess, who lived in Zanzibar many years ago and the *Mfalme*, king, who ruled the Island. One day the princess had fallen into a deep sleep because of the wicked *Gini*, fairy.

Years later, a prince came on a swift-winged white horse. He flew to the palace, found the sleeping princess adorned with jewels and rings. She had a veil over her face. He knelt and kissed her head and she woke up. The whole of Zanzibar awoke and rejoiced. As Grandma told us stories, she would be busy combing our hair or massaging my flat nose, which had refused to grow "high."

"My dear, you do have our Baganda nose!" she observed thoughtfully.

"How I love you Nana, you are the most important person in my life," I smiled.

Grandma taught us folk songs of historical importance which were to be sung before our king or chiefs. We had a harp and a bow lyre, *enanga*, before the age of gramophones or radios. One of the songs that we learnt was about the Battle of Ssese.

Grandma told us how, many many years ago, Buganda had several gods. There lived goddesses called Natwoga and Nakimu. The latter was the wife of Mukasa who was a god known as Lubale. Therefore, our Lake Victoria was called Nalubale.

"The British thought we were dumb and called it after their Queen," complained Grandma.

We learnt about the good gods who brought rain, crops, health and wealth. Grandma taught us about the different clans; lion *Mpologoma*, leopard, Ngo, birds *Nakinsige* and fish *Nkejje*, insect *Kinnyomo*, elephant *Njovu*, *Ngaali*, crested crane clan and many more. We belonged to the *Mamba* lung-fish clan. We learnt to respect our elders; they were our advisers, counsellors, fortune tellers and doctors; not specifically medicinal doctors. These intelligent wise old doctors knew all the names of medicinal plants and what diseases they cured. *Mururuza* cured malaria. Eucalyptus leaves, when boiled if you inhaled steam from them cured colds and cough.

We also learnt lyrics about witchcraft and witch doctors, about marriage ceremonies, about Kabakas, and their lineage. Kintu was our first king, and Suna II the twenty-ninth king. We have had thirty six kings. Our uncle Henry Kimera was named after the third king of Buganda. Another uncle Mawanda was after the twenty- second king. Grandma's brother, Daudi Chwa II, was named after the second king Chwa I, Mutesa II was named after an ever great great-grandfather Mutesa I.

There was a prince Jjuko named after Kabaka Jjuko the tenth king. Whether or not we could store all these names in our young minds at least we associated a known name with our royal relatives who had a similar name when we met. Some songs told us about our great-grandfather Mwanga, how the British took him away from our country! *"Ba twaala Mwanga, tuula owulile ebigambo."* And so we came to know our African history, through songs and music.

It was at this period that Nana gave us our African clan names. I was called Namilimo, a hard worker. Sylvia was named Nantaayi, which meant a person who was swift. Helene was Ndagire, a hole pierced in a canoe.

Sadly Grandma left home for Kenya to visit her mother Nattimba and life became a bore without her. She had acted as a substitute, for the mother I would have loved to have. Why my grandmothers were interested in Kenya was beyond me but Nattimba definitely loved the country. As we were literally housebound, we often sneaked out and found something exciting to do.

Sylvia and I decided to explore the infinite variety of plants in Grandma's *shamba*, garden. A very interesting green short tree, which was covered with lovely small objects of a shades of green, yellow and red, caught our attention. We decided to pluck them, squeeze them then rub them onto our skin. After this experiment our young tender skin began to burn. We screamed our hearts out, rubbing our eyes as we cried. This was a worse torture as our eyes began to burn too. Mother and Aunt Nuru came running to see what in heaven's name had happened to us.

"Devil chillies oh no!" they exclaimed.

Each sister took one baby in her arms and hurriedly gave us a cold bath, grumbling and scolding us as they scrubbed us. When the burning subsided I sucked my thumb and fell asleep.

It was not long after this painful incident with peppers that our spirit of adventure took us again. We again began exploring Grandma's kitchen garden when we came across a bean plant with succulent looking pods. These we proceeded to open, thus exhibiting the young beans of various lovely colours. I thought it would be a very interesting experience if Sylvia and I could see which one of us could push the bean the furthest into our nostrils.

I was a little cunning, I pushed mine just a little up my nose. I then suggested we blow our noses and see if the bean would pop out. Mine did . . . Plop! and we were delighted.

"Now it's your turn Sylvia," I said gleefully.

She desperately blew her nose but nothing happened. She had apparently pushed the bean much further up her nose, probably into her sinus, where it got lodged inside.

Our six year old sister Helene happened to be sneaking a peek at us. She quickly realised what was amiss.

"Sylvia, blow your nose, very hard!" she ordered.

Sylvia blew forcefully but nothing happened. Helene marched us promptly to Mother, who soon decided that Sylvia's case needed medical attention. Sylvia and I were in tears by now. A taxi was called and she was rushed to Namirembe Hospital. After a minor operation, the bean was removed. It seemed like an eternity before Mother came home, carrying Sylvia, who was fast asleep due to the sedation given. She was wrapped in a white soft shawl and I noticed a slight bit of blood near her nose. I felt terribly guilty and unwanted by the family. Not long after this episode Sylvia and I got the mumps. At first our little faces became quite swollen.

"You two look funny," Helene teased us.

We didn't realise we were ill until we looked at ourselves in a broken mirror, which we found in the house. I don't recall ever looking in a mirror prior to this moment.

"Yes," we thought, "something is wrong with us!", conscious of our appearance.

We walked hand in hand towards a lovely green tree, in agreement that "if we cry as loud as we can we may get our faces back into shape." We screamed ourselves hoarse.

Hearing our screams, mother immediately came to see what was wrong. We were quite red and hot as our temperatures must have risen and the screaming worsened the pain around our ears. Mother carried us both, one in each arm, sponged us, and gave us each an aspirin before putting us to bed. We fell asleep snivelling ... the world seemed muffled and far away ...

Grandma Kajja-Obunaku and Great-grandma Nattimba were still living in Kenya. Nattimba had become so much at home there that she learnt Kikuyu, changed her Baganda outfits for *leso* and ate *githeri* and potatoes instead of her former diet of mainly *matoke* and meat. She lived like a simple, unmarried Kenyan woman, no longer like a dignitary in Buganda. King Edward VIII of England gave up his throne for the love of Wallis Simpson. Great-grandma gave up her position in the royal family for the love of Kenya. Her house in Pangani was traded, by the City Council for a new house in Shauri Moyo which she rented out and so was able to support herself. Grandma had a house in Muthaiga an area reserved for Europeans. At this time, lions were a great menace to the people. When Grandma lived in Zanzibar she hardly saw any wild animals, and therefore was unaware of the danger. Once she told us, her servant came running, screeching and screaming,

"Memsaab, a lion, a lion!"

"A lion?" asked Grandma calmly. "Let us have a look at him, Oh, isn't it a beautiful animal! It looks like a big dog," she said admiringly as she looked through the window.

Her servant did his utmost in trying to convince her that the lion was dangerous. Finally she believed all the stories about the man-eating lions of Tsavo during the building of the railway line in East Africa. Hundreds of workers were brought from India and many had been killed by lions. Grandma was advised to carry a weapon to be on the safe side. The lion pranced around for a while and went on his way.

"I kept my sword tucked in my waist belt just in case," she said.

Unlike most African and Arab women, Grandma was quite a tomboy! Entertaining her guests one day, she heard a terrifying roar of a lion. The visiting couple ran indoors.

"Mr. Smith, poor chap, had only one leg. You should have seen how he trembled. I had to carry him indoors," she chuckled. "His wife was in tears begging him to go back to civilisation."

Being tough and brave Grandma instantly got her gun and fired several shots, before killing the lion.

"All the locals fought over the skin. I let them have it although I wanted it," she told us smiling.

We listened with fascination, never doubting a word. She owned a Morris car which she used to drive to Majengo in Nairobi, to buy fruit and vegetables.

"I have a little market shop too," she proudly told us. "But I've employed someone to take care of it." We always enjoyed listening to Gran's fantastic stories. What a great Nana I had.

Grandma would visit us for a short while and off she'd go to Nairobi. It always broke my heart, as she was the one person whose love for me passed through her fingers into my heart when she touched me.

I carried a sour face for weeks on end. Without one word, perhaps because of that, Mother packed me off to Nairobi on the train alone, only asking a man who seemed a complete stranger to me to escort me to my Grandma in Shauri Moyo. Perhaps it was because I could not communicate with her that I remember nothing of the journey or arrival until I got an abscess on my little finger. Grandma nursed me tirelessly. After I had missed my Mother and sisters for what seemed like forever, I was taken back home. Years later I was shown the photograph of an aged man who was supposed to be the one who took me to Grandma. Apparently he was a member of the family.

Aunt Nuru had seemed very attached to us by now, probably because she had no children of her own. Mum, who was about to have a baby decided to get a place of her own at Nakulabye. Her sister begged her to leave one of us with her. Without a second thought I was the one chosen.

"Helene is much too naughty and Sylvia is still a baby. I guess you can keep Mandy," Mum said thoughtfully.

To my puzzled mind, this seemed a very cruel decision. I lived a very secluded life with my strict Aunt. No music, toys or friends to play with. I was literally locked up. One day, Aunt Nuru told me that she was going to the market at Bakuli.

"Can I come with you Nava, please?" I asked.

"The weather is too hot in the afternoons," replied my Aunt.

She decided to leave me locked in the house utterly alone, which was very frightening for a little four and a half year old girl. She had fried some delicious curried liver before she left.

"Mandy, I have left twenty pieces of liver in a dish on the table, now don't touch it!" she said softly as she lifted her shopping basket.

"She's testing me," I figured.

I sat there like an angel for a couple of minutes, occasionally casting an eye on the luscious liver. The delicious smell kept hitting my nose, and making my mouth water. Although I was pretty young, I had the capability of solving my problems. I found a knife in the drawer, cut off a teeny bit from each piece of liver and ate to my heart's content.

The toilet was a pit-latrine, which was detached from the house and I could not get out. Feeling the need to relieve myself, I peed under the bed as my Aunt would not have reacted pleasantly to me wetting myself. Before long, Aunt Nuru came back, counted the pieces of liver and gave me a hug for being such a good girl. Mother came for her weekly visit, and I caused havoc, I screamed and held tightly on to her leg as though I never wanted to part from her again. There was no way she was to leave me again . . I was determined.

"I am sorry Nuru, I'll have to take my baby with me," said Mum.

So off I went home with my Mum. How I loved her. Not long after our move to Nakulabye, Mum gave birth to a lovely eight-and-a-half pound baby daughter, at Rubaga, a Catholic Mission Hospital. Dad named her Berit, after his sister's daughter. I was actually pleased to see the baby. About this time we had a cousin, Emily Bjordal.

31

Berit was soon our new playmate. I spent most of my time with her, while Sylvia played outside looking for some new adventure. Sylvia was now three years old and was quite a spectacle. Very energetic, witty and daring, she was a jack of all trades; Sylvia was also very mature and independent for her age.

One day, Sylvia suggested that it would be a good idea if we strayed a trifle from home and explored the sweet potato plantation. She always advised me to carry a stick for protection. As we were busy on our adventure in the garden, we spied three men stealing mother's clothes off the line and they were actually putting them into a sack! We had quite forgotten Luchiga and had now learnt the Luganda language.

"*Ababbi, Ababbi,*" (thieves, thieves) we screamed.

Mother and some women in the neighbourhood came running towards us. We frantically explained that the thieves were hiding in a nearby out-door toilet. On seeing the group of women approaching, the thieves took off like deer! In spite of our good deed, we were still scolded for walking out of bounds.

"You were lucky you were not kidnapped," said Mother.

We stayed in and would often act as being, Baganda women. We'd kneel and greet each other,

"*Wasuze otyanno Nyabo,*" "Good morning Madam."

"*Burungi Nyabo,*" "I'm fine Madam."

One day, however, we had a lady visitor. She was fussing all over us and we asked her name.

"*Mukyala Namatovu,*" she smiled back as she spoke.

She thought we were most adorable. *Mukyala* ... Mrs, was a new word added to our Luganda vocabulary. We decided to have fun with it. We used it before every name we knew until we ran out of people's names and we thought we'd use animals.

"Mukyala Mbwa" ... "Mrs dog," I said innocently.

The lady's mouth dropped and she immediately ran to mother to complain about what rude little children she had. Mother did not say anything until the following day.

It was a glorious morning in May. The sky was a deep cloudless blue, all the flowers in full bloom, all types of birds twittering upon the green lawns, in nearby trees, colourful butterflies fluttering in and out of sweet scented flowers. The milkman had just come with his tin cans of rich, fresh milk. As mother spoke to the man, she took small steps towards me. I became rather suspicious, and stepped away. I then decided to stop and see what she was up to. To my dismay, she stumbled into me and, as a result, she smacked me really hard. At that very moment in walked Grandma, unexpectedly.

"Stop that at once, Amina," she commended, as she took me in her arms. "You mothers of today have no idea about the up-bringing of children!"

Mother tried to explain how rude I had been to her neighbour and why she had to correct me. Grandma immediately lifted me up and pressed me on her bosom. I was shocked and hysterical, crying my heart out, the more so because Nana was complaining and fussing over me.

"Whoever heard of a baby being rude to a grown woman? Does she consider herself a woman? She probably never had any children of her own," Nana insisted, pressing me even closer.

This incident caused me to develop a sense of insecurity and fear mother for many years to come. After spending the day with us, Nana put me on her fleshy back. I felt a layer of warm air spreading over me, and was carried to Mengo. Here I stayed with Nana and Aunt Nuru for almost a month. I was later re-united with Mother when Grandma decided to visit her mother in Kenya. A couple of months later we moved to Aunt Nuru's house in Mengo.

There was much excitement as we helped mother pack. We watched the lorry take the household goods, trip after trip. Mboni lived with us, although I hardly knew her for the first five years of my life as she lived with Aunt Nuru, Grandma or Great-grandma in Nairobi. She now spent most of her childhood indoors, helping mother with household chores. She cooked, washed piles of clothes, ironed and took care of us, when she was barely a child, just ten years old. Helene, on the other hand, who was a tomboy, was never anywhere to be seen. She was out with her lively friends the whole day.

Sylvia at three years old, was quite independent. She spent a great deal of her time playing imaginative games. When occupied, she did not want any disturbance from any of us, not even me. I respected her privacy, but not so Helene. Sylvia had a little cot which meant the world to her. Helene who was very mischievous, could not resist teasing Sylvia, so she climbed into the cot and began to pester her.

"Helene please get out of my cot," Sylvia cautioned softly and very calmly.

There was just a giggle from Helene. Sylvia walked away and came back after a short while with her hands behind her back, her eyes fixed on Helene. In a split second, Helene jumped up, screaming her head off! Sylvia had heated up a knife and very quickly placed it on

Helene's leg. Sylvia felt great satisfaction, having got her cot back. On the other hand, Helene got a permanent scar where she had been burnt as a constant reminder of Sylvia's wrath.

Berit was now walking and could say a few words with a slight stammer. Sylvia had a new companion and once again I felt as though I had lost a friend. My little sisters were playing guest and host. What a bore! Feeling rather sorry for myself, I walked off. I kept myself occupied by watching safari ants industriously carrying out their daily business.

Suddenly, I saw a single bee lying uncomfortably on its back trying desperately to turn over. I felt sorry for the poor insect as I watched its efforts. I wanted to help it but remembered Mum's warning about how harmful bees were. Therefore I decided to put an end to its brief life with my foot. I loved the feel of the earth beneath my bare feet in spite of the warnings of sores, jiggers and cuts. I crushed the bee very gently underfoot. As I threatened its existence it proceeded to sting me. I screamed, yelled and rolled in the short green grass. Mother with the help of some women managed to pin me down and get the sting out.

Sylvia and Berit were holding each other crying, as was customary in our family. When one of us cried the rest joined in. In no time at all my foot was swollen and I was rushed to hospital to get an antihistamine injection.

While I was at the out-patient clinic getting treated, little Sylvia and Berit continued playing their games. There was a bush, which had exquisite purple flowers and black seeds, the size of coffee beans. It was customary in Uganda to offer your guests roasted coffee beans soon after they had been seated. Sylvia found quite a number of what she thought were coffee beans and placed them on a piece of cardboard, a make-believe plate. She was the "host" in the house and Berit was the "guest". The girls were conversing in perfect Luganda.

"*Wasuze otyano Nyabo*," - "Good Morning Madam," they greeted each other.

Sylvia then brought in the "coffee beans" and offered them to her "guest". Two year old Berit took a bean and ate it, or possibly just swallowed it. On our arrival from the hospital Berit staggered towards Mother and collapsed. Mother picked up the unconscious baby, and began screaming hysterically.

Mr. Jackson, an English gentleman and a neighbour, who happened to be at his house as it was about lunch hour, came running to see what the commotion was all about. After seeing the unconscious baby, he immediately offered to take the child and Mother to Namirembe Hospital, as he realised the urgency of the situation.

On arrival, our panic-stricken Mother explained to the doctor what had happened to her baby. He at once asked Mr. Jackson to kindly rush back home and bring a piece of the plant.

"This is critical," said the doctor.

After looking through all his medical books, it was found that the plant was highly poisonous. Berit was given a stomach washout and was kept under observation for a few days.

In the mean time, Sylvia feeling very guilty, hid herself the whole afternoon. I was in bed with a terribly painful foot, and feeling very lonely without Sylvia. In spite of being instructed to stay in bed, I decided to look for her. I walked limping into the backyard directly opposite Mr. Jackson's house, when I bumped into him with his military moustache! He got hold of me and smacked me.

"Sylvia, you are a very naughty girl. You nearly killed your baby sister!" He said.

*"Si mimi"*- not me, I whimpered timidly in Kiswahili.

We automatically knew that foreigners understood Kiswahili, Luganda was reserved for Baganda relatives. I failed to understand why people always confused Sylvia and me. Do we look identical? I wondered.

In the evenings, we normally sat with the women-folk and had dinner together. When Mother was busy we cuddled up next to Grandma, and listened to fantastic tales about what brave people the Arabs were. She had all sorts of pictures showing men actually cutting each other in half with shining swords. She mesmerised us. One evening, however, when Mother was telling us stories, we noticed that her abdomen was abnormally big.

"Well... I am going to have a baby, come feel it... If you are good, you may feel the baby move," she told us.

Gently, we placed our hands over the big tummy and felt the baby's movements, we were thrilled. My mind unfortunately, seemed to work faster than my sisters'.

"How was the baby put in your tummy?" I asked innocently.

"Now Mandy, you should not ask such rude questions," said my Mother indignantly.

Oh, there I go again, thought my disappointed self, not knowing what I had done wrong, but I did not give up.

"Mum ... how does the baby come out of your tummy?" I asked again, sisters all looking at me with puzzled eyes.

After a short silence . . .

"Well the baby comes out through the mouth," lied Mother.

She seemed pleased with the answer she gave me. I thought grown-ups were ridiculous liars but decided not to give my views.

Our brother was born during the month of Ramadhan and was called after it, but Helene named him Richard. He was soon our live doll. Every time he'd cry we would push a bottle, which was kept in warm disinfected water, into his mouth.

Whenever Mother cooked, Sylvia and I were at her side. I felt sorry for Mum doing all the cooking. She had a big saucepan, heating up oil. The masala fish in the bowl was ready to be fried. I suggested to Sylvia that we could help Mum get on with the cooking. Mum was seated on the low wooden stool, near the sizzling oil, talking to some women, when splash! I threw the fish into the pan. The hot oil poured on her left leg and I saw pink flesh. She screamed and called on Allah to have mercy on her. In seconds I dashed under the bed. I must have been there a whole evening wishing the earth would swallow me. Mum's guest insisted I should be punished by going without food as it was greed that caused this accident. Mum forgave me as she realised that it was an innocent mistake.

After a long absence, Dad came to see us with his brother Svaren, who had decided to return to Norway with his family, his wife and daughters, including my friend Svanhilde, who had been a very good companion at the mine, to bid us farewell.

I was quite untidy that particular day, and wouldn't go to Father unless I had a change of clothes. Mother had just finished making me a white long-sleeved blouse and a skirt but she hadn't done the buttons. I cried and kicked, insisting that those were the only clothes I wanted to wear. Dad was seated holding little Sylvia and the other girls were around him. Grandmother quickly sewed on fasteners but in her haste stitched them the wrong way around and they wouldn't snap.

In the end I was given something else to wear. Dad said I was still his pretty little girl. That was all that mattered. He knew that I fussed about my appearance when he was around. I suppose he was the only person who said I was pretty. I always screamed and cried when he left. He told us later that it really hurt him every time he left us and yet he could not stop himself from seeing us and providing for our needs.

Soon after this visit, Mboni, Helene, and I were accepted at the Gwodino School, a Goan school. We were the only non-Goan, non-Catholic children accepted, supposedly because Dad was a rich man.

Previously I had fussed to go to a nearby nursery but was stoned on arrival by a little African boy. I vowed never to go to that school again.

Father finally decided to build us a comfortable home at Namirembe. Mr. Kamya, who I noted had only one eye, was employed as the sole contractor. As Kabale was three hundred and fifty miles away from Mengo, everything was left to Mr. Kamya. While construction was going on, Helene became ill. The last time I remember her healthy was when she dressed magnificently for the end of term party at school. Sylvia and I watched as Mum dressed our pretty sister and loosened her lovely, long, silken black hair. I was amazed to see it so long! As it was always braided I didn't realise the thickness and length of it. Sylvia's hair was just as long but a light brown shade and mine was ash blonde then, and stringy, so subsequently, it was kept short. I felt quite jealous of my beautiful sister . . . going to a party.

In the evening Helene came back from her party very feverish and ill. As usual, Mum's female friends came at once and gave her advice.

"Someone must have put an evil eye on the child," they speculated, apparently because Mother had dressed Helene beautifully and had loosened her hair.

However the following day her condition worsened. Finally, after trying all the local medicines possible, prayers and sacrifices given to Allah, she was taken to Mulago Hospital and she was diagnosed as having typhoid.

During this period we had a shortage of water and a man called Kapere seized the opportunity and sold us tins of water which he transported in a wheelbarrow. I studied this pale brown handsome man with straight jet-black hair, sharp features and a neat moustache, arriving at our house bare-footed, dripping with sweat. We paid him twenty cents per tin of water. That was how he earned his living. To save water, we normally took our bundle of dirty clothes to a nearby stream to wash. Mboni was with us keeping a very sharp eye on us. We never had a maid to help and of course we gave Mboni no help whatsoever but played as normal children would.

Our curiosity got the better of us and we decided to sneak away and explore the bush while Mboni was busy with the clothes. There were two mango trees at a distance; we thought we might as well get some fruits. I was ahead of Sylvia as we ran. The bush got thicker and thicker as we drew nearer the trees. How excited we were, laughing away, when suddenly my foot landed on a huge coiled-up snake! It spat at me. I shouted *"Nyoka!"* Sylvia and I took off like lightning. We never looked back but ran straight into Mboni's open arms. She quickly washed and scrubbed me where the snake had spat on me. Immediately she packed all the washing and we scurried home. On arrival she told Mother that she would not take Sylvia and me again. All these responsibilities and the poor girl was barely eleven years old!

Helene was still in hospital while Kapere continued, unknowingly, selling contaminated water. I was quite aware that Helene's life was in danger. Grandma never trusted anyone with us, not even the hospital personnel. A nurse came and informed her that Helene needed an operation. She became very suspicious.

As soon as the nurses left, Grandma carried out semi-conscious Helene to a bus-stop at Mulago. She boarded the bus going to town, and yet another to Mengo. Grandma had Helene, a living skeleton on her back. Sylvia and I were outside playing when they arrived. Mother was just about to leave for the hospital and relieve Grandma who had been there the whole night. Seeing her mother and her lifeless child enter the house, mother burst into tears.

"Night is dead," she moaned.

Night was Helene's pet name. Aunt Nuru came running out to see what was happening. Automatically, Sylvia and I started crying, joined later by Berit. Mboni was there, serious but calm.

We watched as Helene was comfortably put to bed. Much later Helene whispered that she was hungry, that at the hospital the nurses were not giving her food. The table had been cleared and I couldn't find any food for Helene. I do not recall where I found a piece of cold cooked banana which I offered to her. She weakly took it and ate. About half an hour later, she had a stomach seizure, and a loose motion with blood. I felt terribly guilty. Why do I always do the wrong thing? Soon Helene started vomiting violently. A taxi was called and she was rushed to Namirembe Hospital.

Every day, I noticed Baganda families sitting in groups mourning, wailing, saying things I did not understand.

"I wonder why they look miserable. Why are they crying? Why are they rolling in the mud?" I asked, baffled.

"Some relatives have died of typhoid," Grandma said calmly, almost absentmindedly, her soft hand holding mine. What a soft, gentle and warm hand Grandma had!

"When people die, do they scream and roll like that woman?" I asked curiously, pointing to some distraught mother.

"No, my little one, now let's visit your sister," she said changing the subject.

Helene was always happy to see us. The children's ward was filled to capacity. Helene looked thin, miserable and her long hair had begun falling out. It broke my heart to see her like this.

Typhoid had reached an epidemic state. I noticed lots of children having the same symptoms as my sister. She stayed at the hospital for a very long time, when finally Mother transferred her to Rubaga Catholic Missionary Hospital. Mother could not cope with her four little girls and a very sick child at the same time. I overheard a discussion indicating that we were to be taken out of school, to my extreme despondency.

An Arab women called Kulsum wanted to adopt me, as she was barren and wanted a child desperately. Mother thought it best to separate Sylvia and me as we always seemed to get into some mischief or other. A decision was made and I was taken away by Auntie Kulsum until Helene recovered. I was actually happy to go, as Kulsum and I had developed a very close relationship. I really loved her. She was exceptionally good to me. Her house lay between Namirembe and Rubaga, a walking distance from home. After nearly three weeks in hospital Helene recovered and returned home. During that period no member of the family visited me. One day, as I was playing alone, I saw Helene walking towards me. Indian music could be heard from my new "home". Helene was wearing a scarf and looked very fragile.

"Would you like to see my hair?" she called. Oh, how happy I was to see her, she thought of me, my dear sister.

"Yes," I answered rather curious.

She removed her scarf, lo and behold she didn't have any hair! I felt a lump rise in my throat, all that hair had fallen out. Kulsum's Alsatian shepherd dog had given birth to a litter of six puppies. Helene loved animals, especially dogs. The puppies were crawling all over the store room where they had been born. Helene told me to put them back next to their panting mother.

"Babies ought to be with their mothers."

I refused, she called me a coward and picked up a pup and placed it next to the mother.

"See, the dog hasn't done anything to me," she smiled reassuringly.          But the pups were restless. I watched Helene enjoying herself with the new born animals. I was suspicious of animals as I was of grown-ups. Suddenly, the mother dog gripped Helene by her dress and really attacked her. Helene was screaming while the dog kept snapping here and there, all over her body with its sharp teeth. Helene's clothes were torn off and she was bleeding and crying. I was outside screaming and shouting holding a stick which I waved frantically. I was hysterical. I could actually feel the pain my sister was going through. Kulsum rushed from her afternoon nap but could not control her own dog.

The next door neighbour on hearing the commotion came with his gun. White people always seemed to have guns. He saw the dog had gone completely berserk. He could not get Helene out, therefore thought it best to shoot the dog. He had to aim pretty accurately as he did not want to hurt the child.

"He is going to kill my sister," I was sure.

I heard six bullets fired, before the dog finally died. The neighbour immediately picked up the panic-stricken child and drove directly to Mulago Hospital where she received anti-tetanus injection, stitches and was bandaged all over. With her clothes in tatters the Englishman took her home. Mother almost collapsed with shock. She could not imagine what on earth had happened to her daughter who had only just recovered from a nearly fatal illness. After this incident, Mother thought it best I come home.

Our new house was ready and we soon moved in. Helene was much stronger and wanted to go back to school. Mother refused to send us back to our former school and we were bored to death.

Father appeared after all these traumas. I kept studying my parents to see some reaction, some concern, some kind of drama about Helene's illness but I could make out nothing. Both met happily and talked calmly. Our education was discussed. Mum was told that Father had applied for places at a boarding school at Kisubi, ten miles from Kampala. So a new era began.

# CHAPTER FIVE:
# AWAY FROM HOME:
# KISUBI AND OTHER SCHOOLS

We joined the Kisubi Boarding School which was run by the White Sisters in January 1952. Oh, how excited I was, we were finally going to school! I had a strong urge towards learning, although we had hardly any encouragement whatsoever from members of the family. Helene, on the other hand was rather upset leaving home. As for Sylvia well, nothing seemed to affect her. Never a word was said by Mboni, she always seemed busy washing and ironing.

Sylvia, who was not yet quite five years old proved to be a very bright little girl. Lack of an outlet for creativity and stimulation made her naughtier, perhaps it was her way of seeking attention. I was the polar opposite, timid, bashful and insecure, a reflection of my parents' separation.

On our arrival, the whole school came out to satisfy their curiosity. Why? I wondered. We noted three Catholic Asian girls in the school, all the sisters, and lots of children of mixed parentage besides the African girls. What was so different about us?

I was extremely confused when I saw the nuns. I could not imagine from which planet they had come. They definitely weren't earthly. All of them were not only white and flat chested, but were covered from head to foot in white. They looked angelic. Grandma and Mum had described angels to us a good number of times.

"Angels watch over little children, angels love good little children."

They wore no make-up, were very serious and seldom spoke. I asked Mother whether they were men or women. She thought I was being rude and smacked me across the mouth. I didn't cry although tears trickled down my cheeks as my lip began to swell. I was never given an explanation, as to who these people were. Consequently, I came to my own conclusion. They were creatures out of this world.

We met the nun in charge, called Sister Felix, and Sister Miriam, the Mother Superior. I took a liking to both women and admitted that they were humans almost immediately. We were introduced to the school assembly. The girls were specifically told to be nice to us. It was a school policy that the older girls were required to mind the younger ones. A girl called Nnassali volunteered to take care of me. She looked like 'Mother frost;' big, long, front teeth with a gap in the centre of her top row. But I liked her because she smiled at me. I was disappointed she wasn't as pretty as my Mum but, I supposed, she'd do. I thought my Mother was the most beautiful woman in the whole wide world.

Sylvia was put in the charge of a flat-chested girl from standard five called Magdalena. Helene was to be looked after by pretty Nosiata. Sylvia took a good look at the three girls appointed to care for us. She was not happy with her mentor because she erroneously believed that the girl's lack of breasts meant, she was too young to mother her.

"I don't want a little girl to mind me. I want a big girl, with big *a'mabere*," she complained.

The nuns laughed as did the whole school. These holy women blushed a little when *a'mabere* was pronounced. Sylvia eventually got an attractive girl with a big bosom.

I gathered courage and asked Nnassali about the white nuns. She told me that they were the people of God. My mind worked again and came to the conclusion that God must have dropped them from heaven, yet I wondered why they didn't have wings.

This first day of school was rather exciting. At dinner time, Sylvia sat opposite me. Helene was at the next oblong table. *Ugali*, a maize meal dish, was served with *maido*, peanut sauce. Sylvia's face was beaming as radiantly as ever.

"Eh Mandy, what is this white stuff?" asked Sylvia in Kiswahili as prayers were being said.

I put my finger across my mouth, gesturing to her to stop talking during prayers. After we were seated, Sylvia put a big piece of ugali in her plate and scooped up a tablespoon full of peanut sauce. This made the girls laugh. Helene, at the other table said,

"Don't eat this food, do you know what this is?"

Ugali was never cooked or eaten by the Baganda at this time. But

Sylvia and I ignored her warning and we filled our plates. Day after day, that was our diet. Occasionally we had sweet potatoes and beans, *bijanjaro*. Next morning, we were awakened from our sweet dreams by the tolling of the convent bell. I opened my eyes, startled and disoriented for an instant. "Blessed be God," was said in Luganda and everyone answered in unison, "For all Eternity," *emirembe ne mirembe*, jumping out of their beds at the same time.

"What in heaven's name is happening? Is there some danger?" we wondered.

The world was still dark and freezing cold as we were not far from *Nalubale*, Lake Victoria . . . that was the spirit lake Grandma had told us about. We knelt down, only because we saw everyone else kneeling, half asleep, frightened and perplexed. After mumbling some words to some Supreme Being, we followed the girls to cubicles. Here we encountered white basins with icy cold water. I dipped my finger into the water and passed it over my half closed eyes, literally shaking from cold, teeth chattering, and my skin turned to goose-flesh, I wondered where my vest, sweater and shoes were. I noticed the older girls brushing their teeth with a *muswaki*, a stick-like tooth brush, dipping it in charcoal ashes to clean their lovely white, ivory teeth.

We then lined up and marched in pairs to the Church, which seemed miles away. Here we were met by these strange, gentle women who lovingly coaxed us to enter this mysterious building known as the *keleziya*, church. No-one uttered a word, all had such solemn looks. I wondered why people always seemed to become sad when they entered these sorts of houses. There was an indescribable serenity within these walls.

Once inside, I was astounded at the sight of the admirable women on both sides of the altar. Where did these ladies come from? There was another most fair woman who had long hair and breasts, unlike the nuns, dressed like our Muslim women, holding a lovely baby. On the right side of the altar was a man . . . he seemed infinitely gentle, loving . . . he was hypnotizing just to look at him. He had features like our Arab men; long hair, a moustache and a beard like a Sikh. He was dressed in a *kanzu*, a long robe, and had white skin and blue eyes just like our Father.

"He belongs to us," I thought.

A nun gently ushered me to my seat. In the church reigned on all-pervading peace and ineffable sense of joy. The air was filled with sweet scent of hibiscus, lilies, roses and carnations. We were later told that the nuns grew these lovely flowers in a splendid garden. My mind went back to this gentle Man looking down at me. His hands and feet seemed hurt. Someone must have pushed thorns into his head as I saw that blood poured from his head.

"Someone must have hurt him," I thought.

I noticed a man garbed in a plain outfit, walking towards the altar, he seemed saintly. I learnt he was called a priest. I was awakened from my trance by one of these gentle white creatures who took me by the arm and told me that mass was over. The nuns had been specifically told not to convert us into Christianity. We were Muslims and had Muslim names too.

My name was Fatma, the radiant light. Sylvia, who refused the name Rukia because it rhymed with the Kiswahili word *mukia*, which means tail, was therefore named Alya instead, the enlightened one.

Breakfast came after church, it consisted of *uji*, a light maize porridge which was served in plastic tumblers placed haphazardly upon the benches, rather than the tables. These were kept outside the dining hall under two mango trees. This substance tasted more plastic than maize and was often cold. It had a few fallen leaves in it, sometimes a worm or two which had dropped from the mango tree. I was taught to use a leaf to scoop up the worms and swallow my breakfast as there was no food until twelve o'clock. By ten o'clock I was so hungry.

"It's break time; maybe I'll get milk and a biscuit," I thought hopefully.

"Out of class! You are all to pick up all the leaves in the compound," the teacher announced instead.

Sundays were always special days. This was the only day of the week that the school provided saffron rice and a light meat sauce. This was also the only day that we had the luxury of a cup of black tea. How we longed for that stale piece of bread which we had to queue up for! How Sylvia managed to be the first in the queue and obtain extra pieces of bread I never found out. To solve the problem of the fungus, she toasted the bread by pushing a long stick through the slice and holding it over the burning, smoky fire.

Being lively and mischievous, Sylvia soon became a favourite of the older girls. She was hyperactive, always on the move, constantly in trouble, or being punished when found in places she ought not to be. Sylvia was very agile and quick in her movements. She often climbed a huge tank which was about ten feet high in which the nuns collected rain water. Then, leaning over the top, she screamed to get everyone's attention. Then, to our amazement, Sylvia would jump down. The girls laughed more out of relief than anything else, then applauded. This gave Sylvia great satisfaction. It was a miracle she never broke a bone. In matter of weeks we were befriended by a very short, fat, old hunch-backed nun called Sister Dorothy, one of the first missionary sisters to come into Uganda. She carried a peculiar horn-like instrument which she used as a hearing aid. Sister Dorothy loved Sylvia, and would look for her almost every day and give her handfuls of delicious toffees, a candy made from a sugar and coconut base. Sister Dorothy and Sylvia became great friends.

We soon learnt our national anthem praising our country and king, which we sang during assemblies. After the curiosity and novelty caused by our arrival had worn off, the older pupils began to mistreat us. When we were introduced to them, the nuns not meaning any harm, told the students proudly that we were from the royal family, and gave them a brief history about us. The older girls didn't like that at all. Hatred began to seethe in them.

"Do you think you are any better than us because your Grandmother is a *Mumbejja*, princess?" they gagged and hit us across the face.

"Do you think you are better off because your father is white?" Smack across my face! *"Kaburu."* I wondered what this word *Kaburu* meant.

"Your Arab relatives sold us as slaves . . ."

I had heard the word slave from Grandma. She had told me that African chiefs in West Africa captured and sold their people to the Americans and that Arabs had introduced this trade to the Africans in Mombasa, East Africa and Southern Africa. Some were taken from Mozambique to the Seychelles, some to America in very dreadful conditions.

As the interrogations continued my nose began to bleed. I already had a nose-bleeding problem and this happened quite easily. Sometimes in my sleep my nose bled and soiled my pillow. I'd be smacked on the head the next morning.

"Do you think your father pays me for washing your dirty sheets! Answer me you little imp."

We stood with eyes cast down before these girls, who seemed transformed into great monsters. We dared not look at their loathsome faces. It was hard to believe that within such a short period, after the fuss made of us, the happy welcome we were given, all that goodwill had fled only to be replaced by unreasonable cruelty. Because many of the girls had no shoes, we were ordered to remove ours, and walk barefoot; we obliged.

At the beginning I didn't mind, as I felt tickled by the gravel. Somehow, Sylvia managed to keep her shoes on, but only during the school walks which were always supervised by a nun, to whom she would cling for protection. Helene developed an abscess on her big toe, and twice lost her toe-nail. She suffered for a long time before it completely healed. How I hated being pricked here and there, to have jiggers removed from my toes. Where are you Mama? She had vanished from our lives.

Our cardigans given to us by Mother were removed and we were told to bear the cold just like the rest. It was quite chilly in the mornings and evenings. I developed asthma due to the constant cold baths, being exposed to the morning and evening chills. The cold was something I could never afford to forget. I became constantly ill and weak. This made the girls very happy as they watched me wheezing, struggling to breathe. They would get me out of bed and order Sylvia to accompany me to a nearby forest.

Exhaustion came quickly and the temptation to just sit for a moment and take a little rest was often overwhelming. The grove was dark, cold and thick. We were tormented by being told that there were lions. Helene warned us that it was true as she had heard them roar at night. Remembering our sister's warning, Sylvia and I would scream and cling to the girls' legs, begging them not to send us into the woods. Helene worried every time she didn't find us in bed. She would hide in a corner and weep as she was never sure she would see us again.

To ridicule us, the older girls enjoyed holding Sylvia and me over a pig-sty. They laughed jubilantly as we wriggled and cried when the pigs snorted under our feet. Not a soul came to our rescue. Tears trickled down our cheeks while the merciless girls laughed and mocked us to their hearts' content.

"Beg for mercy you white ... White people love pigs, don't they?" they scorned. We said "sorry" not knowing what for. It suddenly struck us that it was wrong to be what we were, something that had never crossed our minds. We began to think that if one was not an unadulterated African, European, or Asian, it was sinful, shameful and disgraceful. We felt utterly alone and a sense of being solitary can be frightening to a little child.

Where and to whom did we belong? We thought of the wonderful, loving white father we had, our dear tender beautiful African-Arab mother and our wonderful Arab relatives and esteemed African family and yet we were a disgrace to the world. Why?

We couldn't understand it! We felt alienated and we wanted to belong. We needed help and where were our parents? The older girls took us aside and told us, mockingly,

"Have you heard of a punishing God? He has one big eye in the middle of His forehead, and He is particularly watching the three of you, every time you do anything wrong, He will send lighting from His shining sword to strike you . . . thunder is his voice. This creator only likes pure races, that is, the Africans, Indians and Europeans."

Very strong fear of God developed within me. "He must be different. The God Mother told us about was kind and loved children."

I was so afraid of the omnipotence that I would not even pick up a stone from the ground for fear He'd decide to strike me with lightning. Incidentally, the thunder began to crash and swiftly come closer, with the swollen sky zig-zagging with frightening electrical bolts. That was God wielding his whip; *Boom Boom Boom* raced my little heart, what had I done now?

"See He's getting annoyed. You are wicked and shameful before his eyes, because you're not black or white or brown."

Apparently certain colours mattered to God. I feared the sound of thunder for many years to come.

"We must be horrible creatures," we concluded and decided to suffer the consequences without complaint.

Many times the sadistic girls would take several little girls, chiefly Sylvia and me, to a dark, low-roofed, soot-filled room which was next to the kitchen. There happened to be a loose electric wire which was very much alive and made the corrugated iron roof dangerous. As soon as we touched it, our hands would automatically jerk away as we felt "pins and needles." This made me feel nauseated. I often shrieked, begging the girls not to make me touch the roof. When Helene found out about these dastardly episodes, she smacked and scolded Sylvia and me, and warned us that we could have lost our lives. Where were the school authorities? Help us, save us, please, my heart cried out within me.

"Don't you ever touch any wire the girls tell you to touch. Do you understand?" Helene sternly instructed us.

She remembered Mother telling us about the danger of electric wires. They kill! The torments stopped when darkness covered our world. I actually loved the dark when a black shadow covered all evil.

Lake Victoria was just a couple of miles away from our school. I wonder why Nalubale never called me and swallowed me. There was a forest with thick growth of vegetation, trees covered with rich green creepers, which also filled up the intervening spaces. In the late evening, we heard the incessant sound of insects, their steady beat filtering through the dense undergrowth. The tall trees made this particular area quite dark, damp and cold.

Out beyond the school were silhouettes of small canoes with fishermen, on the placid waters of the huge very blue lake, probably fishing. I peeped through the small gauzed window, gazed at the moon which was as big as a saucepan . . . brightening up the starry sky as well as casting a yellowish light across the compound. Soon a cloud passed in front of the moon, throwing a black shadow over the desolate landscape . . . wish I were up there, wish I could fly . . .

"Time to go to bed, young lady," whispered the kindly voice of a nun. Tired and dejected we fell asleep, sleep my comfort, my one and only escape.

As Sylvia got accustomed to the school, she would sneak to the forest and pick wild, sweet black berries and eat them, or stealthily enter the nun's orchard through a hole she had made through the hedge. She'd steal small limes, tangerines, avocado and mangoes . . . in spite of Helene's warning.

"Do you understand what is done," she persisted, "to children who steal? Their hands are tied with dry banana fibres and set alight, or their hands are slit with a blade and rubbed with chillies!"

I was always somewhere near Sylvia. We were never given any fruit anyway. Hunger made me bold enough to wait for her. The older girls had to collect firewood for cooking as there were no electrical facilities. Everyone used paraffin stoves or charcoal. The younger girls were given duties to perform. To help collecting firewood was one of them. More often than not, when we went into the forest, we came across snakes. These slithering creatures were "devils" that tempted Adam and Eve.

We had been shown a movie on the ten commandments, the most terrifying movie a six and four year old girl could ever watch. The devil was ever behind your back following you, tempting you, we felt. When the older girls came across a snake they'd scream hysterically, running in all directions. Sylvia was nowhere to be seen; when she felt danger was at hand, she took off like a deer! I was slower and always breathless due to my weakened chest. As a punishment for my sister's disappearance I had to carry twice the bundle of drysticks on my head.

On our ritual tormenting day, our prefects came across some green grass-snakes which they knew were neither poisonous, nor dangerous. As always they had all three of us Bjordal girls together! I wonder why other girls of mixed race were not with us. We were given thick sticks and ordered to kill the baby snakes or else they would put them into our dresses! We were frenzied. Helene, being our protector, held her tears back and tried to comfort us. Sylvia who was completely distraught, begged the girls to take her away from the horrifying, crawling snakes.

"Get down on your knees and beg us," we were ordered.

Sylvia and I quivered as we got down on our knees and prayed for mercy. The three of us were taken behind the cubicle and our foreheads shaved and shaped using a razor blade. I closed my eyes as I felt my forehead was being skinned with this sharp instrument. I daren't move for fear I'd be cut.

"You look tidy now," we were mocked "like real Baganda. You must never let hairs grow on your forehead."

"Hair, please don't grow again, I can't go through this yet another time." Bits of hair were then cut off here and there.

"The nuns need your hair to make paint brushes."

A white and blue soap, with a slight mixture of caustic soda, washing soap, was used to bathe us and wash our hair, our skin felt hot, irritated and turned red. Our oldest sister, Mboni, was at day school in Mengo run by an old English lady, but she was made a servant and taught very little. Mother didn't know this. Mboni claimed she was fed on left-overs which were shared with the dog. Were all schools so cruel? We wondered, at Kisubi.

If the girls had nothing to do they would vent their anger on those small girls who had no big sister in the upper primary classes to defend them. A six-year old Muganda girl, also called Sylvia, was made to chew red devil chilies every day just before lunch. Every evening when she was being bathed in open cubicles, two huge girls repeatedly kicked her in the thighs. The poor girl would get on her knees and plead for mercy. They would tell her to kiss their feet. She obliged and wouldn't get more kicks. . .

I felt a sudden familiar gall in my mouth, my heart tore to pieces every time Sylvia was persecuted. I suffered from constant palpitations seeing other children suffer. I failed to see the reason why we were constantly being tortured, in any case Sylvia was not "defiled" like us. As another illustration of their intimidating grandeur, these girls enjoyed making us carry heavy basins of red soil from one stretch to another for hours on end, usually on Sundays when the nuns were at prayer or asleep. When the weight was put on my head I felt my chin touch my chest, when the basin was lifted off, I felt my neck stretch miles upwards.

We were warned that, if any of us squealed to the authorities, severe retribution would be carried out against us. Therefore, for fear of revenge, we never uttered a word to the sisters. These sadistic acts against the younger girls went on unabated. Where is Mama? The school is only ten miles away from home . . . by and by, when our twelve year old sister Mboni came for her weekly visits, we began sending secret messages to Mother telling her of our suffering.

"Mboni help us PLEASE . . ."

"How can l?"

"Tell the nuns that Mother is very ill or dying and needs to see us," Helene suggested.

Permission was granted and we went home on the bus. Soon after our arrival our teacher Teresa appeared there unexpectedly. She found mother as healthy as ever and went back to the school to report about what a liar our sister was! Although Father had been informed of the constant victimisation, he did not want to do anything based on hearsay until he was able to pay us an unexpected visit.

The punishments were worse when we went back to school. The older girls made Sylvia, Helene and me hoe long stretches of land until blisters formed on our hands. Although such tell-tale evidence would have shown up on close inspection, it was incredible that the school authorities never suspected the existence of such cruelty amongst the girls.

During one of these bullying sessions, Father arrived unannounced at the school. Sister Felix received him, then excused herself and went out to look for us. As luck would have it, the person she encountered was one of the ring-leaders, who owned up to what was happening to us . . . How was it the class teacher did not miss us? The Sister became furious and very panicky.

Sister Felix ordered the girl to find us and bring us forth promptly! We hurried, trying to keep pace with the girl, tears dripping down our soiled faces. We were utterly exhausted and hardly had any strength left. When we were brought before the nun, she cast her eyes at our pathetically dishevelled, dirty appearance, and actually wept at the sight of us, her hands literally shaking. She commanded the big girl to take us, bathe us and make us tidy with smart clothes. She promised to deal severely with those responsible for this infamy. But that was all. Nothing was done.

I do not recall seeing a headmistress, nuns or teachers. The school was run by prefects. I saw the nuns at the church or at a distance or at school walks. I remember just two teachers. They had their own teachers 'house! Were they involved? We gave a loving smile to this nun who was going to be our saviour.

After we were scrubbed with washing soap and cold water, smartly attired in new white frocks with black polka dots, socks and shoes, we felt rather awkward; as we hadn't worn shoes for ages they seemed heavy. The nun came to inspect us, gave an approving nod and gestured us to proceed.

We followed the gently swaying white skirts of the nun down the murram lane. We passed absolutely quiet rooms and entered into a partially bare, excessively tidy parlour filled with sweet scented odours of various flowers.

There sat our handsome Father, with his legs crossed, in long black trousers, and an immaculate white shirt with a black tie reading a journal.

"My dad is the most good looking man in the world," I thought.

He carefully placed the journal he was reading on a side table next to him and stood up as we walked in. His face lit up seeing how immaculate we looked and he smiled. We ran into his open arms. Hugs, kisses, absolute silence followed - in that order. Dad, save us . . . can't you see something is wrong . . .?

The excitement and pleasure of Father seeing us looking well produced a kind of euphoria in him, so that stories of ill-treatment vanished from his thoughts. He did not examine our sore hands or feet or shaved foreheads. There was a little talking from time to time . . . we held a cryptic conversation. We were frightened then of telling him anything because of the presence of the nun in the parlour throughout his visit.

"Why don't you leave us alone," I thought in my little mind.

I decided to leave all the questions unanswered. Before taking his leave, Father left a huge box of goodies for us as well as for the other girls. While the chocolates, biscuits and other *tamutamus* (sweets) lasted, we enjoyed a period of peace and goodwill from our erstwhile tormentors. Hypocrites!

After what seemed like forever Mboni visited, to take us for our usual walk and picnic, but found me gravely ill. Being such a loving, wonderful big sister, she was upset to find me extremely pale and thin. I was silent, wide-eyed, full of stunned fascination. Weeks back, for the fun of it, I had had my temperature taken at the dispensary. No-one else had thought of checking it. I was told it was 104 degrees centigrade.

"Helene guess what? My temperature is 104 degrees."

"What?" she touched me. "You are very sick, go to bed at once."

The hunger, cold, unnecessary work and constant brutalities had whittled my formerly strong frame down to a mass of skin and bone. I could hardly move. Mboni immediately rushed home and told Mother about my condition. In no time at all, Mother came with a friend of hers and took me in her arms.

"Mama where have you been all this time?" was a silent question.

Why Mother didn't visit us as often as she should, ten miles away, was beyond my comprehension. She just looked at me and never said a word. She seemed quiet by nature.

Next day, Sunday, was Corpus Christi, the festival of the Body of Christ. It was a Catholic feast in commemoration of the Eucharist. Three-fourths of the school had lined up ready to go to church! The rest of us who were down with chickenpox or some indisposition stayed in the sick bay. Helene and Sylvia were already admitted. I had been ill for so long that days and nights ran together in a blur till the only indication of time was the prefect's or nurses' footsteps, which seemed distant and faint. Any hope of someone saving me drifted away.

Grandma, Mother and one of the Kabaka Mutesa's relatives had come to see us. On entering the sick bay, the girl in charge refused Grandma permission to see us. There was quite an altercation.

"You have no right," stormed one of the girls.

I never saw such hard, cold, cruel, pitiless looks. Grandma lost her temper, and asked the girl, calmly,

"Who are you to tell me I am not allowed to see my sick child?"

In Uganda no one dared talk in such a rude tone to a princess . . . . Grandma report them to the King. My lips tried to move, but no sound came.

She brought oranges as she had suspected we might be suffering from some deficiency. "Jajja" was busy peeling the fruit, saying,

"Unless you crucify me, the way they crucified Jesus Christ on the cross, I shall take my grandchild this very minute." As she said this, she brandished a knife . . .

"Where have you been, my Grandma?"

By this time the hostile girls had quite forgotten about going to church and had collected outside the infirmary. Grandma had aroused quite a stir. The whole school was screaming and shouting and were almost hysterical. During the dispute, Grandma came in and found me lying helplessly in bed. She quickly snatched my inert body and bundled me into a waiting car. The driver, her cousin, was very nervous when she told him to start the engine, despite an attempt by the hostile crowd to stop her. Some dared stand in front of the car.

The headmistress, Mother Miriam, having heard the noise, came out to investigate what was causing the commotion. Soon order was restored and, having heard the cause of the disturbance, Mother Miriam gave her permission for my family to take me to hospital.

I was admitted immediately to Namirembe Hospital and rheumatic fever was diagnosed. On examining me closely the doctor discovered that I was infested with lice which had burrowed into the head sores. He softly explained to the sister that the eruption of rose coloured spots I had was not measles or chicken pox, as the school had diagnosed. The extreme prostration, stupor, delirium and high fever pointed to typhus, a killer disease. A sister watched over me day and night. The family prayed in earnest. Rheumatic fever had been suspected due to stiff, very painful joints, which I was to suffer all my life. My heart didn't escape unscathed either. When I came to, I vaguely recognised the doctor and nurse peering at me.

"Mandy, Mandy, wake up!"

I was spoon fed with some liquid. I understand Mother was there day and night but I saw no-one, not even my Grandma. Where were Sylvia and Helene? Flashes of Kisubi came into focus. An announcement was made.

"All those with non-African hair come to one side."

We lined up just like the Jews being picked up by the Nazis.

"Anyone found with lice in their hair will have to eat them."

An inspection was carried out. The three Asian girls were made to eat a louse each. My turn came, I was given one, my mind worked at a fantastic speed. I held the insect between my forefinger and thumb, pretended to put it in my mouth, simultaneously dropping it to the ground and pretended to chew.

"Now that will teach you to be dirty."

Sylvia, my African friend, who also had the "plague" was punished likewise. The doctor gently helped me into a sitting position and explained,

"We are going to cut your hair off, Mandy, so we can treat the sores."

The doctor personally cleansed me with dettol. I was drowsy and fell asleep, too weak to stay awake . . . There stood the prefect holding our thick leather belts with iron buckles. She had taken my belt too. "Where's your belt?"

I was hit on the head with about twelve belts and I fainted. The girl panicked and carried my body to bed . . . my nose started bleeding, I could hear Helene screaming and crying . . .

"Mandy, wake up we are going to help you walk, all right?" Mother was sitting there, tears streaming down her face. The nurse and the doctor held me. My knees and arms were completely stiff, my back bent. The nurse cautiously moved one leg at a time.

I wonder where my Father is? I remember I had sisters Mboni, Helene and Sylvia . . . Grandma . . . slowly but surely my memory came back. I carefully got out from under the covers, held onto the bed, and tried to straighten out using the wall as support. I ventured to walk. The doctor found me struggling, smiled and said,

"Well done Mandy, keep it up!" I figured out he was approving my action and I too smiled.

"Mum, where are my sisters?" I asked, in Kiswahili.

"Still at Kisubi," she replied.

I wondered if anyone had visited them. I left them ill.

"Where's Papa?" I inquired.

"At Kabale, or probably out of the country," Mother responded, uncaringly.

The nuns wrote to Father and explained that Grandma and Mother were an obstacle towards our education. They advised him to send Sylvia and Helene to their "sister" school in Kenya. Not to have all the trauma the nuns had had, Dad collaborated and gave them full responsibility for the welfare of the children. At this time and age, it would have been considered kidnapping but not so during the colonial era. And so, I lost my sisters.

After my recovery I built an emotional fortress around myself for many years to come and became more of a recluse. I knew our lives were always to be tempestuous but it taught us that we were survivors. After this separation I was not to see my dear sisters for the next two years.

During this period of 1953, Father decided to visit his family in Norway and hadn't been home for over a year, he never saw how ill I was. Great was the excitement when he arrived in Norway. Endless questions to be answered, a collection of geologists to meet. He was interviewed by the Norwegian press and appeared in the newspapers.

54

He later showed us a Norwegian book which contained a photographic map of his mine, taken from the air, and a short history of the Bjordal Mine.

After his stay in Norway, Dad decided he would drive his white Chevrolet rather than fly back to Uganda. It was a very long and dangerous journey. He was well aware of the risk but was determined to give it a try. Dad talked to several Norwegian friends, and two of them volunteered to accompany him. They would become explorers, famous and maybe rich, they thought. They equipped themselves with enough money, food, medicine and clothing to last them, they thought, until they were in Uganda.

They had quite a pleasant journey from Norway to Egypt. When they got to the Sahara Desert it was a different story. Dad and his companions drove into a sandstorm and were promptly lost in the middle of nowhere. They drove in circles, probably in the same area, for hours on end; finally they ran out of petrol. The hot wind, scorching sun, sand and absolute emptiness almost drove them out of their minds. The wind that whipped over Father and his friends was a furnace-like heat. Billions of grains of sand bit at them with hurling velocity. They could not open their eyes for fear of being blinded. The sand ripped into their clothing, ears and soured their efforts to breathe. Sand burrowed its way into their hair, mouth, noses and pitted under their finger nails. The heat was unbearable. Dad passed out from the heat prostration.

During the day, they felt like they were roasted alive and yet the nights were freezing cold. At night the sky was a lovely blue and absolutely clear with a bright, yellow moon.

After two days of sweat literally pouring out of their bodies and enduring extreme hunger, Dad's two friends thought they could see an oasis and palm trees. They even saw Arabs with camels drinking the cool water. They ran as fast as their legs could carry them.

"*Du grunst nicht,* Do not go, you silly . . . It is a mirage." Father cautioned them.

But they kept running and the water kept moving as well. Father remained near the scorching hot car and prayed for a miracle.

"I could not stay in the car as it felt like a furnace. I'd rather the sun roasted me," he told us.

Fortunately, some Arab men riding camels saw Father, whose skin had turned a deep chocolate colour; they knew he was a European only because of his blond hair and blue eyes. Father could hardly talk, let alone stand. His lips were desiccated and his back blistered. These kind men helped Father up onto the camel took him to a hotel and looked after him for a couple of days until he recovered. They exchanged news using gestures, since Father could not speak Arabic nor could they speak English.

Father told them that he was now ready to continue his journey. His car was found. The men had given him plenty of food, medicine, bottles of water and extra petrol and jerry-cans, together with a lot of encouragement.

Father's friends were eventually found dead not far from an oasis. After Father had completed his journey successfully, he was asked to write an article about his travels for the *National Geographic Magazine*, which he did.

He immediately visited me. He seemed very upset to find me in such a pathetic state. Off he rushed to a chemist and bought me all the tonics one could possibly think of. He also made arrangements for Helene and Sylvia to go to school in Kenya.

Although very young, I was aware of the importance of education. My inner urge made me pester Mother to send me to school. I attended one school after another and was more confused than before. All in all I must have gone to five different Asian schools, two African schools and had two years of disrupted schooling.

During this time, there were great political changes in Uganda. Kabaka Mutesa II had refused to unite Buganda with the rest of Uganda. He was therefore deported to England by the British Government. Why were the foreigners interfering with my Uncle? I was more confused than ever. How can the foreigners arrest our King? How dare they come all the way from the United Kingdom to Africa, ordering Mutesa what to do? I wondered why the foreigners always told Africans how they should run their countries. We had our kings for generations; our own government.

Kabaka Mutesa II was not even allowed to pack his things. Absolutely nothing. This is exactly what Grandma had told me they had done to her father Mwanga II. The British smuggled Mwanga II to the Seychelles Islands. Mutesa too, was escorted under security when he boarded a Royal Air Force aeroplane at Entebbe and was flown to Sussex, where it was winter and extremely cold. A Wing Commander met him at the airport, saluted and offered Kabaka Mutesa II a warrant officers' overcoat. At least the British were courteous.

Meanwhile, the whole of Buganda was in shock. The Kabaka's brother, Henry Kimera, was in Bristol studying History at this time, when he heard the news over the radio. He was shocked beyond words. Our King to us was like the Pope to the Roman Catholics. He meant the world to us. Our people in Buganda began wearing bark material as a sign of mourning. Men swore not to shave their beards until the return of their King. It was interesting seeing every man with a beard like sikhs. The Baganda people completely refused to co-operate with the British; all we wanted was to have our King back.

Our family was very involved in the political changes going on in the city of Kampala. Grandma and Mother were at the Lubiiri or at the Bulange, attending family talks with the Katikiiro, Prime Minister, to get any news about the exiled Kabaka Mutesa II. I felt I had lost everything; especially when I came home from school, to find only Mboni. I then understood that the King had been sent into exile in England. Sad songs were played over the radio. Grandma cried for her grand-nephew. I was miserable because the rest of the family was practically mourning. Nobody talked or laughed. Grandma always called me and made me sit on her lap when listening to the news.

At this time, parents rarely sat with a child and explained what was happening. One had to come to one's own conclusions. Once I heard by hearsay that the Kabaka's Lake, a small dam near the palace, had dried up because it was disappointed the British had taken its King. I absorbed everything I heard. In 1955, it was foretold that the *Bassekabaka*, spirits would annnouce when the Kabaka would return to his home-land, and true enough they did. We had three earth tremors that year as predicted. I heard the rumbling noise and fear spread throughout the country sending everyone screaming and rushing into their houses.

Not long after the tremors, an announcement was made that the Kabaka would return on the 18th October and everyone in Buganda was to dress in white. Mother, who was our seamstress, got very busy making our clothes. On 18th October 1955, Kabaka Mutesa II arrived in a BOAC aeroplane. An aeroplane was a rare commodity at this time.

The Baganda people camped at Entebbe overnight. Grandma wouldn't miss this event for the world. She narrated how people lined up from Kampala to Entebbe, a good twenty miles! On the King's arrival a nine gun salute was fired. As the door of the plane opened, the crowd cheered, played the traditional Baganda drums and danced. The Kabaka greeted his family, inspected the guard of honour and was then carried by a member of the buffalo clan, as was the custom, on his shoulders to an open Rolls Royce. Prince Henry was there, dressed smartly in his RAF uniform. I was mesmerised.

57

The route from Entebbe to Namirembe Cathedral was lined with banana trees and decorative arches. People were screaming, singing, dancing and waving branches, cheering the King *"Ye Yekka, Kabaka Waffe,* Our one and only King."* I was up in Namirembe Hill joining in the rejoicing of my people. My ayah put me on her shoulders to enable me to have a better view. The Kabaka went for a service at the Namirembe Cathedral in thanksgiving for his return to his homeland.

The celebration sometimes went on until early morning, and continued for weeks on end. Drums were played for four days. Grandma and I went for parties at the Lubiiri where I played with Kabaka Mutesa's daughter, Omumbejja Dorothy Nasolo, who was recovering from polio. I was exhausted and fell asleep on some *jajja's* warm lap. How I loved all my Baganda relatives, they always hugged and cuddled me. The men shaved their beards and with the hair made stuffed cushions which were presented to the Kabaka.

While I stayed in Uganda, recuperating, my sisters Helene and Sylvia were in school in Kenya. Sylvia suddenly became introverted, shy, timid and clung to Helene for almost two years. Maybe the experience at Kisubi had broken her spirit. Helene too had changed. She became nervous and chewed her nails continuously. She lost all confidence in herself. Here in Kenya they thought it was heavenly; they were never tortured.

One day Sylvia found a tennis ball and decided to aim at the light bulb in the corridor. Probably this was a sign of inner frustration and boredom. Helene was amused watching Sylvia concentrating and gently throwing the ball at each bulb, trying to break them. As she was busy doing this, Sister Mary de Lorette quietly appeared,

"Miss Bjordal, what on earth do you think you are doing?"

Sylvia went quite red in the face and timidly answered,

"Nothing, Sister."

She picked up her ball and hid it behind her back, stood and looked at the nun. Sister Mary very kindly told Sylvia not to play near any bulbs or windows again or she might break them . . .

"All right, Sister," smiled Sylvia.

About this time, the pit-latrines were being built. A mischief-maker, Patrick, took Sylvia by the hand and dropped her right to the bottom. Naturally, when she tried to come up she couldn't. Patrick, who was about fourteen years old, desperately tried to get her out before the nuns found out. Unfortunately, Sister Mary caught him red-handed and expelled him. The workers had to bring a ladder to get sevenyear old Sylvia out. She was full of smiles and happiness when she joined Helene and her friends.

Helene found it a pleasure looking after Sylvia. She believed that Sylvia really missed having a mother around, especially since she didn't understand English. A girl named Sharon Porger made them feel quite at home, because she spoke Kiswahili. On the other hand, Helene felt quite happy in Kenya almost immediately. Anything was better than Kisubi.

Sylvia proved to be very intelligent. The teachers found her a loving child, very shy, yet very smart. The nuns made both girls join music classes. Helene couldn't cope with it but Sylvia did very well. This was during the period when Kenya was fighting for her independence from colonial rule.

Back in Kampala, I had joined a nearby Hindu Asian school. The school had a statue of Krishna and smelt of incense. Practically the whole of Mengo had Asians in their white dhotis, a cap on their heads and a round mark in between their eyebrows. At this school, I went through a very difficult time being the only non-Hindu, non-Asian child, but I was quite used to difficulties by now. I had to learn the Hindi alphabet and prayers by rote without really understanding what they meant. First thing in the morning, after praying to a god with several heads and arms, we were called to recite the *Akara-beka*, the Indian alphabet, aloud in front of the class. The whole class would burst into an uproar of laughter as soon as I opened my mouth. They called me *Chotara*, mixed blood, child of a prostitute, child out of wedlock.

"My Father and Mother fell in love, permission was asked before he took his teenage wife," I knew the truth, the Asians' point of view didn't bother me.

In any case it was Mother who was the rich one not my Father, in fact he was a poor man. In spite of the abuse thrown at me, I was one of the top pupils and surprisingly became the teacher's favourite; this was especially true of the one who had previously whipped me with a thin unbreakable bamboo stick for not knowing the Hindu prayer.

Mother was due to have another baby. I went with her to Nsambya Catholic Hospital to keep her company and was given a bed in the spare room. After what I had gone through she decided to keep me as close to her as possible. Mum stayed in the hospital for a week and then was discharged.

"False alarm," she was told.

After two weeks, she went back with severe pains and was re-admitted. I became bored sitting among all the expectant mothers with their huge, swollen abdomens. I would wander off. One particular day, I landed in a Catholic Church, and felt so much love, happiness and peace. I just didn't want to leave it.

"Oh how I wish I could be a Catholic," I thought as I fell into a trance.

One of the nuns found me sitting in the church and she thought I was lost. Gently I was guided back to Mother.

"My daughter likes your religion," Mother joked with the nun.

"God bless her," answered the nun, also smiling brightly.

After Mother was put on a drip she delivered an eleven-pound, ten ounces baby boy! I was awakened at night and told about my new brother. Next morning, I was very excited to see him.

"Surely, there must be a mistake," was my dismayed thought when I saw him. "He's a complete European and must be at least four months old. He looks like a piglet."

The baby was put in my arms and the weight of him nearly toppled me over, I was still very weak. He was born two feet long with triple chins and a body full of creases. The nuns asked Mother permission to put an account of her baby's weight in the papers.

"No way," Mother objected, "you cannot publish my child's birth weight."

The baby was named Shabaan because he was born in the Muslim month of Shabaan. All this while it was considered advisable, my sisters should not travel to Uganda during the termly holidays due to the State of Emergency that existed in Kenya. I spent alot of time browsing through as many books as I could lay my hands on.

"How I wish I could learn English," was the constant thought in my mind.

I told Mother that I could not cope with an Asian school any more because of the language barrier. She kept me at home and had an Arab private tutor, as a preference. I learned the Quran, Arabic alphabet and basic words but I wasn't satisfied. I complained again. Mother sent me for private tutoring with a Goan girl, who was hardly ever present, though I religiously went for my lessons. An out-of-work uncle of hers occasionally taught me but he wasn't a real teacher. All that I learnt was the alphabet and I quickly became bored again. I wanted to read, so off I went to Mother and again I complained, the more so because the young man held me too close when teaching me, indecently caressing me. I was deeply afraid of him. I didn't tell Mother the truth but I wanted out!

"What in heaven's name do you want me to do? Every school I send you to isn't good enough," she responded in a rather agitated tone.

Yet again, Mum sent me to an Asian home for private tutoring. She did not seem to understand my language problems. The Asian house smelt of Al-houd which were kept burning on either side of the Aga-Khan's picture decorated with sweet smelling white flowers; the Jasmine.

"Wonder if he's Mrs. Ibrahim's God? I better not ask questions . . . don't know what will be done to me . . ."

The teacher was an Ismaili Muslim, and that's all that mattered to Mother. Again I was the only non-Asian child but the Ismaili teacher and children were good to me. I tried hard to learn the language and to be an Asian!

Having mastered the language, I was soon going to Indian movies. *Sujatta* was my favorite movie. I began singing their songs, *Duniya meha meho*, something about the world. English movies did not appeal to me any more. After a while, I was accepted at the Aga Khan School, which I found classy. Was I comfortable? No, not with the children. They teased me a lot.

"Your mother must have wanted a white man for his money!"

Every time I heard the bell for recess, my heart sank, as I knew that the whole school would be dancing around me singing, *"Chotara, chotara"* and saying many other unkind words. Did I cry? No, I wasn't going to give them the satisfaction. I decided to work hard and prove that I was academically better than most.

Unfortunately, Mother took me away from the school just as I was beginning to settle. I was house-bound again. Would boredom turn my brains into mush? I woke up one morning feeling really unwell. What struck me, was that my skin, hands and nails, were yellow. I staggered out of bed and went over to Mother.

"Oh, my God look at you, your eyes are yellow."

As usual the women were called.

"She has *Nkaka* - jaundice."

Off to hospital. Again I do not recall anything until Sister Mary John from Kenya visited and gave us news of Helene and Sylvia and prepared Mother for my departure at the beginning of 1956. She also told Mother that Helene and Sylvia wanted to become Catholics and asked if she minded. Mother said it was up to the children and that the nuns should consult their Father. The nuns having had written permission from Father and verbal agreement from Mother went ahead with preparations for my sisters' baptism. How I inwardly envied them.

"Oh, how I love you sister Mary John . . ."

At the beginning of December, 1955, Mother received a telegram advising her that the girls were coming home after a two-year absence. In her excitement, Mother read "arriving" for "leaving"? She cooked, spring-cleaned, and polished the floors of the rooms where my sisters would be staying. She planned a big welcome party. I had never seen Mother so excited. We hired a taxi, and drove to the railway station at Kampala to meet Helene and Sylvia. I was filled with excitement and anticipation at their arrival. Happy faces everywhere, people hugging, talking and cheering. I stared very intensely at every passenger.

"Where are Helene and Sylvia?" I asked myself.

I was almost in tears when I realised that they had not been on the train after all. We went home with heavy hearts and greatly disappointed. Mother wept and said she feared the children had been kidnapped. I heard her express her fear about kidnapping and as far as I can remember I began to believe her! I finally cried myself to sleep.

The next day we went about our usual routine, but at about six o'clock in the evening an Asian gentleman brought my sisters home! Imagine the excitement that was aroused. The whole house was wild with joy! Everyone was talking at the same time. Apparently, the Asian man was waiting for a relative who did not turn up and was the last to leave the station. Helene went up to him and nervously asked him for his help; Sylvia just held on to Helene. The kind man offered to give them a lift provided they showed him the way. Although Helene had not been home for the past two years, she remembered the way very well.

I noticed that Sylvia had changed. She was tall, very skinny and much too serious. She seemed puzzled and confused. She had forgotten Kiswahili and Luganda and spoke only English. Still holding on to Helene, Sylvia asked in a soft whisper,

"Is that tall brown lady our Mother?"

"No Sylvia, that is our big sister Mboni, Mother is the other lady there," answered Helene, pointing to Mother. Mboni was only fourteen years old.

"Oh," was all she said.

We hadn't seen each other for two years. I thought Sylvia and I would hug, hold hands and talk endlessly. But, she didn't seem to take any notice of me. We could not communicate in the same language. Mother did not know English and when Father was with us he ordinarily used Kiswahili. Most of the time Sylvia kept to herself and did not mix with the rest of the family. She was determined to separate herself and so Helene took food to her, coaxing her to eat.

It took weeks before Sylvia opened up. I tried slowly to introduce her to my ten hand-made rag-dolls I had stitched, the result of utter boredom. Thanks to the dolls, we finally renewed our friendship. I spoke to Sylvia in Kiswahili, sometimes in Luganda, and she answered me in English. By the end of the holidays, we both knew the three languages pretty well.

Not long after my sisters' arrival a disease affected all the fowls at Mengo. Sylvia and I watched Grandma's poultry die, one after the other. I picked up one chick and decided to nurse it. Sylvia brought warm water in a basin together with soap and a towel. We locked ourselves in the pantry and bathed the chick thinking perhaps dirt made it ill. After bathing it, we dried it, sprayed it with baby powder and wrapped it in a towel. Then we watched as it slowly closed its little eyes, and we thought it was asleep, but it was dead. As usual I was filled with guilt.

"I've killed it!" I cried.

Sylvia told me not to worry. She quietly and very calmly lifted the dead chick and threw it out of the window.

Meanwhile, Father had received the news of Helene and Sylvia's arrival and made a special trip from Kigezi to see us. He was very happy to see his daughters looking big and healthy and was surprised at how well they spoke English. Four huge boxes of all kinds of food, tinned and fresh, Ovaltine, Marmite, codliver oil, calcium and malt were bought.

The next day, he came again and took us shopping for new shoes, underclothes and other essentials. At school we wouldn't be in need of anything, since authority was given to the headmistress to buy whatever we might need. The nuns normally sent a stationery list, and one including not only books but personal items we might need, bath soap, washing soap, bedsheets, underwear, socks and the rest.

Towards the end of the month, the Christmas festivities were at hand. Mboni, Helene and I walked up to Namirembe Hill to get a Christmas tree. Mother had made us all dresses of unique colour and pattern. She was proud to dress us alike. It was very exciting time. Helene decided to name me Margaret and I was so called for many years to come.

A couple of days before leaving home we found a lovely stray pup. We took a great liking to it, although it was our Muslim belief that dogs were unclean animals. Unfortunately, our little friend fell ill.

"I know why he's ill," said Sylvia thoughtfully, "he is dirty . . . dirt makes one ill, you know," she explained.

Sylvia was obsessed by dirt.

"Then why don't you give it a bath?" I suggested in my smattering of English.

Tenderly we bathed the weak pup, sprinkled it with baby powder, wrapped it in a towel and put it to sleep comfortably in a box. Well he slept and never woke up. The body was quite puffed up the next morning.

"Let's throw it away," I concluded, rather sheepishly.

"No, no we shall give him a proper Christian burial," said Sylvia firmly.

And we did. Sylvia prayed, "May the soul of the faithful departed in the mercy of God, rest in peace." We then dug a little grave near the *muwafu* or incense tree, buried it and put a cross over it. Twice we had tried to save a sick animal and twice we had failed . . .

# CHAPTER SIX:
# TO SCHOOL IN KENYA

Fourth January 1956 was the most exciting day of my life. Helene, Sylvia and I were travelling together to the Holy Family Convent School in Thika, Kenya. Father had made arrangements for me to study with my sisters; how I loved my Father! There were hardly any passengers other than white pupils going to Eldoret, Nakuru, Naivasha and Nairobi. My curiosity made me aware that the train was divided into three sections. The first class was mainly for the whites. There were "All European Type" signs on their toilets and compartments. These were decorated with light colour formica walls. The flush toilets had soft tissue paper, hand towels and fragrant small bars of soap.

The second class had the "All Asian Type" signs. They were done in wood and had dark green seats which were fairly soft. The toilet, which was really a hole, was designed so that the person using it had to squat over it. If you looked through the hole you'd notice grey loose gravel. The loo paper was like tracing paper. The third class had just wooden benches. These were mostly for Africans or Asians with low income. We, of mixed race, were grouped into the second class compartments mainly used by the Asians.

Every time we tried to cross the "All European Type" compartments to get to the dining room to buy some food or have a cup of tea, the white boys would squirt water at us with their water pistols, calling us niggers or kaffirs and using very foul language. They would also stand with their hands across the passage, blocking our way. We too told them that it was very unfortunate their white men fancied our country and our black mothers.

"What are you doing here in Africa anyway, why don't you go back to England?" one English-Maasai girl asked them.

In our verbal defensive fights we called them *Kaburus* or White pigs. The journey was great fun in a way. I saw beautiful produce farms in the White Highlands, huge dairy cattle, who could hardly walk due to their heavy udders, well fed cattle for beef, lovely green coffee plantations, pyrethrum, neat luxurious colonial houses and an abundance of white people. We did not have many white people in Uganda; probably our weather was too hot for them. How thrilled I was.

As we rode along, other coloured pupils from Bungoma, Nakuru, Naivasha and Limuru got on the train. On passing Nakuru, I saw a beautiful lake which looked blurry pink. I was told it was so because of the flamingoes. This mass rose simultaneously to the sky. I smiled, utterly fascinated. I was extremely short-sighted and everything I saw was indistinct, and I believed that's how the world was. The girls boarding the train were all very curious to see what I looked like.

"Oh, Sylvia, your sister looks just like you," they all commented... "Except for the freckles."

I felt completely out of place as I understood little of what was spoken. I thought the girls were making fun of me, all the more because they giggled so much! Sylvia was a changed girl now. She acted like my big sister, introducing me to all her friends and answering questions for me. I noticed Helene and Sylvia were quite popular.

We arrived in Nairobi quite late the next evening. The nuns were at the Nairobi Station to meet us, their faces beaming with joy. They embraced each child and welcomed them back. Sylvia introduced me to the nuns.

"Do you see my sister?" she asked.

"Yes, dear, don't you two look alike!" they answered with approving smiles.

The faithful bus driver, Morote, also welcomed the girls as they entered the bus. I was introduced to him as well. He seemed an extremely devoted and patient old man. All the way to Mangu the girls were allowed to sing hymns. It was lovely to hear them singing in unison. What a happy atmosphere.

Supper was warm and waiting for us ... food, glorious food. The other pupils from Mombasa, Kisumu and Nairobi were already there. It was quite an experience for me. Everyone was hugging and jabbering. I noted that beside the white European nuns, a priest, our African cooks and workers, we were a race of our own.

A very white girl, almost albino-like, with slightly kinky blonde hair and pale blue eyes skipped past me. A couple of yards away were a number of fair girls, with European colouring, African features and curly blonde hair. In the distance, others a dark chocolate colour with Arab or Asian features with straight, silky, long black hair were linked arm-in-arm talking and laughing happily. The majority were a tanned colour with fairly straight hair which was copper, gold, brown or black in colour. Their eyes were hazel, light blue, brown or dark brown.

I felt like I had been put on another planet, a planet that had gathered the unwanted, the left-overs. I felt a sense of belonging, togetherness and security. I did not hear the word *chotara* for the next nine years.

We had two things in common, a white father and a black mother. The Seychellois were really mixed like us but did not group themselves with us. Their mothers were mixed with French, Chinese, Goan or Indian blood. The black Seychellois were called 'Mozambique'. I was to understand that the French took slaves from Mozambique to the Island. They had a home, the Seychelles Islands, a language, Creole and a faith, Catholism.

After supper, we unpacked, had a wash and went upstairs. The small girls lived on the second floor in the attic, converted into an oblong dormitory. The beds were made of single planks placed on iron rods, the mattresses stuffed with dried maize leaves. The floor was wooden, shining and smelt of fresh Cardinal floor polish. Every corner was spick and span. After we had changed into our nightdresses we knelt and prayed. Of course, I didn't participate as no word made any sense to me. I had my sisters on either side of me, earnest in prayer. I noticed that Sylvia seemed very happy and proud to have me around. A nun walked up and down the corridor until we were asleep. A dim blue light stayed on the whole night. This helped us find the bucket with disinfectant behind a white screen for our relief at night. The next morning at the sound of the bell everyone hurried out of bed and knelt for morning prayers.

"Blessed be God," said the nun.

"For all eternity," answered the whole dormitory.

Standards one to three were not obliged to attend church every day; only classes four upwards did. After prayers we put on our school uniform, a white short-sleeved shirt, a navy blue pinafore, a navy blue cardigan, white socks and black shoes. On lining up we got a pat of toothpaste from the waiting nun. We actually had a toothbrush! After tidying up, we were served with breakfast of a bowl of thick, lumpy porridge, homemade bread and butter and a tumbler of hot coffee. When attending physical education classes, we wore bloomers. These were balloon-like outfits which had elastic at the knees. The older girls wore these under a maroon pleated divided skirt which came down below the knee.

The daily order of our school duties until the end of the term was as follows:

5.45 a.m - time to wake up and go off to church;

7.00 a.m. - breakfast and morning cleaning up;

8.00 a.m. - morning classes;

9.45 a.m. - breaktime and recreation;

10.30 a.m. - back to class - more lessons;

12.05 p.m. - lunchtime and recreation;

2.00 p.m. - afternoon classes;

4.00 p.m. - tea, games and bathtime;

6.00 p.m. - dinner and recreation;

7.00 p.m. - homework;

8.00 p.m. - prayers and bedtime.

The Angelus bell was rung at noon and no matter where we were or what we were doing we'd stop dead still like statues and pray.

"The angel of the Lord declared unto Mary, and she conceived by the power of the Holy Spirit . . ."

Every Monday we assembled and saluted the British flag and sang to our gracious Queen Elizabeth II. I counted myself lucky to have an English Queen and an African King.

An older Goan girl was appointed to take care of me. Oh no, is she going to punish me? My heart sank, my happiness vanished.

How wrong I was. Every morning my fostermother saw that I brushed my teeth, she combed my hair, bathed me in a huge tin bath with hot water using a lovely smelling soap, and scrubbed my nails. Normally we were three little ones in a bath. We played with each other in the water like normal children. Then we were vigorously towel dried and dressed.

The big girls took great pride in their little girl. It was unbelievable. They watched over us when we ate, made our beds, washed our clothes and polished our shoes . . . not all big people are bad after all . .

The food was very different from what we had had at Kisubi. For breakfast there was oatmeal porridge, homemade bread and butter, jam and coffee. At break time plenty of fruit, chiefly pineapple, sometimes we had a sandwich. Lunch consisted of rice and meat or fish and plenty of potatoes, mostly mashed, vegetables and pudding. After school we had a piece of homemade cake or sandwich and tea. Supper might be macaroni, meat or shepherd's pie and pudding. Although the cooking was terrible, it was better than starving, as far as I was concerned. I appreciated my meals with gratitude.

As I mentioned before, I had missed two years of steady schooling when I joined the school. I was therefore tried in standard three with Sylvia. I was sent back and forth between standards one and two whenever an English lesson was taught. It was a great triumph on my part to actually have attained reasonable results against so many odds. The teacher, Miss Hooker, helped me build self-confidence. By the end of the year I stood ninth in a class of twenty.

End of term was always a thrill. We were going home! That first time I was very proud I could finally speak English almost fluently. I was certain Father would be pleased with me. On arriving, we all rushed to the cot to see our new two month old brother who was born while we were away. His name was John Rajab. He was gorgeous, very handsome, with lovely tanned colouring, big round eyes, a pointy nose, a small mouth and dimples! Shabaan was named Frank, probably by Helene as she knew many Christian names. Frank, and I were the only seeming 'ugly' babies born to mother. I devoted every minute of my holidays to my brothers; we played with them and took them for walks every morning. I began to play-act the teacher and mother role whilst Sylvia was always my assistant and nurse.

In the evening we often sat and watched the sky. It was always magnificently black, dotted with millions of bright stars. Every evening, thousands of fruit-bats flew in the darkening sky. Bats are ugly looking creatures that made their homes in the eucalyptus trees in the valley near Makerere College. Sometimes, while on our way to visit some of our relatives near Makerere, we would ask Grandma to stop for a few minutes near these trees. We watched the bats, screeching and quarrelling and blindly fluttering among the leaves. Grandma warned us about how dangerous these creatures were, and we believed her.

One day we found a stray bat in our back yard; it probably was hurt or ill. Sylvia said,

"We've got to kill this wicked creature . . . witches use them to do evil deeds. Do you know Meggie when Jesus, *Nabbi*, was crucified the spider wove a cobweb to protect him but the lizard and bat showed the Jews, *Yawadhi*, where Jesus was with their tongue."

This was one of Grandma's many tales. Believing Sylvia, we stretched out the wings of the miserable creature and stoned it to death.

Although this act was unlike that of most little girls, we were satisfied with ourselves for punishing the bat who deceived Jesus.

When back at school in Nairobi the nuns asked me if I would be interested in learning music. I jumped at the opportunity without a second thought. Sylvia and Helene had stopped taking music lessons due to the attitude of the teacher Miss Eileen. She was a Goan and appeared more patient and understanding with the Goan pupils than with the coloured children.

I practised devotedly, I would not give the teacher cause to slap me across the face or hit my hand backwards across the keys. I did have that treatment several times but I persevered for the next five years and obtained my practical and theoretical certificates. Sylvia decided she'd rather learn ballet with a Russian lady named Miss Sonia. Sylvia proved to be very gifted and became an outstanding dancer. She took part in *Hiawatha*, in which the ballet class performed at the National Theatre in Nairobi. Sylvia appeared in many shows and plays in school. I on the other hand was a stage-freak.

Sylvia talked endlessly about the Brownies' club. Sister Gabriel was Mother Owl. The girls nick-named her the "Owl" because she had round blue eyes. I noticed that the little girls seemed to have a lot of fun. I wanted to participate in all the school activities. I wished to wear the brown uniform and be like Sylvia. She set me an excellent example, but I was still aloof. Lack of communication was my problem. My English pronunciation was terrible and as a result I was often laughed at.

November 5th was Guy Fawkes Day, when there was a big bonfire. All the Brownies and Girl Guides prepared a surprise evening for the whole school. It was relaxing sitting out around the brilliant blazing fire in the evening while the two clubs performed for us, doing Scottish, Irish and English dances and also singing English folk songs. Finally in 1957 I was asked if I would like to join the club. Sylvia, of course, gave me all the encouragement I needed.

"Look Meggie, we go camping, have interesting outings to Thika, picnics, sometimes we go to Nairobi, we play 'treasure hunt' in the woods; it's all so exciting, you must join us."

I could not resist all these tempting opportunities. I felt exceedingly proud, learning the Brownie rules, the British National Anthem . . . "God save our Gracious Queen . . ." saluting to the British flag, and finally wearing the complete Brownie uniform! We had a lot of fun together in this club. Later we became Girl Guides. Sister Mary John was our leader. It was quite an achievement being a Girl Guide.

It was difficult to get the opportunity to join certain clubs. You had to have the personality, your class teacher had to approve your conduct. You had to have certain capabilities, to keep the school rules and be more or less a model of perfection. If you proved otherwise, you were dismissed from the club. We learnt to do a little essential cooking, mending clothes, First Aid, nursing, making beds, practically everything a woman ought to know. One thing that was always emphasised was "Give a helping hand".

That same year, Helene and Sylvia were baptised together with many other girls. I particularly noted Helene's God-mother a lovely Seychellois/Goan girl, called Rosy Pereira. A week later they received their First Holy Communion. It was a great event. Sylvia and Helene wore their lovely long hair in gorgeous curls. They were attired in immaculate lovely, flared lace dresses with long bridal veils. I almost cried because I couldn't become a Catholic until I knew my Catechism well and learnt the mass in Latin.

The little angel-like communicants sat on the front bench. The whole church was decorated with flowers and filled with the fragrance of white lilies and roses. After mass, the nuns took photographs. A huge breakfast party was prepared. It was a great day for the whole school.

Home dresses were worn instead of school uniform on such occasions. The nuns, teachers and the whole school joined in the celebrations. Every end of term was an exceptionally exciting time too. We had about one week off from real school work. Our time was spent on going over examination papers, doing corrections, recovering books and doing general tidying up. The most overwhelming time of all was when we went to the attic to get our suitcases!

We were in a frenzy. The whole school sang without fear of criticism or punishment.

"No more school,
No more work,
No more sitting on high, high benches,
Tralala Boom cia
If your teacher interferes
Box her in the ears
And throw her down
Tralala Boom Cia!"

Sylvia got hold of a group of children and conducted them while they sang. Soon the whole school joined in. Sylvia was the centre of attraction.

71

Although Helene was just two years older than I, she was a great mother to us. I don't ever remember having to do anything. Helene saw to our hair, our ironing, baths and packing things. She kept a watchful eye on us when we got onto the train from Nairobi to Kampala. The nuns gave us packed lunches, dinners and something small for breakfast. Pocket money was given to Helene to buy cups of hot tea or cold drinks, if we needed any. Helene would tell us that as soon as we went over the Jinja Bridge, at Owen Falls, we should prepare ourselves for the arrival at Kampala. Coins were thrown over the bridge into the water as a charm for good luck. We were extremely excited at the prospect of seeing our sisters and brothers. Mother was always at the station, looking as beautiful as ever. I was so proud to have such a beauty of a mother. We were usually very good for the first two weeks of our holidays, but after that mother began nagging and wishing we were back at school. And yet no-one wept more than mother when we were about to leave. Helene was just as bad! They were both in tears. Sylvia and I didn't cry that much. During this December of 1956 the New Bulange was opened.

School was my second home, maybe my first. I felt loved by my teachers. I respected the nuns and the whole school was my family. During the first week, we spent most of our time exchanging news on how we spent our holidays. There was a sort of competition over how much one had done during the holidays. We told our friends of the rock-i-show we attended and watched a live South African musical show where Mr and Mrs Ruchanga danced and we were all frenzied. It was a life time experience. Records of Miriam Makeba were played too.

Sylvia and I had done very well in the third class and we were both promoted to the fourth class. Our teacher, Miss Joyce Hooker, had begged the Headmistress to go up with us for yet another year. Sylvia's work was very good and I was catching up gradually. I was having difficulty seeing the notes on the blackboard and my teacher noticed it, but the nuns did not take her seriously when she brought the matter to their attention. I was much too tall for my age, so the teacher had a problem keeping me in the front row as the other children complained that they could not see the blackboard, as I was in their way. The teacher decided to keep me in after class. She hugged me, rubbed her forehead on mine, saying I was a very clever girl. I actually felt her brains transferring into mine. I was definitely going to be clever.

Sylvia was very confident of her academic performance, in fact she was one of the top pupils. How she did it, was anyone's guess. Sylvia was for ever out of class, training herself to play marbles, she had to perfect herself, to beat the boys at it. Being late for class was no big deal. Often she'd excuse herself in the middle of a "boring" lesson and disappear for hours. Alone in the playing field, she practised netball, batted the ball, played on the swing. In spite of her irregularity in attendance, the teachers didn't punish her.

However, I loved the nuns and the teachers in Kenya . . . they didn't inflict pain, on me anyway. Pupils were punished for a reason. A man named Kamau was employed to whip bedwetters. Had the nuns done any child psychology they would have known better than to inflict pain on such children. There were four children who never stopped wetting throughout their years in school. My soul cried out every time they were whipped with a tyre strip. The nuns believed a heavy dose of discipline administered to a child with any problem soon straightens her out.

On the other hand, when I was ill with asthma, I was kept in a clean fresh infirmary. The nuns gently nursed me and made me as comfortable as possible. They made me a warm lemon drink, rubbed my back and chest with Vicks, kept me warm, added extra pillows to ease my breathing. Grown-ups aren't really bad people after all, I assured myself. Unfortunately my happiness disappeared one morning when Mother Miriam from Kisubi visited me. I believed she was a doctor because she carried a stethoscope but she was not; nuns had to learn to cope with any emergency. My heart sank when I recognised her. Will she punish me? I was so confused.

"How come you have such a bad chest, dear?" she asked with concern.

"The nuns at Kisubi let the girls bath me in cold water. They took my sweater, socks and shoes," I blurted out, wheezing terribly, being unnecessarily defensive.

"No, my dear, nuns do not do things like that."

My mind reflected back to the time when the girls always insisted the nuns ordered them to punish us. I had been brain-washed and had believed them. But it still seemed strange to me that the nuns at Kisubi were not sensitive to the physical condition of their pupils. Thika was different, but still they did not see the need for an eye test.

The following year, 1958, we were promoted to fifth grade, but I had progressed so fast that the nuns thought I should be tried in the sixth class. When the smiling headmistress told me about my double promotion, I was down-hearted because I would be separated from

Sylvia and my friends. I went into the sixth class and crouched in the back row, my heart pounding against my chest. The Maths teacher expected me to be at the same level with the class. Algebra and Geometry were Chinese to me. Slowly but surely I slipped back to standard five. Every time Sister Mary De Lorette saw Sylvia, she'd scold,

"Margaret, I thought I promoted you to standard six. Why weren't you there when I taught Maths?" She accentuated the question.

Sylvia never said she wasn't me. This went on for some time until one day Sylvia commanded me,

"Meggie, you'd better go to standard six. I am tired of taking your scoldings for you."

"Believe you me, I'm not going up," I assured her.

The teacher finally thought it best to leave me in standard five where I preferred to be. This was one of my best years. It was cool and flowers were blossoming in plenty. I was baptised one Sunday morning by Father Lammer, a German parish priest who was a giant of a man. I did not fully trust the man. He was a German. I was told Germans killed Jews and Christians. They were Nazis. I was already brainwashed about the Germans and Russians. They were atheists and prejudice was drilled into me. In spite of this, baptism was a turning-point for me. My original sin was cleansed off my soul. The joy within me was indescribable. I no longer cared that I was ugly and skinny, that my spoken English was not good, that I was a half-caste. I was one with Christ, that's all that mattered.

The Saturday night before my baptism, Helene, poor girl, used dried maize leaves and bits of coloured strings to try to curl my straight hair. Nothing helped. Sunday morning, Sister Mary De Lorette used all the clips she could find to hold the veil, so it wouldn't fall off my slippery hair.

"Why don't you have lovely curly hair like the rest of the halfcaste girls?" I was often asked.

My clothes were second-hand, probably Helene's, but my feet were too long, the nuns hurriedly bought me a pair of white tennis shoes. I was much too tall for the group, perhaps over age too. I was therefore put at the end of the line. After this wonderful experience of receiving Christ, I prayed that no matter what the future might hold in store for us, He would never let go of us.

Being Catholics in a Muslim home could have been unbearably difficult, but we solved our problems peacefully and joyfully. In Kampala each Sunday morning we woke up at 5.45 a.m. dressed silently and crept out of the house before the family was up. We then walked to the huge Rubaga Catholic Cathedral, attended Holy Mass and were back before being missed.

Telling lies was a sin but several times we felt we had to lie, saying that we had gone for a morning walk. This we did unreservedly every holiday without upsetting our Muslim relatives. During Idd, a Muslim holiday, we dressed in our long outfits and accompanied Mother to Kibuli Mosque for the Idd celebrations. We wished our relatives *Idd Mubarak* and joined in all the Muslim celebrations. We bowed and greeted everyone, *Asalaam Aleikhum*, and we loved them. Our Arab and Baganda relatives treated us like flowers. There was always a big Catholic celebration in Uganda commemorating the death of the martyrs of Uganda. The youngest martyr, Kizito, whom we understood to be a distant cousin of ours, was put to death when he was barely fifteen years old by our great-grandfather Kabaka Mwanga II. I learnt such dreadful stories about my great-grandfather, I dared not admit he was my relative. Oh no . . . they might hang me - punish me. When we were at school we decided to seal our lips.

Sylvia wasn't in the least bit bothered.

"We have a saint relative. I'm sure he'll always protect us," said Sylvia. "How many people today can claim they have a saint relative in heaven?"

Many a time we were reminded that the family had never been followers of Christ.

"Your grandfather did not even want this foreign religion," we were reminded.

No matter, we devotedly went for our daily evening walks up to Namirembe Hill to the grand Protestant Church and said our rosary, singing "Spirit of God." There we saw the bronze tablets bearing the inscription: "To the Honoured Memory of the Martyrs Who Laid Down Their Lives for the Sake of Christ - 1885." Here under a lovely green bush we prayed. This gave us a peaceful happy inner feeling. Guilt never crossed our minds for not kneeling or praying at home. Causing disruption, arguments and unhappiness was not our intention. We were happy and only wanted peace. We would do our duty and the Muslims would do theirs. We believed that faith was spread better by good example rather than by a loud voice.

Back at school we prepared for our next religious step . . . confirmation. The Right Reverend Bishop McCarthy was to confirm us.

How I loved that Bishop. The three of us were to be confirmed the same day, in 1958. Although Sylvia told me the Bishop would slap me hard, I was not afraid. After all, it was just a slap, not torture.

Confirmation was to make us truly strong in our faith. We sang "Come Holy Spirit." The Holy Spirit was to strengthen us against temptations. We had now received four sacraments including Penance, which brought me a lot of inner peace. As usual we had a party.

"This school is heavenly!" I used to think.

During the second term of every year, we had the big feast of Corpus Christi, which was one of the most exciting feasts of the school year. Memories flooded my mind of when I almost died on this very day at Kisubi. The upper primary girls were sent a class at a time to collect hundreds of leaves and flowers. Buckets and plastic basins of all colours and sizes were used. The collection was conducted under strict supervision by a secondary girl, as the nuns were very particular about the upkeep of their gardens and did not want them needlessly destroyed. We had to break off flower petals and leaves and put them into the basin, each group doing a certain colour. Sylvia couldn't wait for this event. This meant missing at least two periods of work for almost four days. It was during this period that the bolder girls discussed what nicknames they should give the nuns and teachers.

Sister Mary John was called "Long John" because she was slim and very tall. Sister Robert was called "Bouncing Ball" because she was short and plump and seemed to bounce when she walked. Sister Aristide was called "The Saint" because she was really lovely to everyone. Sister Gabrielle had two names, "Red Tomato" or "Blinking Eyes," obviously, when angry her eyes blinked in an uncontrollable manner, her face turning a bright red. Sister Jijelle was called the "Gazelle" just a word to rhyme with her name. There was a Miss "Marble Eyes," her eye balls seemed to bulge out of their sockets. We laughed at the new names till our sides ached! I couldn't believe that having fun was permitted.

When all the flowers were sorted out into different groups, the green leaves put into different basins, an artistic nun drew all sorts of pictures on the ground depicting the events of the life of Christ and the teachers chalked in the colour they wanted to be filled in. The teachers supervised each group and everything was done faultlessly. On the Corpus Christi day we wore our white dresses, socks and shoes, in contrast to my former school where I wore a sack-like dress and no shoes.

After mass, we had a procession of prayers and hymn singing. Josephine Martin and her twin sister Marie Clare were chosen as the little angels. Both had their hair unplaited. A white Seychellois girl was usually chosen to play the blessed Virgin Mary; she had long hair the colour of gold, which flowed down to her waist when worn loose. A shimmering crown was placed on her head. Two pretty Seychellois sisters with long golden hair were the big angels placed on each side of the blessed Mother. I could imagine no hope for me to take part in such events.

Sylvia and I took a liking to a Kikuyu baby girl called Njeri. Her mother worked at the school. The baby was about six months old and was a most adorable, chubby, cuddly, infant. Every free moment we had, we would ask the young mother to let us have her baby. We played with her and carried her around with us. We decided that during the holidays, we would sew as many dresses for the baby as we could. At home, we tore up old dresses, or bought material, and made about fifteen lovely outfits of different sizes.

Back at school we surprised Njeri's mother. One afternoon, she let us hold her baby. We took the lovely, brown baby to the changing room, but there was no hot water!

"Sylvia, what shall we do now, we can't bath the baby?" I said most disappointedly.

"Of course, we can; cold water won't kill her, it probably will do her more good than all the dirt she has," said Sylvia.

As we bathed Njeri the poor child took short breaths every time we splashed water on her. After wiping her, we put cream and powder on her, combed her short, curly hair and finally dressed her in her new dress. Did she look cute! How delighted we were with our experiment. Beaming with happiness we carried out our lovely "living doll" back to her mother.

*"Ngai, rora mwana wakwa!"* "My God, look at my baby," she said.

She cuddled her baby and thanked us over and over again. We then presented her with the bundle, our dream dresses. From then onwards Njeri was always clean and well dressed. Our dream was to give our lives for the care of unfortunate children ... We would have a big house and adopt a child of every tribe in the world and they'd all grow up as our children. I wanted to protect every child from brutality.

During this period Grandma, Mboni and Ramadhani visited Zanzibar. Grandma told us that she shook hands with Queen Elizabeth who invited her to Buckingham Palace. The person who took photographs missed her shaking hands by seconds. This was in 1958 I believe. In 1981, when I was flying to the U. K. she said,

"Visit my friend Elizabeth, tell her you are my grand-daughter and she'll give you . . ."

The famous, agile, flexible, adventurous Sylvia was called when any mischief needed to be done. The whole school knew her as "the good sport." We had a big orchard at school which was fenced all around. The older girls often persuaded Sylvia to slip in through the hedge and retrieve some of the forbidden fruits. Nearly all the secondary school girls loved Sylvia because she would do anything they wanted. When caught, she was often locked up in the dark, eerie school cellar for breaking the rules. Sometimes she was scolded and smacked in front of the whole school as a punishment to humiliate her. It never worked.

"At least here you are punished after you've deliberately broken the rules," she consoled herself.

At Kisubi we had been punished for no known reason. At Thika, Sister Mary De Lorette slapped her across the face for being disrespectful during prayers and her nose began to bleed. Sylvia smeared the blood all over her face and screamed.

"Look what you've done to me. I shall tell my father!"

She could actually publicly defend herself, without fear of retaliation. Sister De Lorette dragged her away and locked her in the cellar. Helene began crying and shouting at the nun,

"You big bully, don't you see she's only a little girl!"

I just sat quietly and cried my heart out. Although Sister Mary De Lorette was quick-tempered, she had no malice and deep down she was a very soft-hearted nun. She eventually went to see Sylvia, apologised and gave her lunch. Sister Mary De Lorette had a very soft spot for us.

Shortly after this event, we went to Uganda for our usual holidays. Our vacations were spent indoors as mother and Grandma were very strict. Outings were on a regular basis. Shopping at Mengo town, mail to be collected at the Post Office and marketing at Bakuli. Whenever we stepped outdoors we heard the singsong of *Banowe*, the Norwegians. No-one dared to bother us since all the people were afraid of Grandma. She was known as *Mama Mkali*, the strict mother.

We took our little brothers for walks up Namirembe Hill. Sylvia loved talking to an old hunch-backed English gardener who lived on the hill. He looked a hundred years old, something like Shakespeare's Shylock! I never went near him, he was weird! I was even afraid to go into the magnificent Namirembe Cathedral, due to a huge statue of a bird, made of dark brown wood, perhaps representing the Holy Ghost. Although it was very artistically made, it frightened me terribly. Sylvia told me,

"Fancy these people worship this brown bird."

We were becoming like the many religious dominations who believed Catholics worshipped statues. All the same we continued our walks up the hill, visited the colourful flower gardens, and played on the soft, green well-kept lawn. Coming down Sir Albert Cook's Road after a lovely evening we passed Mwebaza House, a newly built complex privately owned by Mr. Mwebaza, rented mainly by the Asian communities. The famous echo of *chotara* was heard from adult Asian women. We did not think we were any different as we had long straight hair down our backs like any other Asian woman. Our staunch Muslim mother always emphasised silence when abused.

"Never abuse people, every human being was created by God," we were told.

But sometimes it got a little too much.

"Wait here," said Helene. "Do you remember Grandma told us the Aga Khan, their Spiritual leader, had married a white woman, a non-Muslim actress called Rita Hayworth? They too are mixed."

I loved my Grandma; she knows everything, I thought.

"Come out, you Indians," shouted Helene.

Out came a Sikh man his huge bare stomach protruding, covered with the open long beard and an abundance of hair down his back. He looked like Goliath. I was sure he'd kill us. The Indian women were peering from the windows laughing and saying obscene words, waiting to see what their colleague would do to us.

"This is our country and I'll tell our King to send you back to India," Helene threatened.

After that day we were never abused by any Indians. Rumour spread that we belonged to the Royal family; after all Mengo was basically the land of the Royal family. All the Indian shopkeepers at Mengo respected us. As years went by our neighbours befriended us and invited us for lunches; how we loved the Indian curries, rotis and chapatis.

Every evening as a ritual six of us dressed very smartly and walked to Namirembe Hill where there was a spacious lawn and played. One of our brothers, Frank, had straight blonde hair and was very fair. The Baganda people would chant,

"What a lovely *muzungu* boy", or, "I wonder where these halfcaste children got this *muzungu* baby."

What a life. When winning one battle with one race we faced another with a different race.

"This is our brother and he is not a *Mzungu*," we told them.

Mothers would marshall their children, "Come here quickly *Abazungu bajja okubilya*,the Europeans will eat you."

Sylvia was once so furious that she went up to the toddler, lifted the frightened, screeching little baby and said, "don't believe your mother, we never eat people."

She then kissed and cuddled the baby. Sylvia walked up to the mother and confronted her.

"Since when do human beings eat other human beings?"

The woman giggled and said, she was only joking.

"That's not a joke, it's fear you are putting in that child!" Sylvia responded.

We proceeded to church, though very upset to think that little African children were made to believe non-blacks were terrible people . . . I wished all people were one colour!

Most times, Mboni and Helene were too busy to join us. In any case they never seemed to enjoy the things Sylvia and I loved to do. We therefore didn't miss their company, as long as we knew they were home.

Anxiously, we went to the post office to collect our reports. Sylvia and I did well in standard five. She stood fourth and I fifth. Father was very proud of us. He hugged us and smiled warmly. My school reports had improved progressively, but I had to work very hard to be an above average pupil whereas Sylvia was at the top without much effort. The whole class was lively and bright. It included a few boys and Sylvia was usually grouped with them. A young Goan teacher called Anita Dias taught us. We almost drove her up the wall. Nonetheless, the teacher-pupil relationship was good.

In February, Josephine Martin, a twin sister of Marie Clare became ill. When we first became friends, she asked me,

"Meggie, do you mind if I call you mummy?"

Her parents had been murdered during the emergency. The six month old twins were brought to the convent by their maid and the nuns adopted them.

I told Josephine I would be delighted to be her mummy. She confided in me about a pain she had in the stomach and no matter what the nuns gave her it didn't help. She rested her head on my lap and asked me to sing to her. This went on for quite a while before she was taken to hospital. An announcement was made that Josephine was critically ill, that we should pray very hard for her. The teachers wrote to Padre Peo, a saintly priest in Italy, hoping for a miracle. Cancer was discovered. Josephine was given a couple of days to live but was miraculously discharged from the hospital. Great was the excitement.

On arrival at the school, Josephine requested to see the whole school. We assembled in the convent compound. Tears rolled down our cheeks on seeing her. She was just skin and bone! Little did I know that, later, cancer would play a role in my life as well. The nuns kept Josephine at the convent. I was privileged to visit and stay with her. Trembling she pulled up her dress and showed me the big operation scar which ran right down her stomach. On 18th April, 1959, during the holidays, I had a dream that Josephine had died, and saw the whole funeral.

At the end of April, we missed the train back to Nairobi. Helene and Sylvia were beaming with joy. I was all nervous about it. Mother had had enough of us that holiday. She booked us for the next day and sent a telegram to the nuns. When we arrived at the Nairobi Station, the nuns were a little late to collect us. Helene decided, we should quickly take a taxi to great-grandmother Nattimba who lived in Shauri Moyo in Nairobi. The old woman was very pleased to see us. She had not seen us for a considerable time. The whole neighbourhood was stirred at our arrival. Meanwhile, the nuns came to collect us as they had received the telegram from Mother informing them of our arrival. They panicked after realizing we were on the passenger list and yet not at the station. Immediately a telegram was sent to Father telling him that they believed we were lost.

After our two-week stay with great-grandmother, I timidly asked Helene if we could go back to school. Great-grandmother agreed with me. She sent for a taxi and asked one of her trusted tenants, Mr. Kamau, to escort us to Mangu. The old woman lectured us on the importance of education, but Helene was in tears on leaving. The nuns were relieved to see us although they gave us suspicious looks. We were scolded and lectured on the anxiety we caused the school. Telegrams were sent at once telling our parents we were safe and sound. This was after two weeks of absence! I wondered if our parents were worried. Did they inform the police? What about the school? Did they look for us? Did they inform the colonial authorities? We were casually told that telegrams had been sent home to both our parents, and that was that. Perhaps the school felt they had done their duty. Perhaps each parent assumed some good Samaritan would have taken us to school.

I immediately asked about Josephine and was told she had died during the April holidays.

"When?" I asked curiously.

"On 18th April," my friend said.

I wasn't alarmed as I had strong faith in God and knew Josephine had wanted me to know about her death when I was on holiday. On hearing this Sylvia was terrified. She couldn't accept the fact that people could die when still young.

Life went on as normally as could be expected . . . Something new was introduced at the school. The secondary school girls were allowed to bathe every day of the week. The primary girls had a bath three times a week - Monday, Wednesday and Saturday - but it was compulsory to have a daily wash and change of underclothes. Sylvia thought that this was very unfair.

"Why should the secondary girls have a bath every day and we can't?" she asked indignantly. "I have an idea. Why don't we have a bath every day? We can carry hot water in a big bucket and have a bath at the toilet every afternoon," she said suddenly.

I was the first person she confided in about her plan. I whispered it to Georgina and she to Jane. Soon, there were four of us in the bathing team. Everything went smoothly for a couple of weeks until Helene found out about our disobedience. She called Berit, who was only eight years old but rather bold and boisterous for her age, and commanded her to report the matter to Sister Gabrielle. The nun was shocked to hear that the four girls were having baths in front of each other in their underwear! Georgina had begun wearing a bra although she was a year younger than I. Being conscious about it she faced the wall when bathing not wanting to scandalize us who were still flat-chested.

Sister Gabrielle sent Sister Jijelle to investigate the crime. Berit had had to direct her to the exact spot! We had just begun our ritual.

"*Bien,* girls, what are you doing?" asked Sister Jijelle in her accented English. We were shocked and dumbfounded!

"Now you may go to the linen room at once, just as you are. *Allez!* You were not ashamed to bathe in front of each other, I am sure you will not be ashamed to walk in your underwear all the way to the office!"

We were stupefied! One can imagine the whole school staring at us as we walked, all laughing at us. How cruel can grown-ups be? What humiliation! I wondered where the boys were? They would have had the laugh of their lives!

"I'll fix Berit, you just wait till I lay my hands on that girl!"

muttered Sylvia.

Poor fat Georgina, was in a worse situation than we were; she had to use her arms to cover her big breasts. We, the culprits, were led to judgement and punishment. We had to bend over a stool and get caned on our behinds with the *kiboko*.

Jane, Georgina and I took our punishment with grace. At least here I knew why I was being punished. Sylvia was another story. When her turn came, she went inside the linen room to the two nuns and created havoc. Just the sight of the stick made her scream.

"Wait, wait sister, let me prepare myself," she said rubbing her bottom.

She then pushed the stool towards the nuns. Sister Jijelle tried to hold her and ended up running round and round, chasing Sylvia, both of them followed by Sister Gabrielle with a raised stick; they made quite a spectacle of themselves.

"Sylvia, you will get more punishment if you don't stop your nonsense," Sister Gabrielle shouted angrily.

"It's not fair, Sister, beating a small girl like me with a big stick. You should get a little stick!" Sylvia pretended to sob.

In the end, Sylvia came out with a flushed face. She always got very red when excited.

"I shall tell my father!" she shouted back.

We later asked her what happened and she laughed, "I wasn't hit at all. You are all stupid! You got to fight for your rights! How could the nuns punish you for trying to be clean? I fail to understand."

We were however relieved that she didn't get hurt, laughing out of relief. Sylvia, typically defiant, told us that she would continue to have a bath the next day and the day after that, but we decided against it. I don't know whether she did or not. I had made up my mind to keep the school rules. From that early age, if any girl broke a rule, no matter in what class, Sylvia would be among the culprits.

In November 1959, a flu epidemic broke out in the Mangu area. We heard the daily wailing of the Kikuyu village women over a dead child. Twice Sylvia and I ran away from school to attend one of these funerals. She told me that I should not worry about breaking the school rules because Christ had said, "Bury the dead." I was my usual nervous self.

Three quarters of the school was ill. I fought the influenza but my asthma grew worse by the day. Valerie Peters, our head-girl, was busy helping nurse the sick, in addition to organising the school activities.

She had no time to think about herself. She was one of our toughest girls in the school. The primary children loved her because she spent a lot of her time with us. She told us that she had never been ill in her life.

One Saturday morning after mass, I looked at her and I thought she didn't look well. She wore a long knitted brown and beige coloured scarf around her neck and had a slight cough. Valerie took us in for breakfast and did her usual Saturday chores. After tea, when all her work was done, I heard that Valerie was taken ill and was in bed. A group of us paid her a visit. She was her usual happy self, talking and laughing. Sylvia and I were with her for a while.

In the evening, Dr. James Winston was called. He confirmed that she had pneumonia. The whole night she was very ill with a high temperature and a cough. Early Sunday morning, she began to cough up blood. Dr. Winston was called at once and said there was no time to waste. Valerie was rushed to hospital. Sylvia, Georgina and I stood as we watched six men carry Valerie to the waiting Plymouth. Valerie, who was a Protestant, asked the nuns for a rosary. She died at Kahawa on her way to the hospital. These were two great shocks we had that year. The nuns visited the Peters and gently broke the grave news.

Our school was now called the White Sisters School, not that it was run by white women but because the congregation were clothed in white. Many people misunderstood this and thought otherwise. Each congregation of nuns had a name. The Consolata nuns, the Little Sisters of Jesus, the Sisters of Mercy and many more. 1959 was my best academic year, I finished third in the class. The teacher's favourite pupil was ninth. The teacher was shocked and went ahead to re-write the exam and made us do it again. I came ninth and her favourite student third. I was very disheartened.

We were now entering our final year in the primary school. In spite of the teachers' and nuns' strict warning about how important standard seven was, we took little notice. The class was more mischievous than ever. Sylvia was always late for classes. If the bell rang summoning everyone to class, she would always insist on finishing the game she was playing. With Sylvia, sports took precedence over studies. She had to finish the game and just hoped there would be enough time for academic pursuits. Her apparent stubbornness should have been strictly dealt with; but the only punishment open to the nuns, short of expulsion, was confinement, which proved ineffective. Her misdeeds were best described as selfish gaiety, the thoughtlessness of unbridled youth, the wish to be happy anywhere, regardless of the consequences. She was a being upon whom the "shadow of the world had not yet fallen." I often waved to her in detention and she would wave back happily.

Although standard seven was hard work, it made no difference to Sylvia whatsoever. When she came late for classes she gave such funny senseless excuses that the whole class laughed. More often than not, the teacher laughed too. Eventually, as she walked into the class late, the teacher would say,

"Don't bother giving me your excuses, just sit down."

Sylvia would smile and sit. Little did the teachers know that's what she wanted. She knew that the nuns and teachers would not punish her. If she did not have anyone else with enough nerve to help her disregard a few school rules, she would do so alone, but her influence was such that there was usually someone to share her prerogative of defiance.

Sylvia soon found a new friend about her age called Penny, who was a little on the plump side. Sylvia played all sorts of tricks on this girl. She would ask Penny to climb through the window of a locked classroom to retrieve something or other. It was always a safe bet that, owing to her size, the poor girl would get stuck! Sylvia would try to push Penny through the window while laughing hilariously. The two became the greatest of friends for a long time. They perpetrated many hilarious frolics. If there ever lived a tomboy, it was Sylvia. The classroom, church, dining hall, playing fields were all the same to her, arenas of merriment and of youthful exuberance, which the school authorities found completely irrepressible.

In contrast, I was friendly with Georgina. Although she was a year younger, she nursed and cared for me whenever I had an asthma attack. She was extremely motherly.

That year we had three teachers. Sister Aristide taught Religious Education and English, Sister Mary De Lorette took over the class when we got out of control and Miss Alice De Souza taught quite a number of subjects, being our regular class teacher. We had a few boys in the class, the most outstanding characters being George Cardovilles and Peter Brown. The latter was a born clown and would send us into gales of laughter till our sides ached. Peter was always being told to stand in the waste paper basket. Every time the teacher turned her face away from the class, Peter would start clowning behind her back, distracting the class. If Miss Alice turned back he would put on an appearance of innocence. But the teacher was suspicious and she put him out of class. God help you if the headmistress saw you out of the class, you would go to the office and write endless pages of Marion Richardson. That however did not stop us from cooking up some new entertainment.

Once we found a porcupine and we put it on the chair of the new teacher, Miss De Mello, nicknamed "Marshmallow." The class really played her up, she sometimes, burst into tears! Just as she was about to sit down, we in pity for the porcupine, shouted, "Don't!" We were detained for two days.

The nuns had a little store where the unripe pineapples were kept. Practically every day, we were given a sufficient piece of pineapple. But because there was a great quantity of the juicy fruits lying in the store for nothing, as Sylvia put it, she, together with some of her friends, decided to have a couple.

Sylvia slid through the narrow opening at the top of the store room and landed on top of the fruit. She began to throw pineapples out to her waiting friends . . .

"How many more do you want?" shouted Sylvia from the dark room.

There was no answer. On noticing Sister Jijelle spying, the whole gang took off, leaving Sylvia without warning. It was quite funny seeing the pineapples falling out of the store and hearing a voice while the nun watched in amazement! Finally Sister Jijelle opened the store door and got the rascal out. Sylvia was asked to name all the girls who had asked her to throw the fruit to them.

"No-one asked me, I just felt like throwing them over," she lied. "I wanted to see if I could make a good netball scorer," she continued, staring at the nun with her eyes full of candour.

"Sylvia, it's not good to lie, now own up," said Sister Jijelle calmly.

"O. K. Sister," agreed Sylvia and gave the names of all the girls which was quite a big gang! Apparently, one of their friends, J. J., had told on them.

Well, some of the girls were locked in the cellar, some in the ironing room, and some in the suitcase room. Every morning the ill-behaved girls had to remove their shoes and use a *panga*, a large working knife, to dig a little patch in the coffee plantation. Some of them had to gather coffee beans. I was worried sick about Sylvia, but her best friend Edna told me not to worry, that they were fine. She assured me that she would look after Sylvia.

Sylvia, on the other hand, said she enjoyed working in the coffee plantation, but she found digging with a *panga* more difficult than using *enkumbi*, a hoe. She always found a philosophical way to accept school punishment.

When the K. P. E., Kenya Primary Examination, as it was known in those days started, we were smartly dressed, all anxious and nervous. The whole examination took a week and a half to complete.

I did not do very well but Sylvia got a second grade. Most of our classmates left either because they did not make the grade for secondary school or they were judged too old. The nuns opened a commercial class for some of these girls and others joined a nurses' training course. Helene had already gone back to Kampala to study nursing.

# CHAPTER SEVEN:
# SECONDARY SCHOOL

About ten of us went on to the secondary school. This year we had an intake of well-behaved girls, who all had a normal childhood and were now old enough to be away from home. They were unlike the rest of us who had been sent to boarding schools at the ages of five or six. The classrooms usually did not contain more than twenty-five girls. We found a whole new life when we joined the secondary school in 1961.

We were supposedly more mature. Childishness was no longer accepted by the nuns, even to the small extent that it ever was. The uniform was different; it consisted of a navy-blue pleated skirt, a blazer, a white shirt, a navy-blue tie, black shoes, white socks and a hat to top it all. Our hats and blazers, ordered from England, were only used on Sundays and big occasions or when we went to the city of Nairobi. Otherwise, we wore navy-blue knitted caps for church and navy-blue cardigans.

We were totally dependent upon ourselves, doing our own washing, shoe-polishing, keeping our lockers and personal belongings tidy, ironing, using flat solid irons heated over a furnace, with padded cloths to hold them. We would change to a hot one when the first got cold. A South Indian girl, Priscilla Jerome, was almost killed when her long hair got tangled in the generator. Someone rushed for a pair of scissors and chopped off a chunk of hair to save her. Each student was assigned to a certain chore, cleaning the headmistress's office, classrooms, corridors or the rest of the school. The secondary classes were known as forms whereas the primary classes were called standards. The church-going days were reduced to three a week. How grateful

Sylvia was for four days of longer sleep in the morning. I was elected the class prefect. It certainly wasn't easy having a sister like mine in the same class! When she came late for class or for the homework period she'd kiss me, tell me that she was my little sister and was sure I wouldn't write down her name, making sure the whole class was listening, and they all supported her! Our regular class teacher, Sister Aristide, was very fond of Sylvia and me; we liked her too. During the year, Sylvia and I dropped History, and took French as a preference. Oddly enough, both subjects were taught at the same period by the subject teachers. Otherwise, I had a great interest in history and would read my friends' text books. Sylvia debated with the class that they need not speak French, just learn a French song and put a real French accent into it when singing. Sister Jijelle taught us,

"*Au Clair de la Lune;*
*Mon Ami Pierrot,*
*Prete moi ta plume,*
*Pour e'crire un mot.*"

Not many girls were interested in the French, especially after learning about the French Revolution and reading *The Tale of Two Cities, by Charles Dickens.*

At this period Sylvia grew at a rapid pace. Her physique was much larger, heavier and taller than mine, she weighed about 132 pounds and was an extremely strong girl. Sylvia, always the extrovert and not afraid of the limelight, was chosen to star in the dramatization of the books studied in English Literature. We had to study Shakespeare, and memorize speeches and poems in addition to the New Testament verses.

"You see, even Shakespeare wrote about me," she joked as she dramatized "To Sylvia let us sing" in front of the class.

How she managed to learn her lines in such short periods was beyond me. In all those years that we had been intimate, I never saw Sylvia with a book. However, she was almost always at the top of the class.

Our prep period was from six thirty to eight thirty. One of the new subjects was sewing. Sister Aristide taught us needle-work, at which she was an expert. We sewed school bags which we later used as our personal bags. One evening Wendy decided to show us what a Giriama woman, a tribe from the coastal area, looked like. Most of us had never seen one! Wendy put the book-filled bag under her skirt and pulled the strings over her shoulder and merrily danced away in the class. How we laughed ... Sylvia kept encouraging her to go on dancing. Jane was strategically placed to give warning if the nun on duty came up. The poor girl was in hysterics when Sister Mary de Lorette suddenly appeared. As soon as we sensed her presence, we bent over our books, pretending to be hard at work but we could not stop giggling as Wendy's false behind was still protruding.

"Right girls, what's so funny?" asked the nun.

There was no answer. Wendy and Alice continued laughing.

"Stand up Wendy, perhaps you can explain what's so amusing," commanded the angry nun.

When Wendy stood up, behold, there was her protruding behind! The laughter began all over again.

"Downstairs to my office!" ordered the furious nun.

"Yes Sister, just let me get this bag down," she responded.

Wendy went down the spiral staircase for her punishment. She was made to kneel downstairs until we assembled for our night prayers, after which we quietly went to bed.

Two weeks later, during one of our evening study periods, a girl gave a loud yawn, a sign of boredom, undoubtedly. The odd sound startled all of us. What followed was unexpected. We screamed and because of this a general panic went through all the other classrooms. Pandemonium broke loose and soon everyone was running wildly for the steel spiral staircase. No-one had stopped to find out what had actually happened. Only the unsuspecting girl who had emitted that yawn enjoyed the results. The commotion was so great that it brought out not only the nuns and other teaching staff, but manual workers as well. They came running from all directions with *rungus*, clubs, *simis*, knives and anything else they could lay their hands on. When we were asked what made us run and scream no-one had any explanation. Despite all the subsequent inquiries it was never resolved what caused that furore. The nuns did not scold us, but only spoke soothingly to the school and assured us that no harm would ever come to us.

"See, even all the staff came because they care for you!" the nuns told us.

They also pointed out that, in the case of any emergency, the school possessed a siren which could be heard as far away as Thika. At these words, we calmed down, said our night prayers, and finally went to bed.

Yet one day, again during the study period, the big shed used in the playing area collapsed. The sound and tremor sounded like an earthquake. We ran like the wind, screaming at the tops of our voices. Sylvia was never seen during these events. She always took off like a deer. She probably was the first to reach the boarding block, all in a matter of seconds. I was surprised to see what people could do when they panicked. Big fat Maria picked up two girls in each arm and ran, shouting at me, "Run for your life!" Some girls fainted and more fell over them. That particular evening many girls hurt themselves. What a stampede! Again we were spoken to, many girls were nursed and bandaged. We prayed and went to bed.

It was at this period that I decided to write down my experiences at Kisubi. We had just read the book *"The Story of my Life,"* by Helen Keller, a blind, deaf and dumb woman. I was mesmerised. If a woman with such disabilities could do it, why couldn't I?. Sister Mary de Lorette found the hard cover black exercise book with all the information, hidden at the bottom of my desk.

"Miss Bjordal, I'd like to see you in my office," she said calmly. "I have read your story, it's very interesting. But leave the nuns out of it. We are people of God and I doubt we were responsible for your suffering."

Responsible? Responsible? It was their school they never checked on us . . . the lice eating me alive . . . it must have taken months for them to cause sores . . . who was responsible for me . . . the school wasn't, my parents weren't . . . let bygones be bygones?

"Yes, Sister."

I took my book and put it back in my desk. The following Sunday I was down with my usual colds and asthma. This made me very unpopular with the girls as most of the students were very healthy and active. I had a feeling of loneliness like one left behind on a strange shore. Sylvia felt she had to let me know when she was about to break a rule.

"Meggie, a group of us are going to hijack a country bus and go to Thika," she said, smiling mischievously as always.

"Really?" I responded, not believing a word she said.

"Actually, we are not really going to hijack the bus, but we are going to board one," she giggled.

"Do you have money for the bus fare?" I asked her, rather worried.

"Yes, yes of course we have the money. We are planning to go to the woods where we shall dress up, lipstick and all. No-one will recognise us once we've changed ourselves," she explained, her face animated.

There was nothing I could do to change her mind. I thought to myself that although discipline is good for the soul, the heart wants freedom. In any case, I felt too weak to argue. I sat and read *Kidnapped* by R. L.Stevenson.

As I was buried in thought, I saw a gang which consisted of a form three girl, Maria, some form one girls and little Berit, who was in standard five. I watched them as they approached the gate, talking excitedly, half walking, half running. One of the girls held a bag which was packed to capacity with clothing, shoes and make-up. They jumped over the gate and disappeared through the coffee plantation. I thought Berit looked out of place as she was much too young. The girls were away for a good two hours. They planned to return at 3.30 p.m. knowing that tea was served at four.

Sister Jijelle was on duty that particular Sunday aftenoon. It was unusually quiet without the gang around. Sister Jijelle was walking with a standard one girl and I distinctly heard her say,

"Sister, the big girls can jump over the gate," pointing at the gate. "Really, have you ever seen big girls jump over that gate?" Sister Jijelle asked most curiously.

Oh yes, Sister, I saw them today. One by one, they jumped over there."

"How many did you see?" asked Sister.

"Six," lisped the little girl.

I began having palpitations. Not too long after that Sylvia and her friends came back after having had a really smashing time. Sister Jijelle had gone up to the attic to watch for them. She probably had spyglasses. As she spied them coming back, she rushed towards the gate to meet them. Although they were in complete uniform, the suspicious nun opened their bag and found shorts, high-heeled shoes, make-up and a camera. Sister Jijelle marched the "rascals" to the Headmistress, who gave them one week's detention! Sylvia begged me not to worry about her as she had had a really lovely time. I later learnt that they did not go to Thika at all but were only taking photographs in the wood, in shorts and bathing costumes.

"It was worth the punishment!" she assured me.

Defiance was an achievement. Thereafter life went on as normally as possible. It was at this period of 1961 that Prince Henry Kimera proposed to Mboni. The two fell in love the very first time they met at home when he visited us. Not religion, family taboo, or age difference could keep them apart. On their honeymoon, they went to Mombasa. Mutesa too visited Mombasa. Henry met the khadi and many Muslim leaders who converted him to a Muslim. Mboni gave him the name Rashid. Hundreds upon hundreds of Muslim nominations attended the ceremony and the story appeared in the newspapers. The Headmistress, who had obviously read the papers, approached me and commented on how wicked Mboni was changing a Christian man into a Muslim. As far as I was concerned their marriage was heaven made.

In 1962, after a lot of persuasion, Sylvia joined The Legion of Mary, as the Girl Guides Association ceased when Sister Mary John left for England. This organisation was started in Kenya by Edel Quin in 1947. The aim of the club was to train oneself to be more kind, charitable and more pure in all that one did. We were to follow the example of the Mother of Christ, Mary. The Magnificat was our daily prayer:

"My soul proclaims the greatness of the Lord
My spirit rejoices in God my Saviour . . .
He shows Mercy to those who fear Him
He has lifted up the lowly . . .
He has filled the hungry . . ."

The prayer filled us with love and kindness for the poor, the hungry, the sick, orphans and all unfortunates. Our former standard seven teacher, Miss Alice De Souza, who ran the club, later joined the convent and became a White Sister. How I cried. She was so beautiful, had lovely dresses and shoes like Cinderella. Miss Almeida, another of my favourite teachers, then took over the club.

We learnt all sorts of things in this club, meticulously laid out the priest's garments for mass, cleaned the altar, arranged flowers, helped the teachers with different chores, played with the small children, visited the sick and mended torn clothes. Sylvia and I usually chose the same duties each week. The little jobs given to us took a little more than ten minutes every day. Surprisingly, Sylvia took her Legion of Mary meeting seriously. Once every first term we went on a three day retreat, that is complete silence, meditation and prayers. Sylvia was a totally different character at these times, serious and devoted to all the religious duties.

The last Saturday of school, there was our once-a-term outing. This term we visited a student's home in Ruaraka. The family took us across some waterfalls to a large dam surrounded by rocks. What fun we had jumping over stones and getting ourselves wet. Dorothy Wilson informed us of a short cut, but wasn't sure whether or not it was safe to

93

cross over the rocks.

I volunteered to be the first to try to cross; this shocked all my friends. Sylvia stood by me smiling with encouragement. Everyone was surprised that she was not the first to cross. Normally she was the leader. That particular Saturday, I took a Saint's medallion and put it inside my bra as protection, praying, "Do take care of me today."

As I crossed the rocks my friends, with the exception of Sylvia, stood at a distance and watched. I carefully stepped on the first and second rock. But when I put my foot on the third rock, down with it I went! Not having any idea about swimming. I remained in an upright position, then sank to the bottom where the water was much cooler and darker. All the while I kept my eyes open as I watched the water suck me to the bottom . . . it looked like a transparent wall. I was very calm indeed; automatically I was drawn up. I took a breath, then down I went again. I never swallowed any water. I remembered tales of drowned people with bloated stomachs. I didn't want to die like that.

At this point, Miss Almeida, our chaperone, told the group to get down on their knees and ask the Blessed Virgin Mary for her help as we belonged to her. The group was instructed to keep away from me as I might pull down anyone who tried to save me. They said the rosary most fervently.

"Meggie is my sister . . . I'm going to help her!" cried Sylvia.

She began moving towards me. No-one else tried to run for help or throw me a stick or do anything to assist me, but my sister did. As I came up a second time I remembered my medallion and thought,

"Jesus, did you bring me here to take me away?"

I was sure I'd drown yet I was very calm. Again I sank to the bottom. My mind was aware of my sister being close by. As I came up a third time, Sylvia screamed frantically,

"Meggie, give me your hand!"

And I did. Sylvia's strong grip saved me! She pulled me out miserable as a wet chicken.

"Sylvia, you saved my life . . .! I shall never forget it!"

We hugged, kissed and held each other close for a while as I wept. Sylvia realised I was crying and immediately made fun of me.

"You were something else Meggie," she said. "How ridiculous you looked when drowning. The only thing that I could see every time you came up were your glasses! Don't you know what you must do when you are drowning? You should float not stand upright, silly."

Mr. and Mrs. Wilson gave me a change of clothes, later we had our picnic. After quite a memorable trip, we went back to the school, exhausted. I felt grateful I was alive.

After this incident, the nuns thought it was wise for us to learn to swim. We had never dreamt of wearing a swim suit or swimming, but when given the opportunity we took it without a second thought. Once a week we were taken to the Blue Posts Hotel, Thika for our swimming lesson and taught by Miss Rogers and a former pupil, Miss Jennings. Sylvia learnt rapidly. I didn't, in spite of, or perhaps because of, my near drowning episode.

During this period, Mr. Jennings was one of the outstanding drivers in the Coronation Safari. How proud we were, he was the father of our classmate Joan. The Wood family's father, Mr. Babu Wood, was a minister in the government. Miss Jennings was one of the first, non-white Kenyan women to join the Royal College, now the Nairobi University.

I must admit, we had very devoted teachers who did their utmost to make our lessons interesting; all except our Asian Geography teacher who came from Thika. As soon as we settled, eager for the lesson, we were instructed to read certain chapters in the text and make notes while she sat busily knitting away! As always, some bright star found a solution. She suggested we copy the text word-for-word in hope that the Headmistress would find out what was amiss when our books were sent to the office for weekly check-up. The headmistress quickly realised what was happening, sacked the Geography teacher and took over the lesson herself.

Sister Mary de Lorette was due to retire, she introduced our new Headmistress, Sister Maureen, whom the girls nicknamed 'Quack-quack,' obviously due to her nagging. She was unpopular with practically the whole school.

The Headmistress changed the school's name to Maryhill. Mary after the Mother of Jesus and Hill as it was on a hill. Every Sunday evening, the nuns organised some entertainment. After much pleading with the Headmistress we were actually shown a movie, had a debate, a quiz, a short play or a social evening. We loved that one! Permission was granted to bring all the rock-n-roll, twist and jiving music. We had a record player for the entire day and danced to our heart's content!

One Sunday night, Doris, who was given the responsibility of returning the record-player to the nuns, was persuaded by friends to keep it for the midnight feast. Doris, one of Sylvia's favourite friends, was given all the encouragement needed. Much as I would have loved to join them I had to refrain, being the class prefect. It wasn't a privilege but an obstacle. The nun on duty did her usual parade up and down the dormitories for an hour reassuring herself that everyone was asleep, and finally went to bed. Unknown to her, dormitory ten remained awake as they excitedly awaited the nocturnal get-together.

After Sylvia and her friends were positive that the nuns had gone to bed, Doris switched on the record-player. Out jumped the excited girls from their beds and began to rock-and-roll, twist and madison. I lay in bed wheezing, nervous just in case I'd be held responsible for this outrageous behaviour. Suddenly, the door swung open. Into their beds jumped the girls, giggling away. Doris had no time to switch off the gramophone but spontaneously threw her pillow over the machine. It sounded like a drunken man humming out of tune. Sister Jijelle switched on the light, looking very suspicious.

"What's going on in this dormitory?" she asked angrily.

"Who is making that funny sound?" she was walking towards the sound.

"Stop it at once!" stormed the angry nun, but the weird noise continued.

In no time at all she found the record player. Doris, Sylvia and those who had been dancing were made to kneel for half an hour outside the infirmary.

Before long, the Princess of Toro, Mabel, a third former, joined the school. We all stared at this six foot tall, majestic-looking girl. We gathered for an assembly and were introduced to the Princess, daughter of the Omukama, King of Toro. She had an exquisitely beautiful sister Elizabeth who was to become an actress in the movie *Sheena* years later. Her brother Patrick, whom Mabel brought home when she visited us, was to become the Omukama, King of Toro in 1993.

"We've had four Princesses in the school and I am sure none of you have been aware of it," the Headmistress said.

The whole school gasped, "Four Princesses!"

"Yes, dears, they too come from Uganda."

Sylvia laughed and said, "Meggie, the nuns mean us. They think we are Princesses and we are not. I wonder what you'd call a *Kiwewesi* in English . . . I should explain it to them. *Kiwewesi* means a grand-daughter of a princess."

The Princess called the three of us together with some other girls from Uganda assuring us that she was going to cook *matoke*, a Baganda dish of cooked green bananas. We had a saucepan and heaven knows how Princess Mabel came to have a bunch of *matoke* bananas. She instructed us to save all our meat at suppertime. Sylvia filled her long plastic-lined pocket with all of the cooked meat she could lay her hands on. There were no restrictions as to when one could leave the dining hall. Knowing what was in store for us we were filled with anticipation. Wood had been kept ready together with three big stones upon which the cooking pot would be placed, not forgetting a box of matches and papers to start the fire.

The Princess had begged for some onions, tomatoes and butter from the kitchen. Cautiously we crowded into a little bathroom busily getting on with the cooking. The stew smell wafted all the way to the linen room where Sister Gabrielle sat busy sewing. Her nostrils picked up the delicious smell, followed it and caught us red-handed in the bathroom just as we were about to start our lovely dinner! We were detained, watching as the saucepan was taken to the convent. The nuns probably had a feast of it, and I am sure a good laugh too. The rest of the school consoled us,

"Bad luck girls, try again another time."

There was much unity in the secondary school. No-one ever gave anyone else away when they knew there was some mischief cooking. At the end of the term Mabel joined us on the train to Uganda.

Having had a good break, we were determined to work really hard; especially me. Third term was my best. Sylvia was chosen to be in every play the school performed. Although she was outstanding academically, she still managed to be caught breaking one rule or another. When rebuked for disobedience she'd defend herself,

"But I didn't hear the bell . . . You don't expect me to be distracted when reading an interesting book?"

She was always prepared when questioned, and would put on a very serious face when defending herself. Some of her excuses were unrealistic yet hilarious, sending the school into uproars of laughter.

"What are you laughing at? I didn't ask you to laugh. What's so funny?"

Our country was liberated from colonial protection on 8th October, 1962. I wondered how Great Britain gave us independence when we were always independent! Uganda had never been a "settler colony." Europeans were not allowed to buy land there. And in spite of the deportations we have already mentioned, traditional forms of government had been preserved. The school was given the weekend off. As it was just a mid-term, we were unable to make it home for the celebrations. The nuns kindly organised a party for us. Mother had sent us a considerable parcel from home; cookies, biscuits, three pink dresses with *Kabaka Yekka* printed on them, shoes, socks, little flags with red, black and yellow stripes and a crested crane at the centre.

In Uganda it was a very big day, mother wrote. The Duke of Kent represented the Queen and gave a speech to the Lukiiko. Grandma, Mother, Aunt Nuru, Mboni and her husband Prince Henry attended a garden party at the Palace. The celebrations went on unabated for weeks on end. How we missed home. Our six-month-old nephew, Prince Daudi, was the centre of attention at all the parties. Great grandma Nattimba, now seventy-seven, rejoiced at home in Mengo. No more colonial comments on us occurred after this when we travelled on the trains.

It was now 1963, the first week of form three. A lecture was given on the importance of every lesson that we were taught. Anything might come up in the Cambridge School Certificate examination. We had a different teacher for almost every subject, unlike the primary school. Sister Jijelle continued teaching us French, Sister Aristide taught Religion, Sister Robert was our Mathematician, and Sister Gaitan taught Art. Sister Gaitan was so determined that practically the whole class became artists. We did a lot of outdoor, still-life and composition paintings. Sometimes she narrated a story and asked us to choose the part which appealed to us most and paint it. This was one subject Sylvia was serious about and she produced excellent work. Her poetry, literature and drama were tops. She talked about becoming a poet and began to laboriously compose short poems, especially when she was bored with lessons like Geography, Religious Knowledge and Church History.

Newspapers were put on a stand for our interest. This was something out of our world. We all crowded to read what was new in the "outer" world as the nuns called it. Martin Luther King led a non-violent march in 1963, blacks confronting whites. We read how terrible the whites were to the blacks. No wonder my great-grandfather Mwanga did not accept foreigners; they would have made the Baganda slaves as they did the West Africans. There was a picture of Black Americans who marched from the South to Washington led by Martin Luther King. Jesse Jackson was in the limelight too. They were fighting for equal rights.

We read that our King, Sir Edward Mutesa II, was made the constitutional President of Uganda. Pictures of the Prime Minister, Milton Obote and the Kabaka were put up everywhere, even in the dining car on the train. Oh yes, we had a Prime Minister, just like the

British. I wondered why he wasn't called the *Katikiiro* like before. Anyway Obote was a foreigner to every Muganda.

## THE MEANING OF LIFE

When I sit myself down and think,
I think that life could be better and I blink.
Yes, we can make it Heaven here on earth,
Where there is hate and dirt.
Love is something that is difficult today,
But learning to love God can make it gay.
With the disappointment of by-gone days,
Every heart-break, every laughter had had its way,.
To make the experience a loving or bitter memory,
Each one being part of our learning tree,
Let's make it Heaven while we can.
Living day by day with no real plan,
Step by step we discover the beauty of living.
Being together, understanding, but most of all giving
By doing so, there is so much to achieve
So let's live
Let's give.

### SYLVIA, 1963

Sylvia seemed utterly bored on Sundays. After some hard thought she persuaded her dare-devil friends, chiefly J. J. and Elvira, to get away from school and have some adventure.

"Why don't we go across to the Kalimino Falls, or over to Mr. Mariani's house? Let's do something exciting instead of hanging about school!" Sylvia said.

Mr. Mariani was the school's former Italian manager and was now managing a nearby farm. He was also J. J.'s godfather and they knew he'd be pleased to see his god-child.

At the farm, the old man was indeed pleased to see them. When sitting in his lovely lounge, they were offered sandwiches and cold drinks. Sylvia noticed some big barrels and asked Mr. Mariani what they were for. He explained that he stored his wine in them, that in Italy there were thousands of vineyards of pale green and purple berries growing in clusters on the vines. Hundreds of villagers gather grapes in baskets, and take them to the presses where the juice is extracted for wine. This is stored in big barrels; the longer you keep it the better the taste.

"Can we have just a little please, Mr. Mariani?" she pleaded.

"Sure, sure, but not too much," he answered in his strong Italian accent.

Well, the girls drank quite a bit of the lovely sweet wine. After having their fill, they decided to return to school. The girls seemed all right till they reached school; then the wine began to take effect. I was just about taking the school in for supper. In walked the group laughing, giggling and really acting oddly. After supper, I asked quite sternly,             "What is the matter with you, Sylvia? Why are you giggling so much?"

Before I could blink, Sylvia's hand smacked me hard across my face, which cost me a stiff neck for almost three days! I was astounded. Sylvia had never as much as pushed me! I was now convinced something was definitely wrong, but I couldn't figure it out. We stood staring at each other, both shaken out of our complacency. Suddenly, Berit appeared.

"How dare you smack Meggie?" she screamed.

She could be as rough as Sylvia when occasion demanded. Berit chased Sylvia around the school block. When she caught up with her, she had a bucket of cold water, which she threw at Sylvia to sober her up. Sylvia tried to fight her sister back but staggered. Berit got hold of Sylvia by the hair and pushed her face into the gutter. Sylvia's face was covered with mud, and she was absolutely furious and quite breathless.

The entire school was excited and completely out of control, screaming and laughing. Being the class prefect, I had to act quickly to control them before the Headmistress found out. Sylvia had gone berserk! Unfortunately, the nuns heard all the din and commotion and came to find out the cause. They took the girls in for questioning. J. J. and Elvira were so drunk that they were immediately put to bed. The other girls told the nuns that they had eaten some nuts! The staff were puzzled and worried, thinking perhaps the girls had eaten poisonous nuts. The girls were immediately rushed thirty-five miles to King George's Hospital, now Kenyatta National Hospital. Here they were met by a very kind, understanding African doctor. He cautiously questioned them and they told him the truth. The doctor promised that he wouldn't tell the nuns their secret but that they should never take any alcohol or wine ever. He instructed the nuns to give them an aspirin every four hours and was sure the girls would be all right.

In any event, the girls were detained for a week. J. J. and Elvira were in complete isolation for two weeks under strict supervision. How did the girls spend their time? They were given old fabrics from which they had to remove the sequins and coloured beads.

"These must have been dresses of the 1920's," one of the girls speculated, "perhaps the nuns had worn them before joining the convent." Giggles followed.

I felt miserable not seeing Sylvia for a whole week. We had no idea what they went through until they were released from detention.

"You know Meggie, we were given an old spinning wheel and we had to spin thread just like in the story of Rumpelstiltskin. Can you imagine that? Sometimes we cleaned windows, polished floors, mended socks and other stuff," she told me.

"Did you get anything to eat?" I inquired of her.

As a child I had suffered from hunger pangs and I was obsessed about food.

"Yes, bread and water."

Unfortunately, this time they were in complete isolation and we couldn't get sandwiches to them. There was calm in the school after this drama. We sat our termly exams, packed and went to Uganda for our holidays.

## HOPE

Oh rain washing away the dust,
God's rain wash away the painful past.
A new day born to let me try again,
Give me joy and take away the pain.
Laughter ringing in my ears,
Singing joy throughout the years.
Wishing for others just like me,
So sorrows you, from us flee.
Bringing love and laughter day by day,
So with us always say you'll stay.

**Sylvia Bjordal, 1963**

# CHAPTER EIGHT:
## HOLIDAY TIMES

Kampala is built on seven hills, like Rome, I was told by some Italian nuns. Kampala Hill is one of our favourite spots for evening walks. We are extremely proud of Makerere Hill, where the first university in East Africa is located, and to the west is Rubaga Hill which bears our Roman Catholic Cathedral founded by the French Missionaries of the White Fathers' Order. The Catholic Cathedral is artistically painted with scenes of the martyrdom of the first Catholic converts, who in 1886 had been put to death by our great-grandfather Kabaka Basammula Mwanga II.

Namirembe Hill is another of our favourites. Here stands an ancient looking copper-domed Anglican Cathedral. The cemetery holds history; here we visited the grave of Bishop Hannington who died in 1885, Alexander MacKay, the Scottish Calvinist who was a printer and mechanical engineer and died in 1890, Captain Raymond Portal who died in 1893 (Fort Portal, a town in Toro, was named after him) and Sir Albert Cook, the pioneer doctor who died in 1951. We noted all these historical events down into our notebooks for future reference.

The Nakasero Hill has the shopping centres chiefly owned by Hindus, Pakistanis, Madrasis, and a few Sikhs. The few Goans we had were school administrators, doctors, lecturers, officers; on the whole they did the white-collared jobs. Their wives and daughters were mostly teachers or nurses. Practically all our tailors were Asians. Many Hindus in their dhotis and white caps built Kampala and practically all the beautiful buildings in Kololo Hill. The Sikhs, *mistris,* as they were known, seemed to be supervisors in big constructions in Kampala and Mengo. Most of our doctors, dentists, opticians were white people from

102

different parts of Europe and England.

Kololo Hill is a beautiful suburb, site of the homes of diplomats and well-to-do Africans, Europeans and Asians. From here we viewed the whole city. We seemed to be on a cloud watching the city lights like stars. Kibuli Hill holds the famous Muslim Mosque. This is where we prayed during the big Muslim feast of *Idd-El-Fitr*.

We had only one community teenage club in Kampala, on Mayembe Hill, organised by the Khoja, and girls had to be escorted by an older brother, cousin or relative. We wore our can-can knee-length dresses, the boys were in suits and ties. No drinks were served, no smoking was permitted. No slow music played, only rock-and-roll, jiving. Elvis Prestley and Cliff Richard songs were sung by a famous Asian/European boy Warren McMohan. Abroad young people had gone on drugs and nudity, and punk styles were introduced.

This was a period when the whole world was frenzied and rebellious about inner freedom, a sense of belonging, loving and peace. These were expressed in music, speech and the way of dressing, wild hairstyles, colours, very strong eye make-up. Pop stars sent everyone crazy especially Elvis Presley, Cliff Richard, Ricky Nelson, the Beatles, the Monkeys and many more. Many young stars who had made it big died tragically due to drugs or motor accidents after wild parties.

Much as we called our parents "squares" they were very aware of what was happening abroad. This made them over-protective to the extent of being almost cruel. The nuns had emphasised that pop-music was the devil's work. Some of our parents forbade make-up until marriage. No going to hair-dressers, that was vanity. Mini-skirts were in fashion, but that showed indecency, no morals. The nuns' restrictions coincided with our own Baganda up-bringing. We found this acceptable without much rebellion. In Buganda no teenager was allowed into dance halls. Movies were strictly censored. The early three o'clock and six o'clock shows were the ones open for children.

When going into Kampala we avoided wearing high-heeled shoes due to the hills. But not so Sylvia, no matter how agonizing it was.

"Father said he likes to see a lady in high heels. One looks smart. I shall wear my heels," she would insist.

There was no arguing with Sylvia once she decided on doing something. Window shopping was our priority, followed by a coffee at Christos, a Greek cafe, thereafter buying a few things, if we had the money. One wasn't given money without a reason. While walking one day, Sylvia suddenly relaxed on the pavement,

"Wait girls, I want to massage my toes."

She then removed her shoes and wriggled her toes almost as if she were doing ballet. Shoppers stopped and stared. We commented that she was making a spectacle of herself.

"Let them stare. What do they expect me to do when my poor toes are hurting me?" she would explain, gesturing while talking.

As we crossed the road, Sylvia suddenly stopped, shielded her eyes and stared at the sky. Berit and I were puzzled and we too looked up. Cars braked and drivers gazed upwards in confusion. Pedestrians, shoppers and shopkeepers joined us. Then Sylvia stopped staring, smiled at the gathering and told us to continue walking.

"You can attract people's attention so easily," she commented.

Sylvia was never a girl to be easily embarrassed by anything. On arriving home we heard that Father was admitted to Mulago Hospital for his regular check-up. Back to town went Sylvia, Frank and I to visit him. Frank not only looked like Sylvia but was of the same character, a comedian. Although it was quite embarrassing going anywhere public with them, it was great fun. Frank always stopped the traffic at a pedestrian crossing to let us girls pass!

As we walked through the city centre, we decided on buying something for Father. I suggested a bunch of flowers, Sylvia and Frank insisted on cream cakes.

"That's best for a sick person."

Sylvia's persistence made us buy a box of cakes at the Kizito Bakery. The bus stage was directly in front of the shop. Unfortunately, when we boarded the bus, there was only standing room. Every time the driver braked or swayed, Sylvia oscillated forward, knocking into the standing passengers. The box containing the cakes which she held burst open. Out fell the cakes. The cream smeared the people in front of her. A few of them picked off bits of cake, handing them back to Sylvia. Sylvia passed such funny apologies in broken Luganda that she made everyone burst into peals of laughter.

Frank was standing just behind me. Although just ten years old he was extremely tall     five feet six inches, all legs and arms and very skinny. When he stood up, people gaped and commented, "Eh, Omwana nga muwanzu . . .what a tall boy."

"Frank, forget about being a gentleman, just sit, for heaven's sake," Sylvia said.

She seemed embarrassed when she heard the comments. Although Father was quite surprised at our unexpected visit, he was happy to see us! He was in stitches when he heard what had happened in the bus.

"Just throw the torn box of cakes into the dustbin, for goodness sake."

Talking to Dad for a while we noticed he seemed bored.

"Eh, kids, I don't think I'm going to stay here any longer. Do you know something? I've decided to run away. I don't see what I'm doing here in hospital anyway. Here take the keys and wait for me in the car. I'll take you home," he said mischievously.

We became quite worried but he reassured us.

"You know your Daddy is a tough man; only my machine goes funny at times, but I'm a healthy man. Don't worry."

He meant his heart. We did as we were told. A couple of minutes later Father came and off we went. Mother was very surprised indeed to see us sooner than expected with Father!

The whole of our December holidays, we found people still very excited about *Uhuru*, independence. The phrase "*Ye Yekka Kabaka Wafe*, our one and only King*," was on everyone's lips. Sylvia and I were invited to an important dinner at Lubiiri Palace. Mboni, Prince Henry, Sylvia and I sat at the same table with the Kabaka and the Prime Minister, Milton Obote, leader of the Uganda People's Congress, UPC, and with diplomats. The reception hall was magnificently set; tall mahogany, cushioned chairs, oblong tables where silver cutlery and crystal glassware glittered in their places, and breath-taking sweet-scented flowers filled this huge room.

We noted the guests were in formal clothes. Most men wore western outfits, long-tailed dinner jackets, suits and ties. Some wore the traditional Baganda *kanzu* and a coat. The ladies seemed to glide in their colourful *Busuutis*. We wore flared plain cotton dresses with can-cans. There were all sorts of people; Europeans, Asians, English and Arabs besides the Africans. Sylvia and I made sure we met and talked with as many foreigners as possible. We learnt a little about them and their countries. A butler offered us a drink. Mischievously we tried a little cider and baby cham. Finally, we were invited to the dining tables.

What was to be served? We couldn't wait to find out. A variety of food was brought and we were waited on by smartly dressed waiters in their immaculate white outfits and caps. Savoury meat, beef, mutton and chicken were served with rice, roasted and mashed potatoes, hot steamed matoke, vegetables and puddings of all kinds.

Sylvia whispered, "Meggie, wait till we go back to school. When I tell my friends that I was sitting next to the Kabaka I'd like to see the looks on their faces."

To prove it, she politely asked the Kabaka and the Prime Minister, Milton Obote, to give her their autographs, which they kindly did. After dinner there was a dance. The Sudanese Ambassador invited Prince Henry and family for a dinner at his home at Kololo Hill the following Saturday. The house was lovely and the garden breathtaking. The whole family was hospitable, making us feel quite at home. The Ambassador's wife was most elegant and their babies adorable.

Although there was difficulty in communicating, we got along pretty well. Mboni spoke Arabic and our hostess answered in a Sudanese language which sounded almost similar. Mboni translated everything that was said, she was definitely a linguist. She spoke and understood English, Kiswahili, Arabic, Luganda, Nubian, as well as a touch of Luo, Kikamba and Kikuyu which she had learnt whilst on holiday with Great-grandma in Kenya.

Nattimba, our Great-grandma, was now too old to live alone and Mother thought it best for her to come and live with us in Uganda. She had lived in Kenya since 1940 taking care of herself. Great-grandma, who was quiet by nature, kept to herself most of the time. I sometimes questioned her about the past but she was reluctant to talk about it. However, I was persistent and she gave me a lot of the early history of Uganda and Kabaka Mwanga, the time she lived in Zanzibar, and how Mother met Father. She often asked me my name.

"Mandy," I answered.

She shook her head, answering in perfect Kiswahili;

"You are not Mandy, I remember her as a big, strong, healthy girl with big brown eyes, blonde hair and fair skin. Don't pretend to be my grand-child. I don't know you."

I called out the names pointing to the girls,

"Kwa sisi sote, nani ni Mandy?"    amongst us all, who is Mandy?

"If you are Mandy, I don't know what these people have done to you. You've changed!" she said.

I excused myself and left feeling terribly hurt. Little brother John was terrified to look at her.

"Don't take me next to Bibi, I'll get all those wrinkles," he'd say. The boys seemed scared of old, withered wrinkled people, but we really loved our Great-grandma. We did practically everything for her including organising her breakfast, lunch, dinner, preparing her bath, helping her dress or taking her for short walks. This interest in the old members of our family was unlike the attitude of most teenagers.

A couple of days after our arrival home Father came with our holiday shopping. As usual we were all very glad to see each other. He talked and questioned us a lot. Did we like Maryhill? Were we given tonics? How did we do at school? In the nine years I was at Maryhill Father paid us one visit, very briefly. He gave us each five pounds for pocket money, which was a lot of money in those days. Berit and I immediately gave ours to Mother for safety's sake. Sylvia explained she was old enough and had to learn to be responsible. Mother didn't insist but let Sylvia alone.

One Saturday afternoon.we decided to see a movie *The Miracle*. The main actor was Pat Boone, a favourite of ours, he was so handsome just like our Father. Mother gave Berit and me twenty shillings each, which was more than enough for the pop corn, sodas and bus fares back and forth. Sylvia securely tied up the five pounds in a handkerchief and held it in her hand. At the interval, Sylvia decided she would go to the "ladies" room to "powder her nose." Unfortunately she forgot her money on the dressing-table. After the movie, she suddenly remembered her money tied in the handkerchief and rushed back to the ladies' room; obviously it was gone.

Sylvia exclaimed that she wouldn't face Mother as she had specifically told her to leave some of her money behind and she had not listened! She had decided to commit suicide by walking in the middle of the road and getting run over. That's exactly what she tried to do, like a girl possessed. Cars honked and swerved trying to avoid hitting her. Berit and I ran into the street, each firmly held an arm and managed to get her home. Mother wasn't angry as Sylvia imagined she would be. Mother always told us whatever happened to us was God's will. Within a few days Sylvia had calmed down and was her normal self.

Although we had studied in Kenya practically all of our lives we knew more about Uganda than any other country in Africa. Out of curiosity I went to Mombasa, Kenya, at the end of 1961. I thought it was a good year to learn about Kenya by spending the holidays with my schoolmate Monica Louis who would be my future sister-in-law. There was so much to see. The big Indian Ocean, beaches dotted with mainly white tourists, Arabs in their kanzus, *bui-bui* clad women, lots of Seychellois people, Asians, hundreds of sailors, it was like watching a movie. The people and customs were totally different from what I was used to.

In April, 1962, Sylvia and Berit decided they too would go to Mombasa Island. They never missed a swim in the Indian Ocean any day. Sylvia really made the best of the holidays. As she watched the sea,

at the age of fifteen, she wrote this poem;
## MY SISTER AND BROTHER

Troubled water, I see the waves everyday,
As if each will get out and go its own way,
As they come to the beach they mellow out,
Like you and me.

I felt miserable and alone at home with just my brothers. Father came to see me and took me out shopping and dropped me at the movie *Blue Hawaii* with Elvis Presley, but it was not the same without Sylvia. I was glad to go back to school. Sylvia talked non-stop about how wonderful Mombasa was. She had been invited by her Somali-English classmate and Berit stayed with a friend of mother's, who was taking care of our brother Frank.

The following holiday, Berit invited her friend Hazel to Uganda. We mischievously rang our uncle, the Kabaka Mutesa II, and made an appointment to bring our guest from Mombasa to see him. He was very kind-hearted.

"Sure, bring her along," he said.

We took Grandma along because once she was seen there would be no questions asked at the *Lubiiri* Palace gates. We met the Kabaka, played his grand piano, danced and had a lovely time. The Kabaka really loved Grandma. He told us he liked to hear her speak Luganda as she "twisted" it a little like a foreigner. The Palace was full of historical artifacts which were most interesting. The elephant tusks arranged according to sizes, different drums, lovely hand-made carpets, and *Ebibbo* baskets were handed down from one Kabaka to another. Each heirloom had a distinct history and beauty of the past. Later, as usual we were driven home in one of the royal Rolls Royces.

A week later we took our friend to Kasubi where all the former Kabakas were buried. Grandma regularly went to visit her father's burial place. When you enter the hut, it is customary to remove your shoes as a sign of respect. The entrance is still guarded by a large stuffed leopard.

We also attended one of the Kabaka's birthday parties which were held at Babunanika, one of his palaces. On weekends we sometimes went on picnics with the Kabaka, Prince Henry and Mboni at some island where Mutesa would hunt. The Botanical Garden near Lake Victoria was of great interest. A trip on the lake in Mutesa's lovely boat for an hour or two was quite a relaxation. We visited Masaka, Jinja or Mbarara on Saturdays and Sundays which was always a treat. We showed our friend Bulange, the King's Court for Justice. It was easy for us to visit Bulange because Prince Henry was working there.

Mother had more confidence in us now that we were older and allowed us to go to town on our own as long as we kept together. We were never permitted to wander off without informing her where we were going, or when we'd be back.

Helene was taking her nurse's course at Nsambya Hospital. She had been a perfect sister and mother when we were together at both boarding schools. I was the opposite. I believed my sisters should be independent and do their own chores. Sylvia was already taller and bigger than I. Berit was much too boisterous to deal with in any case. Sylvia often came to me to do her hair yet she was very polite and gentle about it. That was about all I could do.

One evening Sylvia entered my room, her face beaming, I was busy ironing.

"Sylvia, what's so funny?" I asked curiously.

"Promise me, you won't tell anyone if I tell you something," she giggled.

"I promise," I said, rather impatiently.

"Promise you won't tell Mother or Helene," she asked again.

"I've already promised and you know I keep my promises," I was agitated by now.

"Come over here, I want to show you something," she cautioned. She opened her single long plait of hair, bent over, parted the hair and lo and behold she had chopped all her middle hair right down to the roots! I gasped.

"Sylvia, what have you done?" I was almost in tears. The lovely copper coloured hair was all cut.

"Well it will be much easier for me to comb and manage now. Meggie, don't you understand, my hair is too much. I wonder why God gave me so much hair! I must have taken after Samson." We laughed.

She knew just how to make a joke of everything. True enough Sylvia did have an abundance of hair. Anyway, we kept the secret.

We took hot dinners for Helene almost every day of the holidays. We enjoyed doing this, because it gave us a chance to dress up and wear our high-heeled shoes, but no make-up was permitted yet. We met Mboni and our brother-in-law Prince Henry, who was now called Rashid, after his conversion to the Muslim faith. I recalled the day a nun

Arab relatives, Prince Rashid (Henry Kimera), Shaaban (Frank), Ramandhan & Grandma, 1962.

Form III & IV students at Maryhill Mangu, 1964..

Prince Henry, Mandy & Prince Ronald Mutebi in Nairobi, 1986.

Kabaka Daudi Chwa II

Grandpa Seif Nassor & Mboni in Uganda, 1965

Sylvia at Trafalgar Square, 1972.

Omumbejja Kajja Obunaku, Nattimba,
Amina & Nuru at the Lubiiri Mengo, 1937.

Nuru, Kajja Obunaku & Amina, 1939.

111

Grandma meets Queen Elizabeth II in Zanzibar, 1958.

Sister Maureen, Sister Robert with Ex-Maryhill girls at Hurlingham, 1986.

Michael, Sylvia, Mother, Mandy & Adrian, 1980.

Sylvia Christine Bjordal,
1976.

Cousins & Aunt, Berit (extreme right) in
Norwegian ceremonial outfits, 1962.

Kabaka Daniel Mwanga II

Sister Robert & Ex-Maryhill girls, 1988.

113

Sylvia Bjordal in Uganda, 1962

Mandy and Sylvia in Nairobi, 1966.

Lucy Amina, 1981.

Lucy Amina and Sylvia, 1978.

Ganya Ramadhani, Kizito & Abdul Aziz Bulwada

Sylvia, Dad and Mandy at Nyamolilo, 1963.

114

Harald Bjordal & Amina Nava, 1956.

Nattimba Binti Juma

Sylvia & Michael wed, 1977.

Sir Edward Mutesa II

115

called me over to where she stood.

"Margaret, did you know your Uncle the Prince married your sister and has changed his Christian faith to a Muslim? The shame of it!" The nun was scornful. As far as I was concerned Henry and Mboni were an ideal couple.

They had been married while we were still in school. At times we were driven home in their Mercedes Benz, although we preferred going on the bus or walking back home. During one of our visits, a group of teenage Asian boys followed us and began teasing us. I was always nervous but Sylvia assured me that she'd put them in their right place if they dared come within three yards of us. More often than not, Sylvia ended up telling the boys off. On the other hand, the boys rather enjoyed Sylvia quarrelling as she seemed unbelievably dramatic. We noticed the same group every single day, somehow they knew what time to expect us.

One particular evening, we left later than usual. Sylvia told Berit and me to hold one of our high-heeled shoes in our strongest hand as a weapon. She normally used her left hand for tougher jobs.

"Don't be ridiculous. You mean to tell me we are going to walk all the way to the bus stop with only one high-heeled shoe on?" I asked.

"And why not?" asked Sylvia. "Why worry if people look at us, or if they laugh at us, we've got to protect ourselves, haven't we?" she said, very determinedly.

It was around seven when we left Helene that evening. I was very worried indeed, although it was a clear, moonlit night. The moonlight danced gaily over the tarmac road and made the stones glitter like tiny jewels. Fireflies twinkled in the grass like hundreds of stars. The air was fresh and we took deep breaths as we enjoyed every step we took. Early evenings in Uganda were always fascinating and calming.

"Oh, how I love the world when it is like this, so serene, stars shining, no-one on the road," said Sylvia.

Deep inside I was nervous because it was quite a distance to the bus stop. There was an avenue of eucalyptus trees on either side of the road. It was creepy. I asked Sylvia and Berit if we could start praying. Sylvia suggested singing.

"It's less boring than praying," Sylvia said.

So we began to sing in altos and soprano . . . "soft as a voice of an angel!"

Suddenly, we noticed five strange luminous lights materialize out of the darkness and smelt cigarettes. I warned my sisters that we might be attacked by some unknown gangsters. Sylvia ordered us each to hold our shoe tight and be ready for war! We then realized that these must be the same Asian boys who had formerly been following us. The boys walked right across the road, blocking our way.

"What the hell, let's pass them; if they as much as lay a finger on us, we'll have to fight," Sylvia stormed.

Berit was just as tough and bold and a tomboy as Sylvia was. On we marched, towards our pursuers. It was quite a comical sight as we bounced along. As we drew nearer, the boys passed nonsensical comments.

"I dare you boys, come and fight," Sylvia shaking one shoe across one of the boys' faces as she spoke facing them. They did not answer, but only laughed.

"Why are you bothering us? Why don't you follow your own women?" she screamed at them.

There was still no answer from them, and then, almost like a miracle, a bus appeared along the road and stopped for us. Thank you, thank you God, He must have heard our prayers. The boys ran after us, shouted for the bus to wait for them; fortunately it didn't. Every passenger stared at us in amazement as we were still each holding a shoe in our hands. Realizing how odd we looked, we quickly put on our shoes. Happy that we were going home safe and sound. As we ran down Namirembe Hill from the bus stop, Sylvia thrust both hands high in the air and shouted jubilantly,

"We have conquered!"

That summer of 1962, Helene left for Preston, England, to continue her nursing course. As usual she cried her heart out as we escorted her on the way to Entebbe Airport. Secretly, we envied her.

"Don't worry Meggie, we can wear her dresses now," Sylvia comforted me.

"How will we get them when she's locked them up in the case?" I queried.

"We'll find a way of opening it," she replied confidently.

Working patiently and with great determination she managed to unlock the case. Dressing in Helene's fancy clothes we immediately walked down the all Asian street to the Blue Room Studio, and had some photographs taken which we later sent to her. Helene was shocked and angry to see us in her dresses!

We loved this Asian street, especially the sweetmeat shops, and imitation jewellery shops where we bought ourselves fake diamond crowns. Opposite was the magnificent Khoja Mosque which attracted glamorous high class Muslim Asians clad in shimmering outfits, adorned with gold, going either to pray or to attend fancy celebrations. We didn't notice many black or halfcaste Muslims there, at this time. They preferred the Kibuli Mosque. Years later integration occurred. Previously any Afro-Asian would totally hide his or her African identity. They spoke and dressed as Asians and were never called *chotara* by the Indian community. In fact Afro-Asians would join the Asians to tease the Afro-European children.

# CHAPTER NINE:
# KIGEZI AND ZANZIBAR

At the beginning of August 1963 we received a letter from Father inviting Sylvia, Berit and me to spend our leave with him up at the mine! We were to be with him after fourteen years. He assured mother that he would come down to Kampala to pick us up and buy us boots and coats since it was very cold up at Nyamolilo. We waited full of anticipation for a week but Father didn't come. Mboni saw how disappointed I was and found someone travelling to the Congo to give us a lift. Mother thought it was a good idea instead of expecting Father, who had heart trouble, to travel the entire 350 miles. Mboni described Kabale as a paradise, where she had actually seen the clouds touch the ground below. We didn't believe her, we thought it was a tall story. To be on the safe side mother sent Mboni to chaperon us. Around six-thirty in the evening, we arrived at Kabale, a resort town. The distant mountains formed a picturesque backdrop for the town. The mine was fifty miles away from there.

Instead of venturing into the countryside unknown to us late in the evening, we decided to spend the night at a hotel in the exquisite little town of Kabale, and continue our journey the next day. We were up early the following morning when the world outside was tinged grey with the slight pink flush of dawn. It was freezing cold as the mist had touched the earth. Mother had told us when we reached Kabale not to ask for Mr. Harald Bjordal, but rather for *Kanya-Mugara* or *Kanywara-Musoke* pet names the local people had come to know him by since the early forties when he first went there. One name meant "someone with plenty of hair" and the other meant "someone who smoked a pipe," or something to that effect.

After about half an hour of driving up a winding dusty road, we

119

came across an old sign board Bjordal Mines. Swerving right we followed the road which took us directly down the valley to the mines. We saw the clouds below us, like a soft woolly blanket    it was magnificent!

The weather was bitterly cold, misty and damp. Father had a floating bridge of beaten down grass, reeds and papyrus stems covered with loose clay earth, kept in position by a double reed wall. The man who brought us there was wise enough not to try to cross the bridge in the car. A decision was made to cross the marsh on foot carrying our luggage. How exciting all this was. Our legs kept slipping into the freezing, wet, cold clay, but nearly all the workers came to give us a helping hand. We looked like the explorers in David Livingstone history books as we walked up the five miles to Father's mansion. Mboni boarded a bus and went back to her family.

Father was not there, which was a great disappointment. Barnado and Msererekano, the house keepers, played hosts to us. The beds were made up, the wood in the fire place lit and then after dinner, coffee was brought on a silver tray and placed on a little round mahogany coffee table near the fire place. The fire danced, wood crackled and the smell of pine filled the air. We had never seen such a huge, comfortable sitting-room before. Msererekano told us that he first saw us when we were only babies, and now God had blessed him by letting him see us grown. Both men were kind, polite and affectionate.

We soon felt very much at home although we had neither parent around. Exhaustion overpowered us and we fell into a deep sleep under six blankets. The next morning at 6 a.m. a pot of hot tea and a jug of imported milk, "the milk-maid" was brought to our beds. It was bitterly cold, and we were still exhausted and sleepy; we took the opportunity and spoiled ourselves just a little! Who ever dreamt we'd be served tea in bed?

This treat lifted our spirits. We dressed quickly and went out to watch the magnificent aurora of the red sunrise. It was a quiet, serene morning. The light pink and white clouds below covered practically everything beneath us. Sylvia sat on the veranda just staring at the wonderful view. After a big breakfast we saw her busy writing.

## TO LIVE AND TO LOVE

I dream of a love so fitting,
Yet so calm and so healing.
I dream of love without measure,

When all is lost, I dream of love I treasure.
I breathe this love, it fills me up.
I am alive, I'm free,
The beauty of nature I can see.
Though my eyes blind they may be,
If I have no feet, my heart will still beat.
Until God above takes that from me,
A human being of love I still can be.
But if I cannot love, I cannot give,
Though I have all, I just can't live.
Without love, I cannot exist,
God above count me not on your waiting list.

## SYLVIA, 1963

In the meantime, Father arrived in Kampala, deeply disappointed not to find us there, as he had wanted to buy us warm clothes and accessories. He did all the shopping for the month we would spend with him and he came back two days later.

Father's house was way up the highest mountain at Nyamolilo. We heard the faint distant sound of a car getting louder and closer as it made its way up, slowly climbing the winding dusty road. How excited we were that Father had finally come home? I was to be with my Father after years of separation! We all ran to kiss, hug and help him with his luggage. He looked very tired.

"How are my young beauties?" he inquired with a loving smile. "Now girls, you'll have to excuse your Daddy as I have to dip myself into a warm bath. I usually take half an hour!"

Msererekano and Barnado brought in hot water and filled the bath. After half an hour Father came, all neat and tidy, smelling of Old Spice. Father watched us and smiled as we said our prayers before dinner.

"The nuns have brain-washed you kids," he said.

"Not really," I answered.

"Now girls, Dad is relaxed, tell me all about yourselves," he said with a smile.

His voice was always deep and courteous . . . so different from that of other men I had come across who might be rough, coarse and unruly.

We all talked at the same time. We had so many questions to ask;

how he and mother met, how did he come to Africa, about his family, his home, his country, why he and Mother separated, the lot! And Father answered them non-stop. We began to feel that he must be tired, having driven 350 miles, and we worried about his heart condition.

"Dad, I think you should go to bed now. You must be tired," I smiled trying to act the mother.

"You are right dear, I am tired, but you can stay up as long as you like. I know you love music. I have some nice L.P's you can play and dance if you want. There is Aretha Franklin, Charlie Pride, a few Elvis Presley and Cliff Richard."

"Thanks Dad, we'll read in bed," we answered.

Every evening we looked forward to welcoming Father. After working for almost twelve hours down in the mine, he would spend about two hours doing his paper work, as he had no secretary. We spent every moment with him. It was funny watching him type with six fingers but he coped very well.

Sylvia had almost finished her painting supplies but luckily Father bought more oil paints, easels, brushes and papers. We painted to our heart's content, listening to music by Acker Hill.

Kigezi, my childhood home, is one of the smallest districts in the South Western corner of Uganda. Its beauty is beyond description. There is nowhere in the world with such varied scenery, mountains, valleys, lakes, an abundance of greenery.

Father took us to every corner of Kigezi. From the volcanic peaks of the Birunga Range which is the home of the gorilla, to the soaring Mt. Muhavura Range which is 13,547 feet high and the third highest mountain in Uganda, we travelled to the fertile lava plains and minor craters of the Bufumbura volcanic mountains in the South West, perched exactly on the Uganda-Rwanda border. It was most interesting as we had never seen lava before.

We then went to the broken mountain country around Kabale, the main town in Kigezi. Later we travelled to the scattered lakes of which Buyeni and Mutanda are particularly scenic, with all kinds of birds feeding and preening themselves on their shores. We visited the Ishasha and Mitam Gorges and the rolling grasslands of Ruzumbura in the North. From there, we went from daylight into darkness through the impenetrable forest of Western Uganda. Here we saw great gashes in the earth along the narrow murram road.

"Sometimes there are landslides," Father warned us.

Father told us on our next holiday we would go right into the heart of the forest.

"This world is so fascinating, always green, and natural, it's no wonder Father never wanted to join the 'civilized' world of the city", I surmised.

We noted that the *Bachiga* people built their homes in the valley and on the lower slopes of the hills which they cultivated. *Bachiga*, Father explained, meant "Hill People." I told Sylvia how I used to eat sorghum, the Bachiga's staple food, which is also extensively used for brewing local beer. I had had a taste of it when very young.

Back at home, while we played a Dvorak Symphony, we looked at father's photo albums over and over again. They were most interesting. We found from the albums that he was quite outstanding at sports, swimming and skiing. He had photos showing how things were when he first came to Kabale, Ethiopia and South Africa. I was so proud of my Father, looking like an explorer. He told us about the development of Ethiopia's sophisticated civilization.

"Since you read the Bible practically every day you must have heard of the Queen of Sheba and King Solomon's wisdom."

"Sure we have."

"I won't go into that then."

Ethiopia is isolated due to the mountains so that it is cut off from the surrounding countries. The people are beautiful and have a fantastic culture.

"Just look at these photographs. The people here in Kigezi hardly wore any clothes at that time yet when I put on my bathing suit to swim in the dam they all scream," he said while having a good laugh.

Father always swam after a hard day's work. It relaxed him. Wearing our jeans, shirts, tennis shoes and socks we explored the mountains from bottom to top, venturing into the little caves. It was another world altogether filled with an abundance of the most lovely plants one could possibly imagine. Glistening drops of water clung on their petals so the wild flowers and plants were always fresh. I stood listening to the hundreds of different insects chirp, creak and buzz. I gazed down at the wet clayey ground, up at the stretch of green, hilly mountains, and the bright sky streaked with little white stratified clouds.

In a distant thicket, a bird chirped loudly and very busily. What a world! Slowly sweeping its wings, a hawk flew over the distant forest. We could hear a cuckoo near the water which flowed noiselessly in the narrow winding streams. We smelt the warm fresh scent of plants in the air. Walking through a variety of bushes here and there, over crumbling, sinking loose earth, we were delighted at every bit of plant, insect and bird life God had put into this place. An exquisite velvety green spread before my eyes; even the swamp was green, covered with plants, papyrus and water lilies.

I was happy to return to my childhood home, the only real home I had ever known and loved. The house was different but the atmosphere was the same. In the city, things always seemed to be in a state of flux. Here nothing seemed to have changed since I was just a child. The soft green mystery of the wild plants always seemed to calm me. We collected hundreds of different flowers.

In the evenings, Father would sometimes give us an I.Q. test which we failed most times, but all in all we learnt quite a lot from him. He sometimes told us that we could walk further and see the surroundings for ourselves; he assured us there was no danger. We practically ran down to the house of the Manager, a Greek-Cypriot, Mr. Dimitrius. He invited us to dinner the following evening at seven.

After investigating the centre of the mountain, we half ran, half walked down to the mine. Gravity seemed to pull us further down. Some of the caves were an indentation in the mountain. Others had endless tunnels. It was dark and cool inside with only faint light spilling through the opening. We saw a big, man-made lake which Father had built and we could go swimming or boating in it if we wished. Father had warned us that further down it was very dangerous due to quicksand. He had witnessed a child being swallowed up whilst playing with a friend. He also had another small, man-made lake where he bred fish and wild ducks.

We visited the mine, watched how water-power was used to break rocks and how they were sorted out to the final stage, where little particles of wolfram were sieved out. One needed an abundance of water to do mining and fortunately there was a waterfall near the mine, which helped with the supply of electricity as well.

In the evening we went for the Greek dinner. We had dressed smartly as Father had insisted on it. We exchanged looks every time Mr. Dimitrius talked because of the comical way he accentuated his English.

Mr. Dimitrius had a wild hog which he had raised from a piglet. The animal was tame, almost like a pet dog. Napoleon, as he was called, understood everything Mr. Dimitrius told him in Greek. Sylvia was fascinated with this animal. She pleaded with us to escort her to the Manager's house and have fun with the hog. I did not like the look of him. He had dirty grey-brown prickly fur, made horrible grunts and snorts and had a wet snout.

One day, Mr. Dimitrius caught us on his veranda with his hog. Sylvia was busy stroking him and I was standing watching when the manager grabbed me by my arms and I gasped with surprise.

"Eh, girls, what are you doing here?" he asked teasingly.

"We came to see Napoleon," we answered.

"Ah, you like my old man? Well I am getting quite tired of him."

He then turned to the pig, who was timidly looking at his master, and said in a Greek accent,

"Napoleon, one of these days I'm going to eat you." The poor pig grunted and lazily made himself more comfortable.

One evening, however, we were invited for our weekend ritual dinner out. There was soft music of Nana Mouskouri playing. Mr. Dimitrius, who was a fantastic cook, made the most delicious dinner. He then brought in his Greek speciality stew. We ate until we could eat no more, very impressed with his cooking.

We simultaneously asked, "What's this lovely stew, Mr. Dimitrius?"

Our host said we would get us the recipe after dinner.

"And my dears that was lovely Napoleon," he cackled.

We almost threw up, including Father! How heart-broken we were as Napoleon had become our friend. We never ate at Mr. Dimitrius' place again!

However Mr. Dimitrius was very jovial and comical, and we loved to hear him tell stories. He was much shorter than any of us and as round as a pumpkin. He looked something like Micky Rooney. We noticed a hand with no fingers and we asked him how come? He was ready with his usual tall stories, gesturing with his stump of a hand. Apparently, one day while working on a machine at the mine, busy talking, all his fingers were sliced off in a blink. The tough man pulled off the remaining, hanging fingers, drove 350 miles to Kampala, and went to Mulago Hospital for treatment. The doctors were amazed that he was still alive. We politely thanked Mr. Dimitrius for inviting us and drove home in absolute darkness.

Out of the blue Father told us he had invited a young Dartish geologist and that we should be very smart at around noon the next day.

"He is very handsome. Something like your Elvis Presley."
We didn't take him seriously but continued with our painting, listening to music, copying songs and dancing. Sylvia was busy with her poetry and we forgot all about Father's visitor.

Suddenly, we heard the car come up the hill. Concurrently we rushed into the bathroom to change. Too late, father was already at the porch talking in Danish with his friend. As a punishment for not keeping to his instructions, he came straight into the bathroom with his guest. Looking quite red in the face, he introduced us to the young man, dirty as we were, our hands smeared with oil-paints. We were dumbfounded but not really embarrassed as the man was nothing like Elvis Presley. On the contrary, he had a thick red beard, a face full of freckles, and was short and stocky    Yuk! Anyway, we smartened up and had lunch together. The man hardly spoke a word of English. Whenever he wanted to say anything to us, father translated. Although the man commented we were all very pretty and charming young ladies, we weren't impressed.

Every second week of every month, it was known to the locals that *Kanya-Mugara,* our father, would treat the sick. People came in droves to be cured of their diseases. They believed Father worked magic; and I believe he loved that. He had desperately wanted to become a doctor and perhaps he tried to fulfil his dream.

Father would bring out his First Aid Box, which had Quinine, vitamins, aspirin, iodine, cough mixture, bandages, plasters, Milton and Dettol. The most common diseases were malaria, common colds, coughs and jiggers    insects which infested the toes. Father would sit with a sterilized needle, Dettol and cotton wool and patiently remove jiggers from one patient after another. He would then clean the infected toes and dab them with iodine and bandage them if need be. The rest of the patients told him of their ailments and received free medication for which they showed great gratitude. How we admired Father's strong manly face as he nursed these people, the patience, serenity and kindness he showed    even to strangers. We wondered what made him do this? The people of Kigezi will never forget him.

Father planned a trip to Rubugure, our first home, intending to give us some historical highlights about those days. He parked the car at a distance, explaining how dangerous it was to drive to the mine. As we proceeded toward the mine we noticed a driving white curtain of rain descending over the distant forest, yet the sun was shining brilliantly around us. The air was filled with moisture. Suddenly the calm bright day was shattered by tiny warm drops. The low leading clouds were black, extinguishing the meagre light trickling along their outer edges, and they drove with extraordinarily swiftness across the sky. The whole atmosphere changed within minutes, flashes of lightning brightened the darkened sky. The peal of thunder and the instantaneous chill caused us to race to the pick-up, where we huddled into the front seat.

Thunder, my most feared resonance. . . flashes of Kisubi came back for just a second. Every tree and plant swayed in frenzied confusion. One would have thought there would be an earthquake, then down came the heavy rain. Torrents of muddy rufous water rushed down the hills washing away the loose earth, lashed at the dry, weak plants. There was an abundance of water, but within no time the dry earth sucked it all up.

A group of Bachiga people cut down huge banana leaves to shelter themselves from the rain while they stood gazing at us. *"Mawe nibarungi,"* "Oh aren't they beautiful!" they commented, giggling away. Every move we made, the same comment was heard. The heavy rain did not discourage them from staring at us, as though we were creatures from outer space.

Father suggested we start our lunch as it might rain the whole afternoon. Mother had taught us never to eat alone.

"If you can't feed a crowd, don't eat while they are watching."

"Dad, you don't expect us to eat with all these people staring?" we said in unison.

"Well, if you don't start, I will. I've had them staring at me for over twenty years!" he responded.

Although the wind subsided and the rain stopped, the furious storm clouds still hung in the sky and a calmer rumbling of thunder could be heard. After much coaxing from Father we continued our journey on foot to the Rubugure mine, where he was prospecting for gold. Out of nowhere a little girl about three and a half foot tall appeared.

"How can parents leave such a small girl unattended out here in the jungle?" asked Sylvia.

Father laughed heartily, and said something to the girl in the Congolese language. When she turned, we saw an old withered woman! Father told us she was a seventy-eight year old pygmy, a dear friend of his. He gave her some money and she prayed over us.

We hiked deeper and deeper into the thick vegetation right into the heart of overgrown bushes, weeds, brambles and exotic plants with dark green wax-like leaves. The tree trunks were covered with soft moss of a silvery velvet green. An abundance of insects and amphibians camouflaged themselves within the plants and tree trunks. There were many pygmies, all partially dressed, carrying bows and poisonous arrows. They all knew *Kanya-Mugara*. One man explained that frogs

127

have magical powers and when you hear them croak they are summoning the rain. The king-fishers were a symbol of peace.

Sylvia saw a fallen tree trunk and decided to climb over it. Before Father could say "Jack Robinson," into the disintegrated trunk she fell, up to her neck. We had to pull her out. Father cautioned us to be very careful when we came across such tree trunks as they had been there for years. We were astounded by the waterfalls cascading downhill, drops brilliant as diamonds in the sun. Father proudly told us that nowhere in the world was there water so pure. Thirst made us bend over the rushing cool, sparkling, fresh water and gulp it down. Half an hour later we were at the mine. Father introduced us to all the workers. This was most interesting and an experience beyond description.

We were overwhelmed to see the three little neat huts where we once lived as children. These mud-built homes were in the middle of the dense forest. Everything was still intact, the beds, little dining table, a cupboard. Father kept tea, coffee, tins of milk, sugar, salt, two saucepans, plastic tumblers. Obviously, this had been his second home for years. On another shelf he had a First Aid Box. My green world flashed back, as I momentarily saw myself as a baby. It was a dream come true. Here I was again to peace and happiness. We lit a fire on three stones using dry twigs and made some tea, whilst Father took a nap on the camp bed. This is where the python nearly killed him. We explored every nook and cranny. Never a thought of meeting wild animals or snakes or being shot by any pygmy came to mind.

After a long, exciting, tiresome journey, we were glad to be back home and in our comfortable warm beds. At six in the morning, we had our usual cup of tea. Sylvia did not have just a cup but a whole pot of tea. It was Sunday, and we thought about mass. Unfamiliar echoes of drums were heard. After our curiosity was aroused, we gestured to a passing Muchiga man and asked him what it was all about. He explained that people were being summoned to prayers. Perhaps there was a church somewhere?

We decided to follow the drum beats, walking in and out of the mountains for two and a half hours without seeing a church! Finally, we came to a dead end of our journey, and found a group of men, wrapped in blankets, pipes in their mouths and holding long walking sticks. One of the men was playing a drum. When we questioned them in Luganda they seemed confused; we tried Kiswahili and were given blank looks. They just shook their heads in complete puzzlement. Disappointed we decided to go back home, arriving at one o'clock. All in all we must have walked for five hours. Father was furious, as lunch had already been on the table an hour earlier. This was his day at home, we should have kept him company.

"Where have you been all this time?" he angrily demanded, growing red in the face.

We nervously tried to explain our motives but thought the better of it. He was never angry for long, although he could be worse than the nuns at the convent school about punctuality. Everything had to be done on time! To him tidiness was of the utmost importance.

Father took us shopping in Kabale about fifty miles from the mine. We toured the small neat town and Father introduced us to all his colleagues.

"Don't introduce us to these young ladies, Harald, we can see they are your daughters; especially this one," they said pointing at me. At the White Horse Inn as we had tea to round off a lovely day.

One weekend Father decided to take us to the Congo border to meet his Greek friend Mr. Constantine, who was mining there. We were very excited. Early the next morning, Msererekano and Barnado packed a picnic lunch. We threw a change of clothes in addition to all our toilet essentials into a knapsack. We drove for miles up a winding road till the villages and people began to look like toys below. We seemed to be driving up to the sky. It was breath-taking. We passed through a bamboo forest, the home of gorillas. When Father described the size of these animals and how menacing they were, it scared the daylights out of us!

We were dead tired when we reached the Constantine Mines. The mine was something out of this world, something that you only read about in books. An ancient-looking house was built on the top of the mountain, surrounded by huge trees with weird looking branches, an owl curiously looking at us. A huge rock wall surrounded Mr. Constantine's house.

The whole atmosphere seemed to boost us up although we were so weary. The golden sun was setting behind the bluish-purple mountains and nature was just settling down for a good night's sleep... there was absolute silence except for a distant hyena, a dog's bark, wind softly blowing, rustling the leaves. Sylvia and I didn't want to go into the house, freezing cold as it was. We needed a moment's peace to sit and admire Lake George and Lake Edward in the distance, watch the last of the sun's dazzling rays lighting the surfaces of the lakes, awesome, calm and serene. The plantations way down below were neat, like carpets of various shades of green shrubs, with systematically constructed terraces. Thatched roofed villages laced and embroidered the thick undergrowth. Up in the trees, bees and drones hovered in front of their hives. Bees . . . I was to fear them all my life after my fateful experience as a child.

After sunset, we went indoors to meet Mr. Constantine, a kindly old man with thick bushy eye-brows, deep beady eyes and slightly hunched back.

"Doesn't he remind you of Shakespeare's Shylock?" muttered Sylvia.

"Ssh, Sylvia!" I cautioned.

Our host gave us a warm welcome and after a hot delicious early supper, we went out again to admire the lakes. The full, yellow moon hung low in the clear sky, its reflection on the lake like a mirror. There were all kinds of birds    black storks, marabou storks and flamingoes preening themselves on the shores of the lakes. Sylvia and I took deep breaths of the cool, fresh air. We listened to the wind whistling and thought that God had never created anything so captivating as the place where we were standing. The night creatures started rustling. The birds in the hedges were trimming their feathers and tucking themselves in their nests comfortably for the night. We slept until dawn flooded the sky with ever-brighter colours, from red-purple to red-orange to white-gold . . . the soft warm orange sun slowly rising, casting soft pink colours on the clouds beneath the mountain. Slowly the sky above turned blue, so bright and rich it didn't look real. The whole atmosphere was like fairyland. There's got to be a God. If wishes could come true I would wake up with the sun, animals, birds and nature and go to sleep when they slept.

At breakfast time next morning, we were introduced to a delegation of Greek Orthodox priests. Unbelievably we saw Father bow when grace was being said by a priest. Sylvia was about to burst into laughter when I nudged her. Breakfast was huge. What an appetite these men had. Two or three eggs each, sausages, bacon, toast, cornflakes, a variety of fruits, fresh cool juices    the lot. We sat and ate, and then, together with Father, we excused ourselves and went for a walk.

Two days later, we travelled to the border between the Congo and Uganda. Sylvia remarked that if only she put her foot over the check point, she would claim she had been in the Congo. Father told us that the stretch of land in front of us was called "no man's land," therefore, there was no point in even trying to bestride it. We stopped at a homely little hotel and had a delicious, hot lunch. Father showed us as much as he possibly could; explaining what that part of the world was like when he first came to Africa. I was surprised to see Asian dukas, shops, in the middle of nowhere.

While we were combing our hair before we left, Father remarked, "It's a wonder I have any hair left. I have given all I had to you. No wonder I am bald."

It was during this holiday we first saw Father gently rubbing *Kamwu*, prickly, stinging leaves, on his sparse hair. He believed this would stimulate the cells and his hair would grow; probably some *Mganga*, local doctor, advised him.

"Come girls and have a look at my bald head. Do you notice some hairs coming?" he asked. We agreed, just to please him.

During that December, we had five weeks holiday. Mother said she would appreciate it if one of us would accompany her to Zanzibar. We all gave her a definite no. Mother had not seen her father since she came to Uganda as a child. She had decided to look for him in Zanzibar. I don't know if that was what frightened us off. But I felt sorry for mother and thought I might as well go and meet the Arab part of me. I knew all of my African relatives, perhaps twenty percent of my European heritage.

The girls teased me! "We can imagine you wearing a *bui-bui* and saying *Asalaam Alekhum*. You may become some Sharrif's wife!" That terrified me. Many of my childhood Muslim friends were married off at barely fourteen or fifteen years old. They hardly had time to mature and enjoy their childhood.

We boarded a train to Nairobi, then a bus to Mombasa. Here we stayed with some Arab relatives for a few days before boarding a ship at Kilindini. Mother and I had a lovely cabin and the journey on the ship was quite extraordinary. How delightful it was being in the middle of the blue ocean, not seeing land at all. This time my world was blue, the heavens above and the waters down below, all a pleasant blue, very calming to the eyes and soul, and my whole being. It was truly a wonderful experience.

*Unguja*, Zanzibar, was very hot. It was another world altogether. Most of the buildings were ancient, made of coral, grey, blue and orange in colour, with lovely thick carved doors. They were three-storeyed, shuttered tenements, all crowded together along narrow streets, which were kept incredibly clean. I saw people sweeping and cleaning in front of their door-ways, very similar to the people back home in Uganda. The populace were a mixture of Asian, Arab, African complexions, whether light or dark, very few whites, most of who were British. Most of the women dressed in *bui-buis* and all I could see was their kohl-dressed eyes. Others wore long dresses. A few wore saris. They sauntered by with baskets on their heads. Every woman smelt of *Al-huod* an Arab essence. Majority of the men wore long white *kanzus* and *tarabush*. Muslim turbans, a thin moustache and neat beard.

We stayed with Mother's relatives. Most commented on how Mother had changed. Her complexion was much darker, her long straight, black hair was now short and curly. A couple of days later a party was made to welcome their long lost relative. There was a huge tray of *wali* (rice), curried meat, and salad made of fresh onions, chillies, tomatoes and lemon. All the women sat around a very big *siniya* (tray), ready to eat. The men were already served in an adjacent room. I was very uncomfortable, as I could not sit cross-legged on the mat for long periods of time due to severe knee-aches, an aftermath of my childhood illness. I could not eat gracefully with my right hand as was the custom, due to lack of practice. One of the ladies noticed my awkwardness and brought me a spoon. I was perspiring in the black *bui-bui* which mother insisted I must wear when we went out. It was unbecoming for a young girl to expose herself!

Mother's relatives told her that her father had gone to Pemba to see about his *karafu*, clove, farm. All in all we had an interesting time in Zanzibar    visiting places, meeting relatives and friends. In the afternoon we had spiced tea and *mahmuri*, buns. Mother told me we should visit the Sultan, and see if the Princess whom Grandma had grown up with was still there. Fortunately, she was at the palace. It was magnificent. I was afraid to meet all the royal family although they seemed friendly enough. I found it difficult speaking or understanding the Kiunguja-Kiswahili but it sounded lovely!

We visited majestic mosques with Lamu-style carved wooden doors as high as fifteen feet! The people are very religious and polite, similar to the Baganda people; everyone who passes, greets you: *"Asalaam Aleikhum."*

Every morning at five-thirty we were awakened by the sound of the *muezzin* announcing prayers, *Fajir*. By eleven o'clock, we experienced a tremendous driving rain, coming down with terrible force on the corrugated roofs, the noise quite deafening. The rain was warm and stopped as suddenly as it started. The island is basically all tropical forest, chiefly coconut and baobab trees. We passed little mud houses with thatched roofs dotted about. The beaches are lovely with soft dazzling white sand full of varied coloured shells. Mother and I collected quite a number, as there were no restrictions at the time.

On 10th December 1963, Zanzibar became independent. Thousands of people gathered at the stadium. Luckily Mother and I were at the front with the invited guests. The handsome Prince Philip, Duke of Edinburgh, and important diplomats sat on a grand platform. I sat almost directly opposite Prince Philip. How I longed to go and shake hands with the Prince . . . just to show off to my sisters . . .

The fireworks, musical bands, army parades, in fact the whole ceremony, was just marvellous. I was glad I had come after all. On Independence Day the whole palace was lit with many coloured lights and their reflection on the ocean was gorgeous! In the evenings the Islands of Zanzibar was just out of this world. The dhows and ships peacefully sailing on the sea. The gentle swaying of the palm trees, the night sky and the bright moon, were enough to take your breath away. I could have sat by the sea the whole night.

We were invited by our Arab relatives practically every evening. I felt my life begin to change, because of the strong Arabic influence on feminine behaviour. I learnt a lot, and appreciated every moment of it. It was an experience in a lifetime. How I loved the Arabic music and danced. I met a beautiful Arab aunt, Zulekha. She told me she was married off at only thirteen. We had a lot of fun together visiting places, having lunches. She showed me how to dance the Arabic dances. The end of our visit came all too quickly. Surprisingly, I was quite sad to leave, but anxious to get home for Christmas. I was utterly disappointed not to have met our Arab grandfather, Seif Nassor.

In Mombasa, we stayed with Mr. and Mrs. Bensted. I had hoped to spend Christmas on the Island as my friends had promised to take me out dancing on Christmas Day. On 23rd December, Mother asked our hostess if she could listen to Radio Uganda. We heard an annoucement that the *Muzana* Nattimba, one of Kabaka Mwanga II's wives, had passed away! Mother was very anxious to be present at her grandmother's burial, but it appeared she could not, as Muslims are buried immediately. Great were the burial conflicts after the death of Great-grandmother was announced. Her cousins from Seta wanted to bury her. Other relatives wanted the *Muzana* to lie with the rest of the deceased royal family at Kasubi.

Our grandmother wanted a small, private Muslim burial at Bombo. Prince Badru, a staunch Muslim, wanted the burial ceremonies held at Kibuli. Grandmother's wishes prevailed. Mboni and other Muslim women prepared the body for burial. Unfortunately, Sylvia and Berit were up at the mine, Helene was in England. Practically the whole family was away except for Grandma, Aunt Nuru, Mboni and the boys. Seventy eight year old Great-grandmother, Nattimba Binti Juma had lived to see two great-great-grandchildren, Daudi and Jasmine, Mboni's children.

Meanwhile Mother and I had quite a rough journey on the United Tours Company (U. T. C.) bus from Mombasa to Uganda, due to heavy rainfall that year. The bus kept skidding all over the road. Mother prayed to Allah whilst I silently prayed to Jesus. We found all the relatives were at home wailing, crying and saying what a good woman Great-grandmother had been. So it was a miserable week we spent together before returning to school.

# CHAPTER TEN:
# THE LAST YEAR AT SCHOOL

It was now 1964 . . . the last chapter of school life. What difference did it make? Sylvia continued her mischievous pranks. Much as they tried, the nuns could not bring home to her the importance of school work. In contrast, the more I thought about facing the world, the more nervous and frightened I became. I was voted head girl by the school. Prior to this I had won first prize for the most popular girl in the school. I hadn't the slightest idea what responsibilities awaited me.

We were surprised that the nuns had bought a small-screen black and white television. We watched Dr. Kildare weekly and all fell in love with Richard Chamberlain.

One Sunday, Sylvia persuaded me that it would be an exceptional achievement if some of us could walk seven miles to Thika, a small town near Mangu.

"It will be fascinating, exciting, most important educational and physically good for us," she persisted.

Later on in the day after much persuasion she managed to get a group of girls and a nun, Sister Alfred, to accompany us on our walk!

"See, I'm not breaking the rule; I even got the Sister on duty to escort us, O. K?" She was bursting with anticipation.

Sylvia's charm always attracted a clique of girls of varied characters. The quiet ones, the witty ones, the mischievous ones— none could resist her entreaties. On this particular outing, the advance guard was composed of the chatty, impatient girls, full of adventure and reluctant to dally. The slow quiet ones brought up the rear, perhaps feeling the effect of their bruised toes, blistered, and aching feet. Surprisingly, I was in the front with Sylvia . . . she had tied her cardigan around her waist and held a stick. I observed, as I had done all of our lives, that Sylvia never walked, she always ran or danced wherever she went. She seemed to take life on the tips of her toes. Was it the ballet training she had had when she was younger? I wondered. And that stick; she was just three years old when she waved the stick at thieves.

It took us one hour forty-five minutes of half run, half walk to cover the seven miles to Thika. The father of one of our Asian day-pupils owned a shop in the town and we were invited for soft drinks, cakes and Indian food. Afterwards, we played music and danced.

Sister Alfred, who was rather lenient, kept saying, "Girls, come on, let's go back," but we were reluctant to leave.

It was unfair to take advantage of Sister Alfred's kindness. She had been exceptionally good to us. Finally we decided to walk back at six o'clock, just as the twilight was fading into darkness. Sister Alfred was very nervous. Supper must have been served, and I was supposed to be on duty. Trouble was in store for bringing the girls back late. Fortunately, the school manager, Mr. Parson, passed by in the school lorry. He stopped and took as many girls as the lorry could possibly carry.

"Let the weak and tired girls go on the lorry, we'll walk," Sylvia exclaimed.

Sister Alfred decided she'd walk with us. All the way back, another seven miles, the nun exhorted us to say the rosary. "I believe in God Almighty..." Darkness increased by the minute. No one had a torch. For safety's sake, we kept to the edge of the murram road, it felt as though we were blindfolded. It was quite dark on the "White Sisters' Road!" Frogs and crickets filled the air with their music; *croak croak, crick, crick.* We had no street lamps in those days, except for the fireflies that twinkled in the grass. We linked our arms together, praying sincerely as we marched; *crunch crunch* went our feet.

The Headmistress, Sister Maureen, was furious with Sister Alfred. She was actually ordered to explain herself to the Mother Superior at the convent. We were scolded a little and had a cold supper. The next day we all had diarrhoea; this was not surprising as we had stuffed ourselves with countless cakes and other food while in Thika. The secondary school girls congratulated us on our achievement!

Out of defiance of the nuns' absolute authority, Sylvia loved to dare them by sending letters to Father to be posted by the Asian day pupils.

"Why should a stranger read my father's letter?"

Every letter we wanted posted had to be read by the headmistress. The first time I ever tried to sneak one out to Father, I was caught red-handed by Sister Mary de Lorette. I wished the earth would open up and swallow me alive. She spoke harshly to me as she took the letter. I complained in it about the music teacher who slammed my fingers on the piano and smacked me across the face every time I touched the wrong key. I told him I was contemplating leaving music, and I stopped music lessons thereafter.

Sylvia begged the day-pupils to buy her knitting needles and blue wool as she had planned to knit mother a sweater. I wondered where she got the money? After receiving the needles and wool she laboriously started knitting. How the whole school made fun of her! As far as we were concerned, knitting was for grandmas. Sylvia had no idea how to hold the needles, leave alone how to read a pattern. She often missed classes, busy teaching herself how to knit.

The work-load of her final year was of no importance. As her knitting progressed, she began hiding in places where no-one could find her. We had no idea what she had knitted until she presented the long shapeless sweater to mother during the holidays. The arms were way down to the knees, the width was enough for two adults. She had the satisfaction, however, of having made something and that was all that mattered. As with every holiday, seeing movies was our priority. *Ben Hur* was the greatest, Charlton Heston the second most handsome man on earth. I still considered Father as number one.

That year, we had difficulty in getting a science teacher. The nuns managed to accept a student from the University of Nairobi, who was doing his practicals, to teach us twice a week. Early one Monday morning, we heard the zooming of a motorbike and beheld, a young handsome Englishman arriving. The whole school was overwhelmed, making the young man quite nervous. We soon took a keen interest in science, a subject we had formerly despised. Our general appearance improved whenever we had science classes. Our dreams ended when Mr. Reed left, to be replaced by a Goan teacher, Mr. Fernandez from Thika. He had deep-set grey eyes, a neat beard and a very tanned complexion. He was much like the teachers of *Oliver Twist*. His voice boomed as he spoke, walking up and down the wooden platform, tapping his ruler. He explained what was expected of us.

"If you do not want to work, just stay out of my class. No-one is to be late, homework should be done, notes studied." At the end of term, much to our relief, we all passed our exam.

On 12th December 1963, we rejoiced for our many Kenyan schoolmates who had received their independence. Back in Kampala Grandma was glued to the radio listening to Voice of Kenya. Mzee Jomo Kenyatta was sworn in as Prime Minister of Kenya.

During the holidays, we received a telegram from Grandfather Nassor in Zanzibar, informing us that he would shortly be in Uganda. The excitement that was aroused in the house was indescribable; mother was to see her father after nearly thirty years. Nassor was to see his daughter, a young thirty-eight year old grandmother of three children. What a hustle and bustle there was in the house in preparation for Grandfather's arrival!

"Oh, how nice it will be to see Grandma and Grandfather together," we said happily. "What will he look like? Will he accept us as his grandchildren? How will Nassor feel seeing his daughters after so many years?"

Making sure we had long-sleeved, ankle length dresses and a head cover, we rode to the railway station to meet him. Seif Nassor still had good posture, and was very handsome. We curtsied and kissed his hands.

"*Asalaam Aleikhum,*" we politely greeted him, just as any Arab girl would have done.

Mother was overjoyed to see her father, and made a great fuss over him. How happy and proud we were to have a grandfather. We invited him on our regular walks all over Mengo and Namirembe. He loved Uganda and thought it was a beautiful country. Later in the week we took him on bus rides through Kampala. Sometimes Mboni and Prince Henry invited him for outings to Entebbe, Bombo, Jinja and many other small towns. Fridays he went with the family to the Kibuli Mosque for prayers. We kept our heads covered whenever we were in his presence. Although the mini-dress was in fashion, it was not permitted in our home, certainly not in front of our Arab or Baganda relatives. The end of our holidays came all too soon and we were back at school. Grandfather stayed on for another month or so before returning to Zanzibar.

Sundays were still Sylvia's special days. One Sunday morning Sylvia and her friends were caught red-handed in the nuns' little farm. This area was their escape from boredom. Sylvia loved listening to the turkeys gobbling and watching the piglets, perhaps recalling the punishments at Kisubi many years before. These animals were truly harmless, not the terrifying huge monsters we saw as children. But, we were not allowed to wander into the nuns' private property. There was a man-made dam, I understand the water was collected from a coffee bean washing machine. The nuns would collect litters of kittens and drown them! Some of us cried when we heard of such a disastrous episode.

In the afternoon, Sylvia and her friends decided to go out of the compound yet again. On seeing Sylvia I called her and restrained her from joining her friends.

"Sylvia, you had better listen to me this time. You are not going out of school!" I sternly said.

"But Meggie, we were just going around the church, that's all," she pleaded with me, as she had done many times before.

"You are NOT going and that's it," I retorted linking my arm in hers and holding her firmly.

We walked back to school together, both happy at having solved our differences. Well ten minutes later, the bell rang summoning us to line up. Sylvia's group was called up to the front and me too! Why in heaven's name? I wondered.

"Sylvia," began Sister Maureen, "count your lucky stars you were not with this lot. Tomorrow they are all leaving the school."

As a head girl, I was included amongst the culprits; this was one of the most humiliating moments in my entire life.

"Ah, that's not fair, Meggie wasn't with them," sighed a few girls. I tried to explain myself, but Sister Maureen would not listen.

"If I say you broke the rule, that's it, as from tomorrow you are no longer the head girl. Now go back to your line."

The nun in-charge, Sister Alfred, intervened, pleading with the headmistress that I wasn't anywhere near the girls who broke the rule. The headmistress realised her misjudgment, swallowed her pride and let me go.

Next morning, I walked up to the headmistress and gave her my head girl badge, but she completely ignored me. I too had a streak of pride and stubbornness and repudiated any head girl duties, such as handing out the mail, taking in the school for their meals, supervising study periods, daily jobs and so on. I had been publicly humiliated and falsely accused. I expected justification in front of the school from the headmistress. This misunderstanding between the headmistress and myself was not solved for three weeks.

Finally Sister Maureen apologised, in private of course. Why couldn't she admit she was wrong? All my life I had tried to understand grown ups and I just couldn't.

Sylvia was very grateful to me for saving her from being expelled. Her six friends, unfortunately, had been literally thrown out of the school the following day. They were huddled into a car with no money, food or extra clothing.

"Find your way home," Sister Maureen ordered.

All the six girls were dropped near the New Stanley Hotel. The leader begged some shopkeeper for ten shillings, got on a country bus and returned to school. The nuns detained her in the convent for the night and threw her out the next morning. She found her way home to Bungoma. Georgina got her fare from an uncle and went back home to Meru. Mary too was helped and boarded a bus to Naivasha. The rest were helped by good Samaritans. Some went to Dr. Barnardo's Home for the night, at least they were given shelter! Maria, who had been adopted by the White Sisters since babyhood, had no one to turn to. The old nuns were very hurt at losing Maria but had nothing to say to their superior.

Where Maria lived we never found out. I met her almost five years later working at a supermarket in Nairobi. She was still her jolly self. She told me she had rented a room in Nairobi and was fending for herself. What a shame! Maria was an "A" student and would have made herself a better life given the choice.

Sister Maureen wrote to Father telling him what horrors Sylvia and Berit were, that she would have expelled them, had it not been for me. Father wrote back that he did not think what his daughters had done merited expulsion from school. They had done what any normal child might do. Sister Maureen handed me Father's letter and asked me what I thought of it. He wrote that he thought single women had a problem in understanding children. I read it and thought to myself, Father has got some guts! The headmistress watched me as I read the letter, waiting for my comment. I had none. As always I feared anyone who had no compassion for children.

At this period we had many African girls of important families. Tom Mboya's daughter, and Pamela Mboya's identical twin nieces, Mr. Mathu's daughters, the daughter of Mr. Muli, the future Chief Justice of Kenya, Dr. Kiano's nieces, the daughters of Mr. James Gichuru, Minister for Finance, and Mr. Ambunya's daughters. I was later to teach President Kenyatta's two nieces, the daughters of Mr. Muigai. We also had a Yugoslav Ambassador's daughter. This was a period when integration was just beginning, slowly but surely.

Getting over the trauma of the expulsion sooner than expected, Sylvia came sneaking into line as the school assembled for dinner and I reprimanded her,

"Sylvia do you mind explaining why you are late?" using my authority as the head girl.

"Can't you discriminate in favour of your sister at least? O. K., I was in the loo," she said pretending to be serious.

"Couldn't you have gone earlier?" I demanded.

"I didn't feel like doing anything earlier, but as soon as the bell rang, oh, I had such a severe stomach ache. I had to run to the loo," she replied, smiling sheepishly.

The whole school burst out laughing. I quickly controlled the girls, called Sylvia aside and warned her not to be late again. I would not tolerate her excuses. She took advantage of my headship practically the whole year through.

Afternoon classes were her periods of relaxation. Not long after the lesson started, Sylvia would fall asleep, unless the lesson was exceptionally interesting. Sister Aristide taught us religion and did everything possible to stimulate our interest. During the lesson on the Church History or Acts of the Apostles, Sylvia actually snored, causing the class to giggle. Sister Aristide repeatedly questioned Sylvia and there was no response. A friend nudged Sylvia and she jumped up.

"You are always picking on me, I know you think I was sleeping."

Guilt makes one defensive! Perhaps Sylvia didn't care because there was no future for women. For years throughout East Africa very few girls made it to the secondary school. The highest class one got to was Form II. Complete education was primarily for boys, the future bread-winners.

At the beginning of the third term we began our preparations for the end of year examinations. Every weekend we worked on past Cambridge papers. A few of us dropped Maths— I was one of them. Sylvia took all subjects except for General Science. To my amazement, she actually took her studies seriously. Early in the morning she got up and studied.

School leaving examinations were a terribly frightening experience. I started developing boils all over my body. The headmistress personally nursed me for over a month. Without consulting me, Sister Maureen wrote to Father, saying that I was under stress and that she thought it best I did not sit my exams. In the first term I lost half my History marks because some girls broke a school rule and Sister Maureen told me as the head girl I should not have let that happen, therefore instead of getting 78% I was given 34%. Instead of being fifth, I was almost bottom of the class. In the second term, I still came fifth and I wondered why the headmistress didn't want me to sit the exam. I wrote to Father and told him I was determined to sit the exam even if it killed me. He was extremely pleased with my decision.

Father asked the nuns to buy us Sanatogen, a non-prescriptive drug, to calm our nerves. The nuns encouraged the whole fourth form to take it once a day, just before we went to bed. It did me a lot of good, I wasn't as nervous as I normally was; perhaps what Sister Maureen had done had given me more courage, more determination. I had written to Padre Pio, a holy priest, in Rome asking him to pray that I'd get a second grade. Fortunately, he did answer my letter advising me to pray and leave all to God. If He thought I should get a second grade, He'd give it to me. Deep inside of me I had made up my mind to become a nun if I had a first grade, doubting at the same time how my Muslim family would have taken that. I fancied the little Sisters Of Jesus. I'd work with and for the poor...or shut my life away as a Carmelite.

When the examinations started I was surprisingly calm. Sylvia seemed a little nervous. I found the papers quite pleasant. I continued my Novenas and studies without fail. Helene, who had completed her nurse's course in Preston, England came to Kenya to see us, together with mother, Mboni and Prince Henry. Sylvia and I were in full concentration doing our last Art paper when we heard the girls calling from downstairs.

"Meggie, Sylvia, your sister from England is here."

I was all excited. I hurriedly finished my paper and rushed to see Helene, after two years of separation. Wow! How smart and elegant she was, and her accent had changed. The nuns gave us permission to go out with the family. Our friends were all eager too meet them especially to shake hands with the Prince, Henry Kimera.

After the Cambridge School Certificate Examinations, we planned to go camping at Mr. Lawrence Brown's farm at Athi River. There was a strong bond between all the mixed race families. Elvira Ferrucio wrote asking permission to camp at the Browns' farm. Mr. L. C. Brown wrote back to the nuns indicating that he'd be delighted to have the class at his farm. We borrowed three tents; two from the nuns, and one from a day pupil from Thika. Pots, pans, matchboxes, tinned and fresh food, drinks, plates, cups, bedding and a first aid box were all packed. Morote, our driver, was responsible for the bus. Thank heavens there was no nun or teacher! Elvira and I had assured the headmistress of our full responsibility for the group.

Filled with ecstasy, we sang tirelessly, for almost all the three hour journey to Athi River. When at the farm we had a warm welcome from Mr. and Mrs. Brown. It was great seeing our old classmates, Mary and Peter, and the rest of the Brown family. Mr. Brown kindly informed us that we could have anything we wanted, milk, eggs, bread, fresh vegetables and fruits, all for free! They extended their hospitality to the use of their whole farm. Great! As daylight waned, we fixed the tents, made the beds, and started cooking. Great enthusiasm and co-operation was shown. After an early dinner, we went hill climbing and had a treasure hunt. Peter took us on a farm tour and helped us with rides on the pony.

It was very cold at night on the Athi plains. When all was quiet, as everyone was utterly exhausted, Sylvia started her mischievous pranks.

"Eh, girls," she whispered, "I can hear a hyena walking around the tent." Some timid girls started screaming, jumping into one another's beds.

"Continue making noise girls. You will attract them . . . Listen, listen, can you hear them calling?" she continued.

"Stop it Sylvia, you are only making everyone panic," I urged.

"Oh, I was only trying to prepare everyone just in case of an emergency. Have you thought how we would handle a hyena, if we're not prepared?" she asked.

She made sense. After listening intently we did hear the whooping cackle of a hyena in the distance. Several girls began to pray.

"Good night girls, make sure your toes are well tucked in, otherwise you'll wake up with them in the hyena's mouth," Sylvia started again.

"That's enough now, Sylvia," said everyone simultaneously.

The next day, after breakfast and general tidying up of our camp, the Brown family invited us for morning coffee. We listened to pop music, Little Richard, the Monkees, the Shadows, Harry Belafonte, we danced and had Peter to entertain us just like the good old days. How we laughed till our sides ached. Later, we walked up the hill to visit the Dunman family. These folks always included us in their family picnics when they visited their children on Sundays.

On Sunday afternoon we packed and drove back to school. The school was overwhelmed on our return. You'd have thought we had come from outer space! There were endless questions asked. Indeed, we had done something new in the history of the school.

A week before the holidays, several professionals from Nairobi gave us career talks. Sylvia and I wanted to become air hostesses but the nuns discouraged us. Sylvia was persuaded to choose nursing. I was talked into teaching. The nuns made the necessary arrangements at the Nairobi Hospital and Highridge Teachers' College for the following year.

Our last Christmas holidays together were spent at Kabale with Father. He decided to take a week off work and take us to Katwe, to show us his mine at Itama. A Jewish family, the Rolands, Father's visitors, joined us. We passed through the "Impenetrable Forest" of Uganda, full of towering trees, braided with moss and lichen and vines. The entangled trees were gigantic and the foliage so thick that, to someone standing deep inside the forest, the sky was almost invisible. It was dark, cold and damp as few of the sun's rays pierced through. Father continued uphill with the car. We laboured up the trail through the dense forest undergrowth, fighting brambles and creepers which festooned the trees like ropes.

Beneath our feet was a carpet of colourful butterflies and numerous other insects which sprang to life, flying from flower to flower. We could hear the chirping of hundreds of colourful long-tailed birds, chiefly the touracco, the white cattle egret and the heron. The leaves rustled as the birds flashed their bright plumage and sang. Some of them were suspiciously peering at us.

The forest was unbelievably massive. There were scattered thickets of bamboo... the floor was covered with various ferns in different shades of green and clumps of wild celery. Huge leaves had drops of water on them like pearls. Hundreds of orchids could be seen, some of them growing on to the tree trunks. As we continued to labour through the forest, we inhaled the fresh smell of damp earth and the faint scent of wild flowers. The grass seemed like a glistening green carpet. What a world of beauty!

In the depths of the forest, we heard the slow passage of a jungle fowl foraging through the bushes, the crackling of twigs beneath our feet and the swishing of disturbed branches. A bee began to buzz round my head. Bees can never leave me alone! The sun crept further up in the sky. The forest seemed to calm me with the soft green, silent mystery it carried. What peace, what creation... how I wished I could live here forever, away from the turmoil of the city. My nostrils expanded to smell time-worn plants and the mushy odour of the river bank. Bending over we looked at ourselves in the sun-mirroring water, dipped our bare feet into the crystal water and sat still for a couple of minutes.

A safari ant crawled across the upturned sole of my foot. Luckily I was not bitten. Here was Father's picnic spot. We noticed the powdery touch of the loose dried earth on the rocks; yellow and orange pollen of some wild flowers kept softly falling upon the large leaves. A mouse turned and darted back into the foliage. A shy mongoose changed his mind on-seeing us and hid back in the earth. Squirrels scampered up the gigantic tree. We heard some mysterious drums of the forest which echoed in the bamboo thickets, across glades and clearings. Out of nowhere, partially naked pygmies appeared with bows and arrows and silently passed us. I glanced upwards, the sky turned stormy, foreboding, heralding rain and wind. Suddenly there was a flash of lightning, a clap of thunder and down came the pestering rain to drench us. Sheets of rain beat on us as we hurried up the hill to the car. We saw unfamiliar monkeys chattering and trying to find shelter among the thick leaves.

The road to Itama was extremely slippery. Father and George Epaminondas, Helene's fiance, had to fix chains around the wheels to steady the car. The Rolands helped as well. The rain stopped as suddenly as it had started. The sun took up a fugitive position behind a passing cloud. We arrived at the mine after a while. The workers all came to meet us, helping us with our picnic baskets. After a change of clothes at the huts, we climbed further up the mountain. The fresh fruit smell from Father's orchard filled the air. Littered with broken twigs and fallen leaves, the vegetable beds had been lashed mercilessly in the short storm. We tasted the most delicious fruits, had our picnic lunch, rested a while and set out again for Katwe. All this while the Rolands were busy filming everything.

The heavy rain had delayed our arrival at Katwe. Weeks earlier, Father had booked a guest house which belonged to the Queen Elizabeth Park Hotel. After a good hot, relaxing bath, we went to the dining hall and had a delicious dinner. Here Father introduced us to his associates, Greeks, Danes, Africans and a few Englishmen.

The next day after breakfast, we visited some monuments and museums. We saw fantastic art displays, batiks, curios made from ebony, monuments made from ivory, rhinoceros horn, purses and handbags made from leopard, lion and zebra skins: these were to be banned in years to come. Although the nuns had taken us to the Nairobi Park, we had never seen such an abundance of wild animals as we saw at the Queen Elizabeth Park. Here, the tall elephant grass grows in great stretches of open bush, broken here and there by termitara, towers of dried red mud built by thousands of white ants, my most dreaded enemies.

Hundreds of species of herbivorous animals were grazing peacefully in the open countryside. They were camouflaged so well by the background that predators must have had quite a hard time finding them! We watched elegant graceful impala which are high jumpers; and have remarkable leaping powers. The tallest of all living land animals, the gentle giraffe, were peacefully feeding on leaves of thorn trees; the massive African elephant, the largest land animals, lazily lumbered about swaying their trunks. We read a sign "Elephants have the right of way." Father stopped the car and let a herd pass. I was scared out of my wits. There were hundreds of dik-dik, antelopes, zebras and eland — the largest antelope in the world, an amazingly powerful animal. Father stopped driving for a while and we walked, barefoot, over the ruts in the dry uneven ground. A gentle placid breeze blew in our faces. Our nostrils picked up the faint smell of dung.

The next day we went to the Salt Lake at Katwe, where salt deposits and carbonate chloride are found. It was like a mirror, and way down the valley the scene was quite blinding. No wonder light-eyed Europeans always carried sunglasses. Farther up the hill the grass sparkled with dew, but below the heat was unbearable and the air heavy. Later we went into the Kazinga Channel on a big launch. Father and Sylvia jumped in for a swim. In the distance, I spotted hippopotami by the hundreds popping their heads up and down. Sylvia rushed back into the boat. Father speculated that perhaps the poor animals were more frightened of the boat than we imagined. We had a memorable time at Katwe, and felt rather sad to go back to Mengo.

The rest of the holidays were spent with Mother. In the first week of January we received our school certificate results. I was overwhelmed with a second grade which was just like I had asked Padre Pio for. Sylvia only just made it. Although she had done extremely well in all other subjects, she unfortunalety failed the English grammar paper. Sylvia was very upset, and decided to commit suicide, the only solution she could think of. Father had absolutely no doubts that she'd be top, now he'd be terribly hurt, that's what she thought.

That night she went to Mother's first aid box and retrieved about ten different tablets. I argued with her that she was being childish and unreasonable. She said she didn't care. We shared a bedroom which had been formerly occupied by Helene who was now married to George Epaminondas. Sylvia brought in the ten tablets, placed them neatly on the side table, next to a glass of water, knelt down, said her night prayers and after praying fervently, swallowed tablet after tablet. I had noticed five different kinds of tonic tablets, an aspirin, a malaraquine and three others. I thought these would not harm her. Sylvia came over, kissed me goodnight, bade me farewell and then calmly got into her bed. I was pretty worried, but I did not show it. Sylvia was soon fast asleep. Every now and again, I'd check to see whether she was still breathing. I'd touch her to feel whether she was still warm. I hardly slept a wink that night.

Next morning, Sylvia woke up languorously stretching like a cat, as fresh as anything, back to her old self, studying herself objectively in the mirror. However, Father was very pleased with both of us for our performance. The nuns urged Father to let Sylvia do her Cambridge again, convincing him that she had the ability to obtain a first grade. Father reasoned with Sylvia but she was reluctant to go back to school alone. She continued with her favourite hobbies of art and poetry.

## THE GREATEST LOVE

What can I compare to the Greatest Love?
The most purest, most wonderful love.
There is nothing in creation,
Not all the nation.
That stimulates a creature,
Not even a preacher,
Like the love of God above.

**Sylvia, 1964**

# CHAPTER ELEVEN:
# GROWING UP

Sylvia had made up her mind to become a nurse and the nuns confirmed a place for her at the Nairobi Hospital. But as she was only seventeen years old she had to wait until the September term. After nine years of our being together I was to travel back to Kenya alone to start my teacher training course. The nuns took me to the college and introduced me to the English Principal. In a navy-blue suit, hair done and sprayed, she looked very dignified, like England's future Prime Minister, Mrs. Margaret Thatcher. Miss Hall welcomed me to the college and I earnestly began my studies.

Sylvia decided to do something in the meantime. She persuaded our brother-in-law, Prince Henry, who had studied Oxford English and was a typical Englishman except that he was a Muganda, to draft an impressive letter to Hunts Motors as she had seen a job advertisement, and had hoped to get a well paid job.

"After all, Dad has a share with the company," she said confidently. "I'm sure Mr. Hunts, dad's lawyer, won't turn me down."

Father did not want her to get involved with his business associates, therefore, he took her back to the mine and trained her in typing. She soon became his proficient secretary. It wasn't long before I received Sylvia's first typed letter. She told me all about what she was doing and how she enjoyed complete peace up at the mine. I really envied her. Here I was a total stranger in Nairobi, with no family or close friend.

## LORD JESUS

When every soul had left a sword in me,
I find my world back in thee.
When all have let me down,
You make me laugh like a clown.
I know you are always around,
I bless the day when you I found.
**Sylvia, 1965.**

147

After spending some time up-country, Sylvia decided to come back to Kampala to do a proper secretarial course and get a certificate.

My first term at college was utterly miserable without my sisters around. Mrs. Nazareth, who noticed how lonely I was, often called me to her house and gave me some of her lovely cooking. Mrs. Dudgen too would sneak me into her place and give me tea. A six and a half foot tall Frenchman, Mr. Michelle, encouraged me in my Art lessons. Befriending the second year students, I felt a little more comfortable. There were three Asians, three Africans and one Afro-American lady, Mrs. Akumu, the wife of Denis Akumu, on the staff; the other fifty-five percent of the teachers were British. The white tutors had an air about them, always very critical and full of sarcasm.

"Miss Bjordal how much time do you spend on your hair; are you sure you aren't wearing a wig? I wish you could give me some of that hair."

This was said almost every day of every term for the two years I was there. Was it envy or admiration? After a written examination I went home to Kampala to spend half of my holidays with Mother and the second half with Father. I normally hitch-hiked three hundred and fifty miles to Kabale. On arriving I was completely exhausted, when I literally bumped into the Bjordal Mines German manager, who drove me up to the mine. Father cried when he saw me.

"Why didn't you let me know that you'd be coming?" he asked sadly.

"It's O. K. Dad, I enjoyed the trip," I said.

"God gave me many children and I am not blessed to have one of you with me," he said and it hurt me terribly.

"Don't be upset Dad, I wanted to surprise you," I responded.

"You kids must blame me for what happened," he continued.

"Of course not Dad, we love you."

We had a quiet, peaceful holiday together. All too soon I boarded a bus back home. A day before my departure to Kenya I felt feverish. In spite of being ill, I boarded the train for Nairobi. Sylvia and I were in tears as we said farewell. On arrival I had a bad attack of malaria and was off sick for a week. The headmistress and matron nursed me endlessly, changing my clothes when I sweated, cooling me when the temperature was high.

Great was my excitement, when Sylvia came to Nairobi in September. At least now we'd be visiting each other. At Nairobi Hospital, Sylvia became very popular with the girls but not with the staff and the Matron. Every Saturday when she visited she'd tell me all her difficulties. Every member of staff seemed to be hostile to her. Their biggest complaint concerned her hair.

"Why don't you do something about your hair, cut it, get it thinned for goodness sake!" What a coincidence?

148

"The Matron keeps telling me off because of my hair. What does she expect me to do when I have so much hair," She would complain and then say sweetly, "Eh, Meggie, why don't you comb my hair for me please?"

We laughed then I would get a comb and brush, Sylvia had only combed the top of her hair, the rest she tucked under her cap. I carefully brushed her tangled, curly hair until it straightened out and reached down to her waist.

"Sylvia, why don't you plait your hair or make a bun?" I often asked her. "I can't be bothered," was her reply.

Then dressing smartly we boarded a bus at Highridge to town for coffee at the Coffee House. Sylvia particularly liked to admire the paintings on the wall. She often remarked that if someone approached her to complete what seemed like incomplete paintings, she would have loved to do it. I wouldn't have been surprised if she did, with her daring quality and entrepreneurial spirit. Back at the hospital Sylvia wrote to Father telling him that she was settled at the hospital but that the "whites" were picking on her.

4 September 1965

Bjordal Mines Limited
Wolfram Mine Kabale
P. O. Box 50,
Kabale, Uganda.

My dear Sylvia,

Thanks a lot for your letter of 4th September which I have just received. I am glad to hear you've well settled in Nairobi Hospital. Very good for you!

I am sure you will learn a lot ... You should be proud of your nationality. Few people in this world can show such variation of different blood so nicely mixed! It is your personality that counts in this world, not your colour. Don't think that people are against you and don't take whatever they say as an offence. It really means that they are just admiring you for your beauty. Just tell them the truth that you are half Norwegian, a quarter Arab and a quarter Muganda of royal blood. That will make them think.

You show such a mixture of blood, on top of it all being beautiful, having character and intelligence! You are very lucky indeed.

Love you.
**Dad.**

The past kept playing her up. I told her that I never felt, at any time, that people were against me because of who I was. What we went through as children was over. I was proud of myself; I had the assurance from Father. Father was very worried and concerned about Sylvia's resultant depression and unhappiness. He felt she needed us to support and encourage her. He gave her every encouragement he thought she needed. After receiving his letter, she seemed pleased and self-confident. I noticed it when we met one Saturday.

"Isn't it funny, Dad wrote and gave me the same advice as you did."

Come November, Sylvia seemed a lot happier. Her letters to Father were much more cheery.

"I am quite settled and enjoying my nursing career. I have cut my hair short to please the Matron." Father wrote to her and supported her decision.

After her hair was short, she went to the hairdresers' on a weekly basis. She looked very sophisticated and elegant with a full figure. She often dyed her hair dark brown or sometimes black. She detested her golden hair, because a woman once remarked in Luganda that our hair was like *enfufu*, red soil. Sylvia turned to the Muganda woman.

*"Sigwe weka amanyi oluganda"*— you are not the only one who knows Luganda," she said.

The whole bus full of Baganda passengers turned to look at us in utter amazement. They were dumb-founded, that we could actually speak their language.

At the end of every year, Nairobi Hospital held a social evening, quite a big party with all the delicacies, drinks and music. I had to ask for special permission from the headmistress to sleep out. I was cross-examined about my night out and made to sign a special book. Sylvia re-assured me about where I'd sleep. I should concentrate on having a wonderful time and when the dance was over, she would then tell me about her arrangements. Most of the nurses went to the hairdressers' and sported beautiful hair styles. Sylvia was glamorous. She wore a shiny golden dress with a pair of high-heeled sandals to match. Her spectacular looks startled everyone with their impact. She had an innate sense of personal style, the instinctive flair for selecting and wearing with great panache the most eye-catching of clothes. A cinderella in a magnificent outfit, she was spellbinding.

What a lovely evening! I was introduced to practically every nurse at the hospital. The crowd was mostly white. I was quite nervous, perhaps due to my sheltered life, but I began to feel more at ease when some of the nurses began to call me Sylvia. Sometimes I pretended to be her, just for the fun of it. We danced till midnight then we walked down an absolutely quiet corridor. Sylvia ushered me to her spacious, tidy and comfortable room. I was to share her bed with her. I hardly slept as she had convinced me that she would be expelled if I were caught in her room at that time of the night. On the other hand, she fell asleep within no time at all. At dawn I dressed quietly and decided to sneak out of the hospital but Sylvia cautioned me.

"Eh, Meggie, do you want everyone to be suspicious? You'd better stay here! You are not going without your breakfast either."

I nervously waited, watching her calmly get ready for her breakfast. About an hour later she came back with a sandwich for me which she had hidden in her pocket and a flask of hot coffee. How memories flooded back. Sylvia will never change.

"I'm off duty; we should go for mass at the Holy Family Cathedral and spend the day in town."

Sylvia took me for lunch, a movie, *Lawrence of Arabia* with the handsome actor Peter O'Toole, and after a lovely time we parted. At the end of the year I was almost reluctant to go home without my sister who was truly a dear friend.

At the beginning of 1966, Sylvia was due for her second examination. We did not see each other as often. She would cut short her visits as she had quite a lot of studies. On getting her results she was very pleased and came over to tell me about it. We decided to go to Nairobi to celebrate. Sylvia wrote to father and gave him the good news.

"Congratulations! Have you thought of becoming a doctor?" he inquired.

"No, it has never crossed my mind," she replied.

By and by Sylvia became very popular indeed at the Nairobi Hospital as she was a friendly, happy and apparently a carefree young woman. I came back for my second term in May. I found Sylvia very depressed. She began to probe into her past, asking father why he left mother, blaming her unhappiness on not having a mother and father together. She felt at a complete loss, unwanted and unloved. Father explained that his childhood had not been easy for him either as he hardly knew his mother. He lost her when he was only a boy, and he had a terribly strict father. Although he toiled from an early age helping at home, he had no grudge against the world nor his father.

You've got to fight for what you want in this world. Life is not easy for anyone. Just hold your head up and keep on walking. You must remember one thing, never take counsel with your emotions and I think that you are apt to do that. Learn to adapt yourself to the hardships of this world, learn to be grateful for what you have and make your life the way you want it to be, not a model of somebody else's wrecked life.

Not long after this, Sylvia met a handsome twenty-one-year old Englishman named George Albert at a dance held at the Nairobi Hospital. The two fell in love at first sight. She at once brought him to college to meet "big sister." Since she seemed very much in love and serious about marrying him, I advised her to write to father. Quite honestly, I thought she was too young to marry and was worried that she wouldn't finish her nursing course. Taking my advice, she wrote to father and he replied.

My dear Sylvia,

Many thanks for your letter of 28th July. I feel so tired at times that I forget what I'm writing. I think a lot of you Sylvia. You girls are very dear to me. I know at your age you feel very uncertain and insecure. Have courage and faith in yourself and learn to stand on your own two feet.

Now Sylvia, about your boyfriend? Please be sensible enough not to make any mistakes. If he is a nice man I shall know. What I would like to know about him is:

a) What does he do?
b) Where are his parents?
c) Has he got a job?
d) How old is he?

There are very few men in this world who can be trusted. Remember that Sylvia. You may have found a good fellow and I wish you the best of luck. Many attractive girls, like you get into hooks of wrong men. So don't forget that.

Lots and lots of love my dear,
**Daddy.**

Sylvia was filled with joy on receiving father's letter, and persuaded George Albert to write to him as well, both asking permission to get engaged.

Although father gave his consent, he thought she was a very emotional girl. However, he was very careful how he handled his teenage daughter, especially where her boyfriend was concerned. He therefore placed his full confidence in me concerning Sylvia, asking me to talk her out of marriage, at least for the present. Sylvia was still a teenager straight from thirteen years of convent life; he thought it wise for any girl to be at least twenty-five years old before committing herself into marriage. Marriage is a commitment, a vocation. He had learnt that the hard way.

George and Sylvia were happy together. You never saw a better suited couple. I often met them at luncheons, dances and movies. When I was at home, Sylvia wrote about her expected wedding, telling me that I should return to Nairobi as soon as I received her letter.

I quickly packed and set off, with brother John, a favourite of every member of the family, who was due to return to school in Kenya. Sylvia had written that she had made arrangements where we could stay and she would meet us at the station but she didn't turn up. We took a taxi to the Nairobi Hospital. Sylvia was beautifully dressed when I arrived but seemed confused and agitated.

"Meggie, I'm so glad to see you. I'm sorry I didn't meet you, but something has happened," she told me. All her friends were around her with faces as long as fiddles.

"What is the matter?" I asked, I thought maybe George had met with an accident.

"Meggie the wedding is off. I'm going to break off the engagement. I'll be back in an hour," she mumbled nervously. She was very confused and sad.

"Sylvia, what am I going to do here with John, and our cases?" I asked, feeling disappointed. I had come all the way from Uganda for a wedding that was not to be.

"Let's see now. I'll keep your cases in my room and you go with Pat to Hurlingham," she answered after thinking long and hard.

John and I went to Pat's. Her father wasn't amused when he met us.

"Pat you aren't old enough to pick strangers from the street," he boomed.

In the evening I went to Nairobi Hospital to spend the night and John stayed with Sylvia's friend. The next morning I collected my brother and left for Eastleigh to spend some time with my Ethiopian friend Georgina.

Apparently, George Albert was shocked beyond description when Sylvia gave him back his ring. He almost went out of his mind! Two weeks later he went back to England and was never heard of again. Later Sylvia came and explained the whole situation and apologised for having upset me.

"Meggie, I don't know what I have done except that I've hurt Albert terribly, but I had to break it off and continue my studies. I know Dad doesn't want me to marry yet."

I told her what she did was unreasonable and unnecessary and that I was sure if she had told Albert to wait he would definitely have waited.

Our brother, together with the rest of his school, was collected at the Nairobi Railway Station and they went to Mangu.

## MY DEEP EMOTION

I've got to run before the storm starts about me
Each thing I do, wherever I go your face I see
Can't touch you now, your love cannot be
Let me be the girl that I am, always afraid
In case I hurt, In case I lose my head
For it's better to love, and lose, that's what's said
I'll never find true love until I'm dead.

## Sylvia, 1966

I had been elected the Social Secretary at the college. This was the year I had the opportunity of meeting Margaret Kenyatta when she visited Highridge Teachers' Training College. Whenever the committee organised a social evening, I'd always invite Sylvia to boost up our spirits. She was the centre of attraction. She performed ballet for the staff and students and in spite of not having practised for two years she was still very good. Late at night, after our late evening, I sneaked her into my room. We again managed not to be caught. On sports day, I would persuade the tutors to let Sylvia play in my place and usually she did. Sylvia, a born athlete, helped our team win most of the events.

Life went on as normally as possible for both of us, until we read in the papers that Milton Obote and Idi Amin were accused of smuggling gold from Congo. Disputes between Milton Obote and the Baganda grew very intense. Soon our King was overthrown on orders of the Prime Minister. During this period the political situation in Uganda was deteriorating.

Sylvia would run to me for comfort. We had not heard from home for what seemed a long time. We concluded that every member of the family had been killed. There were four of us in Kenya at this period. Berit was in Meru doing a Montessori course, John was in Mangu, Sylvia and I in Nairobi. Father was the only person who kept in touch with us.

"I hear it's terrible in Kampala, your uncle, the Kabaka, has disappeared," he wrote. Apparently, gunfire had been heard in the early hours of the morning of 24th May 1966. Your Uncle Sir Edward Mutesa was attacked at his palace in Mengo. What has happened to your Grandma, Kajja-Obunaku, Mother and brothers, I cannot guess. I understand any royal relative is being arrested."

We listened to Radio Uganda and read the newspapers every day. The Uganda Army, on orders of the Prime Minister, Dr. Milton Obote, had been sent to arrest the Kabaka. This act was unheard of in Buganda. Mutesa had never for one moment suspected anything like this might ever happen to him. He was therefore unprepared and in no position to defend himself. He was completely surrounded by the army. Mutesa and a few of his men quickly decided to hide among the eucalyptus trees which covered *Nalongo,* a white wooden gate, and there they waited for the least glimpse of light. Prince Henry was to give me all these news when we met in Nairobi. He had visited his brother Mutesa II that very day when he was overthrown.

While hiding out, they were enveloped by the usual Uganda morning mist and the air felt cold. Fortunately, the gods were on the Kabaka's side and sent a torrent of rain, boisterous thunder and gusts of wind! It poured as it had never done before in Buganda. The fighting and gun shots subsided for a while, until the rain stopped. Mutesa watched from his hide-out as the women of the family, wife, relatives and maids were taken prisoners. Mutesa decided to jump over the wall, as his special escape gate was locked, in the confusion and panic he couldn't remember where his guard normally kept the key.

Unfortunately, he landed on a jutting stone and dislocated his back which caused him agonizing pain. We read the papers and listened to the radio religiously. From there he disappeared and for almost two months not a word was heard about the Kabaka's whereabouts. He seemed to have vanished into thin air. Some of his family believed Mwanga's Spirit had taken him. This caused endless worries. Unknown to us, the Kabaka had tediously walked miles on end towards the Congo. He passed through forests, marshes, mosquito-infested swamps, hid among bushes and hills covered with wild animals, all the time praying earnestly that they would not attack him. He went without food and water, experiencing extreme back-pain and fever. He occasionally hitched a lift. He miraculously passed road blocks, army and policemen, all of whom were watching for him! Sylvia came to the college to see me one Saturday afternoon. She seemed very worried and thoughtful.

"Meggie, what if every member of the family is killed? What are we going to do?" she asked me. I had no answer. I was the oldest of the four of us in Kenya    my thoughts were in turmoil.

Meanwhile, our brother-in-law, Prince Henry made it to Nairobi and came to the college to see me, with Mr. Charles Hayes and a close friend of his. Miss Hall, our headmistress, told me rather suspiciously, that there were some "gentlemen" to see me. Henry gave me the latest news from home. He hoped Mboni and their four babies, all under the age of five, would soon join him and that they would all go to Britain. Two weeks later Mboni arrived with little Daudi and a week later Grandma Kajja-Obunaku came to the college with baby Feizal, who was about eight months old. I was relieved to see them safe and sound. Eventually, after all the arrangements for political asylum were completed, they left Kenya for Belgium.

An announcement over the radio confirmed that Mutesa II was at Bujumbura, a town in Burundi, a small country west of Uganda. What a relief it was for all of us. The British Government helped him travel to Brussels where he was met by Prince Henry who had arrived a month earlier. They then flew to London.

Our little three year old nephew, Daudi (David) and his one year old brother Feizal were sent to France to be cared for by a famous French/American lady called Josephine Baker. The little boys soon learned to speak French. After almost two and a half years of separation, they were finally re-united with their parents. Jasmine, our niece, stayed with Mother at Mengo, Kampala and two year old Henry Jr., was cared for by his paternal grandmother.

I was now due for my final examinations, written and practical, and despite all the distractions Sylvia and I made it through our final exams. By the end of 1966, I was a full-fledged teacher. Kenyatta College offered me a place to train as a secondary school teacher. Unfortunately, I did not feel able to take up the opportunity, as I wanted to fully support myself. The family in Uganda were having enough problems of their own. The nuns offered me a job at Maryhill as a secondary Art and Science teacher for a while, as there were no vacancies at the primary school. I had a trying time with my pupils, the fourth formers who were formerly my schoolmates. I was glad I had this opportunity as it toughened me. They often played me up but I held my place. Sylvia and I kept in touch as much as possible. Sometimes during the week she would come down with our friend Georgina to see me, or they would stay over the weekend. Other weekends were spent with Georgina and her young family, three lovely girls.

As time went by Sylvia suffered from frequent depression. The first person she consulted was Father. In March of 1967, she expressed her inner feelings. He promptly replied.

My dear daughter,

So many thanks for your kind letter. You have not deserted me just because you haven't written for a long time, don't ever think that way. You must realise that you have had to face one of the crises in your life, like the rest of us. We all have these kind of trials and despair: our dreams gradually take the form of reality as we grow older. If I had to live all over again, I would never want to be a teenager. It was such a cruel period, and so full of despair. One is torn to pieces by one's emotions all the time and one feels so lonely.

So, my dear, forget about your misery and cheer up. I love you as always and think you are a very nice, intelligent, young woman. You certainly have a lot of talent and you should start utilizing your ability now and be the master of your surroundings. You need not be a nurse all your life. It is just a step to further betterment of your position in this world. Believe me, Sylvia, to be born in this world is not easy for anybody. You have to fight your way through it and the going can be pretty rough at times.

I went to Norway for medical treatment. They came to the conclusion that I was suffering from an ischaemic coronary heart disease, which is a strain on the left ventricle of one's heart. When I was in Norway, I longed to be back in Africa and see the sun again. Helene told me you had a nervous breakdown after you broke off; count your blessings my dear.

When I was in Norway, I saw the girl who broke my heart when I was young. I nearly died of shock when I saw her. She had turned into a fat, old, grey-haired slug without teeth, and her appearance was enough to frighten the devil himself on a dark night! I counted my blessings!

    **Love, Dad.**

## I'M LOST OH LORD

Oh what am I looking for, for so long?
I need someone to time this song,
Someone, somewhere to ever belong.
Where or when or for how long can this journey go on?
My heart so many times torn,
With love again I'll be born.
Arguing I'll start to blow the horn.
True love will die once more,
He'll leave me stranded on the shore.
When my love to him becomes a bore,
My heart so sore will once more.
Just like the same old song,
To whom, to where, do I belong?

## SYLVIA, 1966

I invited two of my close friends, Mary Brincat and Priscilla Hughes, to spend their December holidays with me. Mary was full of anticipation, eager to see the real wilds of Africa, to experience adventures in the forested up-country region of Western Uganda. We decided to hitch-hike the three hundred and fifty miles to Kabale.

After riding over ten lifts in all on our trip, exhaustion overtook us. We couldn't take a step further, thirst and hunger made us stagger into a grocery store. The heavens be blessed, we bumped into my Norwegian cousin Berit, who was working with the Peace Corps at Kabale. Berit, who was overjoyed to see me, excitedly explained that our German manager was in town.

"He's leaving right now, we've got to find him before its too late," she said hurriedly.

So, we were to get a free ride up to the mine. What a relief! Father was overwhelmed to see me. After all the evening formalities, I dropped into bed and was out like a light till I heard the morning birds chirping and cocks crowing at dawn.

By coincidence Father had planned to spend Christmas at Katwe. My friends were to see the Queen Elizabeth Park. Mary was thrilled to see hundreds of different animals at first hand.

At Katwe, we met all sorts of people, Greeks, Norwegians, Italians, an occasional English couple. There was much to learn in just a weekend. The weather was extremely hot.

"This is the first time I see a dark-skinned person peeling," Berit exclaimed, observing me.

I was terribly sunburnt. The whites did much better in this respect than me. We spent about two weeks with Father but things were not the same without Sylvia around.

Mary, Priscilla and I decided to hitch-hike back to Kampala but Father seemed against it, advising us to board a bus. Unfortunately, all the buses were fully booked. We learnt that there was transport leaving for Kampala at noon. Father instructed us to wait while he went about his business at Kabale, assuring us he'd be back in an hour or two and that if we had not boarded a bus he'd take us back to the mine. We decided on the spur of the moment to leave soon after Father was out of sight. We walked on a deserted murram road for about an hour, suffering occasional showers of dust from a passing car. Then, in the distance we saw a car approaching at almost walking pace and we put our thumbs out, looking for a lift. A policeman stopped. Oh, no!

"Going somewhere, are we?" he asked rather suspiciously.

"Yes we are," and I nervously named the nearest town.

"Hem, do you happen to be Mr. Bjordal's daughter?" he asked, peering at me. My heart sank.

"The old man," I cursed, "he must have sent a policeman to catch us," I could feel my heart racing against my ribs.

"Yes Sir, I am," I answered with a stammer.

"Well jump in, I am going to Mbarara. My name is Lionel and Mr. Bjordal is a great friend of mine," explained the young officer.

Meanwhile Father came back to the bus stop, and smiled when he found we had already left. The officer met Father the following week and told him he had given us a lift up to Mbarara. Father thought we were rather disobedient. Anyway, we had had a lovely holiday and enjoyed every moment of it.

Back in Nairobi, I found Sylvia had taken Father's advice and was doing a couple of things, not only to better herself academically, but to help her fight boredom. She took private swimming lessons and became an excellent swimmer. To refresh her French she bought herself *Teach Yourself French*, hoping to work later as an air hostess for Sabena Airlines. She read an advertisement in the *Nation* from someone teaching music and she applied. She wrote to Father and gave him the news. This is part of his reply.

"So glad to hear you've become an excellent swimmer. That is a good sport and, as you say, improves one's general health. I am glad to hear you are growing up and have learned to control your emotions. This is indeed an important step in life. Don't worry about having a steady boyfriend, you have all the time in the world. Never be in a hurry. You can now choose the sort of life you want in your time. Yes, I think it is wise to get a good grip on nursing no doubt, but you can in the meantime prepare yourself for another job, for instance, an air hostess. You should polish up on your French. You were quite good at that, learn a phrase a day. You are very talented Sylvia! Especially in your drawing and paintings and I would not be surprised if you are talented in music! Good luck with your music lessons.

I gather you are suffering from some spells of depression. Yes, we all go up and down in moods. It applies to everybody I am sure. So glad to hear you are serious about your French. I hope you get a good grip on the language. I think your handwriting and English are super!

I shall not be able to write you another letter before your 21st birthday but here is the best of luck and may you enjoy good health in your coming year. Sorry to inform you that my Father, your Grandfather Bjordal, died at a ripe age of 84 years!"

We were sorry not to have met our grandfather. My working in Thika meant Sylvia and I could only get together over the weekend. One weekend she'd visit and the other I'd go to the Nurses' Mess at Kenyatta Hospital where she had been transfered. She'd proudly introduce me to all the doctors, nurses and some patients. Sylvia claimed she had never seen so much human suffering as she had witnessed at the casualty department.

Sometimes, Georgina and I would wait in the parking place whilst Sylvia worked for an extra hour or so, attending many sick patients. She seemed near breaking-point, as she was completely exhausted by the end of the day. I really felt sorry for her and often wished she hadn't taken up nursing. She appeared very strong but deep inside she seemed weak.

She told me about the mysterious pains she was having, and was admitted at the Kenyatta Hospital for observation. The doctors were confused and thought her condition was due to exhaustion. Bed rest was recommended for a couple of days. At times, we would not see each other for a week, since my time was fully occupied with my job at school. I felt very uneasy if a week passed without visiting her. Although we both lived in Kenya, I'd get a letter saying,

"Sorry for not visiting. I was ill but I am much better now. Will see you soon."

At once, I would board the bus and visit her. I was rather worried as I had never known Sylvia to complain of pain    not even a headache. Finding her apparently well and healthy I decided I was unduly worried.

Father wrote that his heart didn't feel as good as before. This made us very concerned. Sylvia would look into the medical books and diagnose exactly what she thought was wrong with him, and come to her own conclusions.

"Dad should not live in such high altitudes."

Then she stopped writing for a considerable time and Father became rather concerned about her. In December, he wrote to her again:

My dear daughter,

It is such a long time since you wrote to me. I am a bit worried that you may not be well. I wanted to send you some money but this is difficult if you are in the hospital. How is the position for Christmas? Are you coming to Uganda? I would like you to come up here and have a real rest. You must be tired, you poor girl being on night shift. Console yourself with the fact that it will soon be over.

I am not feeling too well myself. Please write to me dear, and tell me what is troubling you. Don't be afraid to tell me your problems. Everybody needs somebody to talk to. I hear quite often from Mandy. She told me that you seemed very tired.

I am worried about you dear and I hope you are not suffering too much. If you've got an ulcer you have to get proper treatment at once. I will pay for the treatment. I told Mandy the same thing. She never told me why she gets high blood pressure.

Helene is fine. Please write to me dear.

**Love, Dad.**

Sylvia was due for her final exam. Father wrote giving her his moral support.

1968 was a great year for Maryhill. The father of our nation, President Jomo Kenyatta, was to visit the school. I was eager to personally see the great man whom Grandma had so often talked about ever since I could remember.

Being the Art teacher, the idea of a fantastic display in the school hall flashed into my mind. I asked the Headmistress, Sister Gwendoline, if I could use the hall, giving details on how I'd decorate it. A total of over two hundred girls from standard four to form four were doing art with me and I promised each one to have a piece of their work on display, still life, nature, composition and various kinds of mosaic work, imaginary portraits, using geometrical figure designs, block, string, leaf and potato printing from the lower classes. Oil paints, powder paints, water colours, tie and dye were used. We worked endlessly, mounting each pupil's best piece on black sugar paper to give it the best effect. There was a wonderful happy relationship with my pupils and we did an interesting display. The hall was then cleaned to be spick and span.

I wrote to Sylvia to get time off from Kenyatta Hospital and be present at Maryhill. Luckily, she was given a day off. Parents were invited too, after which they would take their children home for mid-term. The teachers decorated their classrooms and pupils had to place all their exercise books on their desk for parents to view. Teachers had to be present in their classrooms to answer any queries from parents. The workers cleaned the school compound. A platform was built and canvas put up. A long table with a lovely white table cloth was placed on a carpet. Tea cups, tea spoons, side plates, serviettes were laid out. School chairs were neatly kept near the dining hall in a semi-circle; this is where the parents, teachers and pupils were to sit. The nuns were to sit with the President and invited guests. Teachers were specifically told that we would not meet the President. What a disappointment, I had only wanted a handshake.

The dormitory floors shone like mirrors. White Sunday bedcovers were used. The girls wore their Sunday outfit, navy-blue pleated skirt, a white shirt, navy-blue tie, blazer, hat, shining black shoes and white socks. The choirs practised the songs they were to sing.

An announcement came that President Kenyatta, unfortunately, would be a little late. The teachers took their classes for relaxation and we gave them a drink. It was a surprisingly bright, hot day in June.

We then heard a distant motor-cade coming closer. The school rushed into their prepared seats. Parents were already there. Hundreds of people had lined up the Mangu Road for almost two hours to cheer Mzee Jomo Kenyatta. The police were already there to control the populace of Mangu and stop outsiders from coming into the school.

Then came our long awaited President, his elegant wife Mama Ngina by his side, and all the dignitaries. We stood at attention, eager and anxious to see this great man. We sang the National Anthem.

*Ee Mungu Nguvu yetu*
*Ilete baraka kwetu*
*Haki iwe ngao na mlinzi*
*Na tukae na undugu*
*Amani na Uhuru*
*Raha tupate na ustawi.*

*Oh God of all creation*
*Bless this our land and Nation*
*Justice be our shield and defender*
*May we dwell in Unity*
*Peace and Liberty*

Our Kenyan flag was flying gently on the high post. After the guests were seated Sister Gwendoline welcomed the President, his wife Mama Ngina and guests. It was the first time I heard that Maryhill was opened to cater for orphans and later, when the nuns found that there was no school for mixed race children, they decided to make it a school for such children. Later the Asian looking Goans were taken as they were practically all Catholics and later Seychellois. It was not until just before independence that African and a few Asian children were accepted. Mzee gave his speech and was later invited to visit the school. He had little time and only visited our art exhibition. Whilst in my classroom talking to parents, I was overwhelmed to meet Mr. Muigai, President Jomo Kenyatta's brother. I was teaching his two lovely daughters.

After talking to the last parent, Sylvia, and I literally ran down the school path to the bus stop as we had planned to go down to Nairobi. Parents by the dozen waved and passed us. Mr. Muigai in his majestic car stopped.

"Would you like a lift? You are my children's teacher and I will not let you go on the country bus. Where are you off to?" he asked.

"Thika," we answered almost in a whisper.

Well we had a comfortable seven mile journey. We were very grateful to Mr. Muigai. He was going to his home at Gatundu and we boarded a bus to Nairobi.

I was soon to be married to my childhood sweetheart. Sylvia gave me all sorts of ideas on how I should dress, helped me to choose the outfit and even advised me not to forget the camera as photographs were memorable.

"Oh Meggie, I am so happy for you," she said.

Sylvia was my maid of honour and one of the witnesses who signed the marriage register. Berit, now working in Uganda, came down for the wedding. Sylvia was my regular visitor, helping me organise the house. We were now much happier as we were nearer each other.

In February 1969, Father became very ill and was almost at the point of death. Immediately, we heard the news we wrote to him. Surprisingly enough we received a letter from him, sooner than expected.

My dear daughters,

Many thanks for your letters of 8th February. I had not received any letter from you for a long time. Oh yes, I was very sick a little while ago. The doctors at Mulago Hospital thought it was my heart because my blood pressure was 180/120 but I thought it was a mysterious lung infection which had turned chronic and I was right. I was given antibiotics. I am much better now.

**Love, Dad.**

In March 1969, Sylvia became very concerned about the mysterious abdominal pains she felt.

"Perhaps it's an ulcer."

She casually told me how a young English girl had come to Nairobi Hospital with cancer of the stomach.

"Meggie, it's an awful disease. Within a month this poor eighteen-year-old looked like a skeleton and, Meggie, she suffered so much and in no time at all she was dead."

Sylvia didn't complain much about her pains. She looked very strong and healthy. Father had decided to go to Norway for his leave.

Dear daughters,

Just a word to tell you that I am leaving for Europe on the 18th June. I shall be away for three months. I wish things will go well with you during my absence and I hope life will treat you well. I am in a flap at the moment as I have to fix many things before I go.

Many thanks for the birthday card. I'm off to Europe tomorrow and I am going to say goodbye to your Mother before I leave.

All the best my dears and I hope you will be O. K. Till I see you again.
**Love, Dad.**

It almost broke our hearts when we read his letter.

"Three months!" we exclaimed.

Father went to Hangesund, Norway. We wrote regularly, throughout his stay abroad. After a good relaxation with his family he wrote that he would be back by the 16th October 1969. He wrote that his family was O. K. though his brother had had a stroke and was bed-ridden.

Sylvia went for an eye check-up after reading Father's letter and was told she had to use glasses. Father encouraged her, saying that he was sure she'd still look beautiful. Anyway we decided to treat ourselves to the movie *Dr. Zhivago*, temporarily falling in love with the handsome Omar Shariff.

Grandpa Nassor made a second trip and visited mother and aunt Nuru. Sylvia and I were in Kenya at that time. Leaving for Zanzibar, after his stay in Kampala, he had a severe asthma attack and unfortunately died at Mtito Andei Kenya. The Muslim community took it upon themselves and fulfilled the religious requirements concerning a dead brother. We felt terribly sorry having lost him so soon after we had got to know him.

As soon as I found out I was pregnant, I rushed to give Sylvia the good news. She looked at me seriously and told me about all the abnormalities found in women who suspected they were pregnant but they were no more pregnant than a man with a beer pouch. Sometimes she created gruesome pictures. I begged Sylvia not to tell me any more stories.

"Well, my dear, you've got to be prepared," she would joke.

She was as wonderful as she was occasionally exasperating. After my baby was born, you've never seen a more excited and happier person than Sylvia! She made almost the whole of the Nairobi Hospital staff send congratulatory cards. A huge bouquet of flowers and a box of assorted chocolates were presented to me. On seeing me she kissed me over and over again.

"Daddy should see the baby    it's a real Norwegian," she observed.

She took the first photograph of my little girl and me on the second day after delivery. During my confinement at the hospital we became closer than ever before. Later Sylvia visited me at home, usually with Georgina Zamamu. Sylvia would scrutinize the baby and tell me that she thought the baby was either abnormal or a genius.

"Why do you think so?" I asked suspiciously.

"She's only a couple of months old but looks like she thinks I'm quite a fool!" Sylvia said as we all laughed.

On July 5th, I was home with my two-month-old baby, waiting for Sylvia's visit. Getting a little restless I switched on the radio and was shocked to hear that a well-known Cabinet Minister Mr. Tom Mboya, had been shot by an assassin right outside Channis Pharmacy on Government Road, now Moi Avenue. I wondered whether my schoolmate who was working there had been present. Apparently not, as it happened after working hours. In 1969 and earlier, all shops normally closed at 1 p. m. on Saturdays and the city populace practically disappeared. I heard that the Minister was rushed to Nairobi Hospital.

"Lord help him recover," I prayed.

No wonder Sylvia didn't come home. The Minister was pronounced dead on arrival. Sylvia told me that it was frightening. Hundreds of people had gathered at the hospital and were grieving. Tear gas was used to disperse the crowd.

Next day Sylvia visited us and told me that she'd make it a point to go for the funeral service. On July 8th, a requiem mass was conducted by the Reverend Archbishop John McCarthy who had confirmed me nearly eleven years before. Sylvia was unable to enter the cathedral due to the massive crowd of mourners who had gathered there. The doors had been closed. There was a riot as President Kenyatta's motorcar arrived. Agitated people threw stones at it and tear gas was fired to disperse the crowd. One tear gas bomb fell right next to Sylvia and she collapsed. A good Samaritan picked her up before she could be trampled on and drove her to Nairobi Hospital where she was treated.

After almost two weeks of not seeing Sylvia, I visited her and found her weak and pale. Not long after this I had to go into hospital myself for suspected apendicitis. I came home and was resting when I read the headlines that Sir Edward Mutesa II had died of alcoholic poisoning in his London apartment. What a shock that was. Mutesa had only been ousted three years earlier and was just 45 years old. I was beside myself. Dad wrote and gave his condolences. Sylvia visited me and we cried. Prince Henry wrote and said that the British Government were to see to the funeral. All the Baganda in Uganda and England were in mourning.

Sylvia applied for a job at the Nairobi Hospital in September 1969. She was given a book to record her practical instructions and ward experiences in preparation for the Certificate of General Nursing. Against each item in the book, would be placed a tick in the column headed "demonstration." After a student had gained proficiency in any procedure the ward sister or clinical instructor signed off in the book. It was very important to have that book after you had completed a particular nursing experience.

Between 1st September 1965 and 1969 Sylvia had received instruction in Medical Nursing, Surgical, Paediatric. Gynecological and Obstetrical practice, before concentrating principally on the operationg theatre work. Later, she did Public Health Nursing with the Nairobi City Council. Here she worked strenuously, attended lectures, and carried out visits. She finished her practical course on 20th March, 1969 after completing her Ear, Nose and Throat, Orthopaedics and Infectious Diseases Hospital work which took five months. These were done at Kenyatta Hospital.

Sylvia went to Uganda for her annual leave when baby Helen was about five months old. After spending half her holidays with mother, she visited Father at the mine. Sooner than expected I received a letter about the highlights of her journey; the rattling of the bus with chickens cackling and flying all over it, tons of luggage tied in bundles, some toppling over, banging heads, tobacco smell from pipe smokers, occasional spittle on her face when some passenger cleaned his teeth with a *muswaki* or chewed tobacco leaves. She spent a quiet holiday typing, reading and painting. After her holidays father brought her home to Mengo. They did shopping, and had a few outings before father dropped her at the station on 26th November. On 27th November, 1969 my family and I waited anxiously at the railway station to meet Sylvia. I learnt that father was well as ever and they had had a lovely holiday together.

In the early hours of 28th November. I had a strange dream that Father had died of a heart attack alone in his car with no-one there to help him! I woke up suddenly with terrible palpitations and sweating.

"Lord don't let anything happen to Dad," I prayed.

Whilst having breakfast I told Sylvia about the dream.

"You and your dreams, Meggie! I left Dad as fit as a fiddle."

However, on Ist December Helene rang an Asian family in Parklands whom we did not know begging them to get in touch with either Mr. Louis at Text Book Centre or with me at Westlands Primary School and give the news that Father had died on 28th November at II a.m. suddenly from a heart attack at Masaka on his way to the mine.

Father was driving when he felt unwell. Knowing that to get help was almost impossible, he parked his car on the side of the road, placed his passport on his chest and put his arms up and died. A priest passed him thinking he was waving and waved back. This was around 11.30 a. m. At three in the afternoon the same priest saw the car and father in the same position as he had left him. He became suspicious, stopped his car, and saw father dead. Immediately, he drove to look for a telephone and called the police. An ambulance was called and father's remains were taken to Mulago Hospital for a post mortem.

My husband concluded that we would want to go to Uganda. Immediately, he collected Sylvia at Kenyatta Hospital after which they came to Westlands Primary School to pick me up. I was completely distraught when they arrived as the Headmaster, Mr. Mcdonell had already broken the news to me. Packing a few items, we left for Uganda and arrived in Kampala eight hours later. We went to Mulago Hospital and viewed the body. In spite of being at the mortuary for six days and dying of, presumably, a heart attack, father was not blue but had just his usual colour even sunburns on the cheek. After the official formalities father was cremated at the Hindu Crematorium. We did not have to make any funeral arrangements what-so-ever.

Mr. Hunts, Father's lawyer, and the Manager Mr. Dimitrius did everything. We were told that the cremation would take place at two o'clock sharp. My husband and I, Helene and George Epaminondas, Sylvia and Berit all dressed in black and drove to the funeral. Mother didn't have the heart to watch the remains being burnt. No member of her family had ever been cremated.

Not another soul was there except the Norwegian Ambassador, who arrived after the cremation and gave us his condolences. We stood in silence and watched as the body was cremated to ashes.

My husband, with the baby and Frank who was to baby-sit, returned to Kenya a couple of days after the funeral. Sylvia and I stayed on another week. Dad once told me when he died he'd want his ashes spread over his home garden at Kigezi, but it was never done.

The loss of our dear father was a great blow to us. Our pillar of strength, our advisor, our guide and mentor was gone. We no longer had a strong shoulder to lean on. He was someone with so much love, patience, understanding and wisdom. Suddenly he just melted away from our lives. It seemed that life wasn't worth living any more . . . But the love and wisdom he had given us was to strengthen us to face the world alone. As I sat stunned, I could hear his voice.

"If one loves anyone, one loves the whole person just as they are and not as one would like them to be, therefore I love you as you are."

Perhaps the advice he gave in each letter did not mean much to us then, but as the years passed by we have seen the reality of life that he so often spoke of. Life on earth wasn't easy, we realised, for you've got to work hard to live comfortably and stand up for your rights. He was a great loss to us; we knew it. Now we had to stand on our own two feet and fight our own battles without him.

Sylvia became more lonesome than ever. She probably was hit harder than any of us, but all the while she cloaked her true feelings behind a rigid self-discipline; she laughed, had the art of adroit repartee, was a master of funny stories and jokes. She continued to exhibit an insatiable zest for fun and practical jokes. During all of 1970 we remained very close. She adored my baby and would spend hours with her. However, Sylvia kept on saying,

"I don't know what is wrong with me, Meggie, but something isn't right somewhere."

She kept feeling nauseated for no apparent reason. This was complicated by mysterious back and side pains. After trying all sorts of doctors, she thought that perhaps if she went abroad something might be found. She also believed she had contracted bilharzia in Uganda when she went swimming in Lake Victoria with father. This did not dispirit her, she continued going out for movies, parties and her dances. At one of the dances she met the young man Patrick who had put her in the pit at school when she was little; she reminded him of the episode and they had a good laugh. She tried to achieve as many goals in life as she possibly could.

At the beginning of 1971, I invited Sylvia to live with us. She happily accepted the invitation. At least she'd have a homely environment. In the seven months she lived with us she helped me furnish my home and contributed fifteen pounds per month towards the rent. We stitched the curtains in the sitting room and matching seat-covers for the arm chairs.

We soon received the money father had left us in his will from our lawyers in Uganda. Sylvia knew a good lawyer, Mr. Gautama, in Nairobi who signed the discharge voucher. When the cheques arrived from our lawyer in Uganda, Sylvia advised we cash them. Off to Barclays Bank we went, signed the formal papers and handed in the cheques.

"Are you sure you want to carry all this money on you?" the man at the counter asked.

"Of course we do," replied Sylvia, beaming with anticipation.

I was a little nervous. Sylvia had pre-instructed me to wear a dress with big pockets, a convenience to carry all the cash.

"No handbag, once that is snatched you lose everything," she warned. Wonders never cease. Sylvia loved clothes with pockets from youth. The bank clerk piled the money on the counter. When all the bank formalities were concluded and the money safely in our pockets, we retired to the Coffee House and relaxed over a cup of coffee and a roll. As we sat, Sylvia complained of severe backaches which she assumed were due to lifting heavy patients onto the operating table. I never took her seriously as she appeared very tough and healthy.

I hadn't been too well for over two months. My left side was excruciatingly painful and I was admitted at the Aga Khan Hospital for suspected appendicitis but was discharged due to very low blood count which I was to build with prescribed medication before I attempted to face the operation.

"What's the matter with you Sylvia?" I asked.

I hoped she would confide in me as she always did but she was reserved, perhaps confused.

"I don't know. It must be these anti-depressant pills I'm taking," she replied somewhat doubtfully.

Doctors could not diagnose what the problem was and she was constantly given medication to calm her nerves. Nothing seemed to help her. Her doctor finally convinced her that she needed a psychiatrist as he believed Sylvia's physical health was directly related to what was happening to her emotionally. Therefore, someone who understood the relationship between the body and the emotions could perhaps help her. Sylvia spent almost six months getting psychiatric advice. I once accompanied her to see a psychiatrist but whatever he advised her was of no help to her physical condition.

Towards the end of 1971 Sylvia moved back to Kenyatta Hospital. Then news reached me that she was hospitalized. I immediately visited her. She was still cheerful and taking walks in the ward.

"Oh Meggie, it's so nice to see you," she smiled. "Don't worry, I'll be all right, nothing serious is wrong with me," she assured me in a soft gentle voice.

My sister seemed pale and weak to me, but she convinced me she was just over exhausted. The backaches continued endlessly but the doctors assured her that this was quite normal with nurses.

Because she had a happy character no one suspected she was ill; not even me. She always managed to get people into roars of laughter and, amazingly, never missed her Saturday dances. She was always being invited to parties. Every May 17th she joined the Norwegians for Annual Independence celebrations.

"Meggie, why don't you come to these celebration parties? You are not patriotic to your country. There are so many people who knew Dad," she said.

"I will one day," I answered but I never did.

Sylvia then decided she must learn to drive and took driving lessons. After a month she was given her licence. Then she bought a second-hand mini. Unfortunately, she crashed into some Asian's Mercedes when coming to visit me. On arrival she was quite red and shaking from the shock. She told me the police had come and recorded all the details. The Asian man assured me that there was nothing serious.

"We've settled everything," she said very apologetic, but thankful for the lift they had given her.

At this period, the Kabaka's body was exhumed in London and flown to Uganda for a Royal Baganda customary burial at Kasubi. Prince Henry, Mboni and their children, the Kabaka's son Ronnie Mutebi and all the members of his family who were in exile in England came at the invitation of Idi Amin. Sylvia too went home for the funeral. Unfortunately I was in confinement as I had just given birth to my second daughter, Jacqueline.

After all the formalities, Sylvia and Mboni visited me. I was thrilled to see Mboni after nearly six years. She was still elegant, five foot ten inches with a youthful figure after having five children. She scolded me for having a tiny pot.

"You must exercise," she advised me.

Mboni and I talked non-stop of the past! She was a great help where my baby was concerned. She did practically everything for me. She cooked, bathed and fed my baby. How grateful I was for the two weeks rest.

"Meggie, I am still very mad with you for not consulting me before you got married! I hope you still remember I am your big sister!" she joked.

Sadly for me she left and joined her family in Uganda. They later returned to London. I missed seeing David, Jasmine and Henry.

# CHAPTER TWELVE:
## SYLVIA STARTS A NEW LIFE

Sylvia had been saving hard for seven years, determined to go to Britain to further her midwifery training. With the money saved and what father had left her in his will, she was confident she could fully support herself abroad. She made all the necessary arrangements entirely on her own.

A day before she left Sylvia came to Parklands to bid us farewell. In no time she was in London. What a change that was!

"The city is enormous, there are millions of people, the traffic is gigantic, the weather depressing!" she wrote.

She spent about two weeks with Mboni before joining Luton and Dunstable Hospital at the end of July, 1972. Here she trained for a year, receiving her Certificate in September 1973. A letter arrived filled with great excitement. After qualifying, she was sent to work at the Enfield District Hospital, Chace Side Village. Here she worked with people of all races. Being sympathetic and kind to all Sylvia was greatly loved by all the staff and patients.

After Sylvia was well settled, she got in touch with many of her old pals from Kenya, who were now either working or living in London. The White Sisters nuns organised an Old Maryhill Girls get-together every year. This was a time when all past pupils met, hugged, talked and had a happy re-union. Sylvia was delighted to meet many old friends. She had hoped to meet the Cardovilles, the Baronets, a Badier, a Hartman who was at some British University, a DeSouza, a lawyer, the Chans, the Nunes, Andrade, a Vidot, a Remedios, the Sequieras, the Agards, Dora Mann. She had heard from Wendy Harris, whose sister D. Harris was a lecturer at a university in the States, the Rivers and many more.

When she got her first pay cheque, my children were at the top of her shopping list. She sent us the lovely red striped pinafores and white, long sleeved tops, perfumes and necklaces for me. She met our ex-schoolmate Priscilla Hughes, also a nurse, and she invited Sylvia to visit Ireland where her aunt lived.

"Ireland is scenic and the Irish people quite different from the English. They seem more friendly, while the English appear to be too busy to notice anyone; the only problem is the religious conflicts between the Protestants and Catholics," she wrote.

Sylvia had hoped to get a job in the Irish countryside but it was only a dream. The staff and nurses at Enfield Hospital found her charming and a very likeable, interesting person. She seemed to radiate peace, love and understanding all around her.

A year went by and Sylvia progressed in her nursing career, working in the operating theatre, assisting surgeons during all kinds of operations. For her next leave, she went with a couple of other nurses to Tunisia, in North Africa. She visited many historical monuments and places.

"It's great feeling like a tourist," she wrote. "Tunisia is hot, full of Arabs and quite a number of white people chiefly French. Even the Arabs speak French. I didn't feel out of place as I knew a little of the language."

All this time, she continued going for check-ups as she still suspected she had bilharzia. The doctors had given her various tests but were unable to diagnose her problem. When doctors failed to come to a conclusion she continued working, going out, visiting friends, attending occasional parties at Mboni's house, and being the same cheerful girl she had always been.

Sylvia seized the opportunity of her annual leave and went to Norway with the hope of meeting our relatives. But since the tour was planned by travel agencies, she did not find time to visit the Bjordal family.

"Meggie, Norway is picturesque beyond description just as Dad told us. There are high mountains everywhere. It is so much like Kabale; only that it's much more developed and advanced. Wish you were here," she wrote.

How I envied her. After her visit to Norway she decided to teach herself the Norwegian language and bought a copy of *Teach Yourself Norwegian.*

As time went by, Sylvia's health didn't get any better. She felt easily tired and very depressed. She kept to herself and became rather quiet. One Saturday, when off-duty, she thought she might as well visit Mboni. On hearing the door bell, Mboni opened the door and boom! Sylvia collapsed in the corridor, at her sister's feet.

"Sylvia, Sylvia, what's the matter with you?" asked our shocked sister.

Mboni became terribly worried and anxious, but Sylvia re-assured her it was nothing, just exhaustion.

In 1976, Sylvia wrote that she was to undergo observation in hospital.

"Nothing to worry about; just routine medical check-up," she wrote.

She constantly complained of stomach pain. Finally, the doctors decided to do a thorough investigation. She had a slight operation and her small intestine was examined. Growths were found and burned with some medicinal chemicals. She was told that she'd be all right. If nothing happened in the next five years then she could consider herself cured. About a month later she complained of a side ache. Appendicitis was suspected. Again she underwent an emergency operation. Growths were found on the appendix. Two months later she had a disc removed by a very experienced Chinese doctor.

"Meggie, I am now a quarter of an inch shorter," she joked.

I began to ponder about all these operations following closely one after the other. Sylvia's health began to occupy my mind.

Five years went past very quickly! Sylvia was still working at the theatre at Luton Chace Farm Hospital. She had learned to live with the pains she had gone through all these years as nothing more could be done.

"I'll just keep on swallowing pain killers," she wrote.

It was hard to believe she was ill as she appeared extremely strong and healthy. One day Sylvia was invited for tea by her friend Linda who lived at Brentford, Middlesex. She had rung a car service at Enfield for a cab. A young man, Mr. Michael Hart, came to pick up Sylvia. He stopped in his tracks when he saw this incredible lady. She was very well dressed; a white blouse, a pair of blue slacks, a leopard skin coat and was carrying an umbrella as it was raining that particular day. She looked very much like a film star. A combination of Diana Ross and Sophia Lorraine!

Mr. Hart was overwhelmed, and was at a loss for words. He got his breath back and asked her politely, "Excuse me, Madam, are you the lady who asked for a cab to Tower-block?"

"Well, yes . . . I would have waited for the bus but I'm running short of time . . ." she calmly replied.

Mr. Hart was out of his car in a flash and was holding the door open for her. Sylvia got in gracefully and he shut the door. "This woman has some class," thought Mr. Hart.

They went to the North Circular Road which is a very fast road and drove towards the West of London. Sylvia and the young man sat in silence for some time.

"She certainly is a foreigner," his thoughts raced.

He finally gathered courage and asked, "Do you mind if I ask you where you come from?"

"Well, I was born in Uganda, a country in East Africa and I grew up and worked in Kenya which is a neighbouring country," she replied, smiling at him.

"My name is Michael Hart, what's yours?" he continued politely.

"Sylvia Christine Bjordal. I am a nurse here at Chace Farm Hospital and

I work in the operating theatre." she smiled.

She explained how hard a nurse's job was and that she was on her feet for practically fourteen hours a day. He in turn told her a little about himself, that he loved music and dancing which were two things she also loved. Gathering courage, he asked her if she would go to a dance with him when she had a day off. He was delighted when she said she would.

Michael couldn't stop thinking about her. The following Wednesday he decided to ring Sylvia up. She was called to the phone by the matron, and agreed to meet him two days later. It was November 1976 and the weather was cold, dark and miserable. When he went to collect her, she was smartly dressed, with her long hair worn loose.

Sylvia told him that her grandmother was an African Princess, her grandfather an Arab, and her father a Norwegian. She explained that her father had been a miner and had done extremely well at Kabale but that he had died unexpectedly of a heart attack in 1969. She showed him a few family photographs, which she always carried. He noted that she came from a big family. She told him of her brothers and sisters in Africa, her sister Mboni who lived at Barnet, her brother Rama who lived in Canada and another brother Frank who lived in Dallas, Texas, in the United States. He in turn told her about himself that, he had a twin brother and that his parents lived in the country, about a hundred miles away from London. After a meal and a dance he took her back to the hospital.

The next time they met, Sylvia told him she was shorter than she normally was because one of her discs had been removed and that she had had two other operations. It seems that she wanted to make clear from the beginning that she had doubts about her own future health.

The romance developed for several months before Michael asked her to marry him. She agreed. Michael immediately drove to his home in Suffolk to tell his parents about his girlfriend. His mother took an immediate liking to her. At this time Sylvia wrote this poem:

## WHAT YOU DO TO ME

Like the roaring sea, like the wind blowing
through the trees,
Like the humming of a bee you'll give your love to me
Each morning sigh, the bed on which I lie
Each laughter high, is yours,
Oh me,
Oh my,

Let the storm torment, let sorrow lament.
Let colours blind, this Love is Heaven sent.
When in your arms I am, meek as a lamb
Never let your door slam, just love me for what I am.

## Sylvia, 1977

I heard about Michael when Mboni came to Nairobi for a short visit. It was almost five years since I had last seen her.

Meanwhile in London, Sylvia and Michael had given four months notice at the Marriage Registry; most people normally gave three weeks. Sylvia and Mike changed the marriage date, not once but twice, since the preparation of their house was not quite as Sylvia planned it to be. Michael felt a little embarrassed the second time they were at the Registrar's office.

"Don't tell me we've come to change the marriage date again," the old severe looking man asked sarcastically.

"Yes, we have," answered Sylvia and Mike in unison.

They finally decided on 6th April, 1977. Sylvia wore a short, off-white dress for the wedding, white high heeled shoes and of course her leopard-skin coat to commemorate their first meeting. She rolled her long hair in a bun and made up her face. Michael wore a black suit, white shirt and a tie. While they were waiting for two friends to drive them to the Registry Office, they regaled themselves with sherry. When Sylvia saw the short, heavy-set man with a strong face, stormy eyes that radiated power, his glasses at the tip of his nose, peering at them every time he asked a question, she dropped her eyes and burst out laughing. Of course, the old Englishman wasn't amused at all; he wanted to get on with his duty, that's all that mattered to him. But this was the same irrepressible Sylvia who always loved a joke.

"Do you, Michael Hart, take Sylvia Christine Bjordal as your lawful wife. To have and to hold, for richer or poorer, in sickness and in health, from this day forward till death do you part?"

"I do," answered Michael.

"Sylvia Christine Bjordal, do you take Michael Hart, as your lawful husband . . ."

Sylvia was laughing hysterically, perhaps because of the sherry, which she was not used to, and she didn't answer him. He posed the question again, rather impatiently, and there was still no answer. At the third time Michael nudged her.

"Y-y-yes," she answered, much to the bridegroom's relief.

The newly-weds went back to Palmers Green to celebrate with Prince

Henry and other friends. The same day Mboni arrived back in London without knowing it was the day of the wedding. When she phoned Sylvia to find out why her husband and children were not at home, she had hastily got dressed and went to join the party.

For days Sylvia and Michael went back and forth between Chace Farm Hospital and Palmers Green collecting her belongings. When unpacking, the first things she took out were her two candlesticks which she put on the mantelpiece over the fire place.

## MICHAEL

**M** - Must I tell you how much you mean to me?
**I** - I know you have an idea, I can see,
**C** - Cause you make me feel so special,
**H** - Holding me and telling me I'm your girl.
**A** - All I want is happiness with you,
**E** - Even through the ups and downs we'll get through,
**L** - Love is the reason, hope all gone.

### Sylvia Hart, 1977

Sylvia and Michael were both very keen on tennis and the Swedish tennis champion Bjorn Borge. They watched every tennis match on the television. Both had an interest in art as well and would sit and draw each other's portraits, or play music together    pop and classical, dancing away. Sylvia loved dancing, chiefly rock-n-roll, jiving or she'd play classical pieces and do ballet.

They bought a second-hand piano and Sylvia was filled with a desire to learn to play it perfectly but much to her disappointment she had to give it up as her joints became unbearably painful and sometimes she could not use her fingers at all. It was not arthritis, she was told, but was given pain-killers. Sylvia and Michael were as loving a couple as one would ever wish to know. They went for evening walks together, holding hands and sometimes called in at a pub. They would often go to Palmers Green Field and watch people play tennis and never missed the re-construction of Elvis Presley's concerts at the Historical Theatre near Charing Cross Road. They heard 'Little Sister Don't You', 'Jailhouse Rock', 'Don't be Cruel'.

Sylvia was an exceptionally tidy woman. In spite of her long working hours and the pains she was suffering, she vacuum cleaned the house every day of the week, washed and ironed the clothes and mended them if necessary. After she had done all the household chores, she'd work in her garden. She was creating a home. She would prepare lovely dinners for her husband; usually a curry like back home in East Africa, and he loved it. Sometimes, he'd cook her English meals.

She sat at the electric sewing machine, and sewed non-stop until the curtains were made, then re-covered a sofa set, making cushions to match the curtains. Coming home from work, Michael found that she seemed completely exhausted and insisted she resign from her nursing job. Sylvia was relieved to hear Michael say this and resigned without a second thought.

They wanted a baby. Therefore they attended lectures for intending parents at North Middlesex Hospital, Edmonton. Two months after her marriage, Sylvia rang me.

"Hello Meggie."

"Hello," I answered rather dubiously.

"This is Sylvia, how are you? It's so good to hear your voice after all these years."

I was rather confused about the person who was talking to me. I thought it was Aunt Sylvia from Mombasa.

"Hello Aunt Sylvia," I answered wondering why on earth she could be ringing me.

"I'm not Aunt Sylvia, I'm your sister," she chuckled.

"Sylvia, Sylvia, how are you my dearest? It's five years since I last heard your voice. You sound so English," I exclaimed. We both lapsed into laughter.

"Meggie, I'm going to have a baby," she sounded excited.

"That's wonderful, Sylvia, but why the rush?"

"Well, I'm getting on in age and I must hurry before it's too late," she said lightly.

"Too late," I thought to myself. "What an odd thing to say."

Sylvia was ecstatic about her coming baby. She put on weight rapidly and in nine months she was 175 pounds. She kept herself busy stitching clothes and decorating the baby's room. When she was seven months pregnant, she experienced excruciating pains in the back. X-rays were taken and it seemed that she might need to have a caesarean section. When the time came, Sylvia was in labour for more than twenty-four hours. Michael visited her constantly and was allowed to sit by her in the labour ward. At last their baby girl was born and the parents were overjoyed.

"Lucy Amina, that's what we shall call you," Sylvia said.

Michael rang his parents in Suffolk and Mr. Stanley Hart came to see his grand-daughter. He hugged and kissed Sylvia.

176

"Thank you very much for my grandchild," he said.

They were very happy together, but as time went by Michael began to see a decline in Sylvia. She began to forget things very easily and at times was irritable and frustrated because she wasn't strong enough to cope with the baby.

One day she took Michael's hand and said, "Mike, do you see your life line? You have a long life. Can you see mine, there are lines obscuring my life line. I am going to have problems in the near future," she predicted.

"Oh come on Sylvia, you're a tough one." said Michael giving her a hug, remembering how they used to do arm wrestling.

Sylvia had told him previously how tough we girls all were and how we would hand wrestle with our father, brothers-in-law and brothers. He had thought she was an extremely strong woman.

About eighteen months later, our brother Frank arrived from Dallas to visit Sylvia. They were overjoyed to see each other after nearly eight years. At this time Sylvia had developed a reddish rash around her neck, forehead, and cheeks. Frank was shocked to find her looking haggard and weak. He remembered she used to have an absolutely clear skin.

"Don't you think you should see a doctor and find out what these rashes are all about? I'll pay for the expense if need be," he said.

Sylvia took his advice and they went to the clinic and were given some ointment but it did not help. The rash continued to spread fast right down to her finger tips. This made them very sensitive and painful. Sometimes when baby Lucy grabbed her roughly, Sylvia would scream.

"Lucy darling, that hurts Mummy," calming down, she would quietly say. Her joints constantly ached. In spite of it all Sylvia remained calm and gentle.

Michael had been studying for a London Cab Driver's Licence, which required a thorough knowledge of all the routes of London. To get a Cab Driver's Licence one had to do a practical and written examination.

"Sylvia," Michael said to her one day, "Give me two years of your time. I shall be away most of the day and maybe driving practically the whole night. I know it will be hard on you but I have to do this."

"Mike, a man has got to do what a man has got to do," she responded.

He seemed satisfied with her answer and vowed to improve her life in every way possible. When he passed his exam, Sylvia was overjoyed.

"Mike, honey, now you can get me better," she reminded him.

Michael soon bought a lovely black London cab and brought it straight home: full of excitement. Sylvia ran out to see the car. Michael looked at her face and he could see how ill she was. He couldn't figure out what was wrong with her.

"Come on, Sylvia, let's go to Chalk Farm Pharmacy and buy some herbal medicines," he said.

They bought a considerable amount of carrot juice. Sylvia then decided she'd like to stay with Mboni for a while. All this while I kept receiving letters from Sylvia telling me that she was having some medical investigations carried out on her.

"What for?" I asked a friend. "I have a strong feeling my sister has cancer," I said pensively; it was just a thought out of the blue.

"God forbid! Don't ever say things like that," my Muslim friend sternly replied.

They went to see an acupuncturist. Those techniques didn't help much. Sylvia became restless, always walking from one room to another trying to keep her mind off these mysterious pains. She had a swab from her uterus taken for analysis but the results were negative.

Two weeks later more investigations were done. Finally, carcinomatosis in the epithelial pathways was discovered, which in ordinary terms is cancer of the cells that cover the skin. Two days later she was admitted to Chace Farm Hospital. Her worried husband was called by the doctor.

"Mr. Hart, I have some bad news to tell you. Sit down please . . . Would you like a cigarette?" he asked.

"No thanks, I don't smoke."

"I'm afraid, Mr. Hart, your wife has malignant cancer," he said.

Michael was shocked. He looked as if a hammer had hit him on the head.

"Your wife will receive the best treatment we can give her," said the doctor.

"How long does she have to live?" inquired Michael.

"Years," the doctor reassured him.

Mike was relieved. Sylvia then had a very major five-hour operation for the removal of the rectum which was completely cancerous. She did not regain complete consciousness until three days later. When she came to, she pleaded,

"Please bring me my baby."

"Oh my baby Lucy. Mama is going to die . . . do you know that? Of course not, you are too young to understand," she said helplessly as Lucy was brought.

She was in hospital for five weeks and her weight fell to ninety-six pounds. She was then transferred to the Royal Free Hospital for a year's fortnightly radiation treatment. Sylvia felt a great deal better after this operation. The steroids given to her helped her gain weight rapidly, but she never felt completely well again.

# WHY NOT KNOW YOU

Oh what a life of trifle?
Why not read the Bible?
You'll find the complaints just the same,
Men are always putting God to blame.
For the bad times, they've had,
But never thanked Him when glad.
We're the same all over the century,
Nailing Christ again on the tree.
If we blame Him,
At least we acknowledge Him.
Although only calling Him in trouble it may seem.
He doesn't mind at all.
We are blind and we may fall.

**Sylvia, 1980**

# CHAPTER THIRTEEN: CANCER

All this while it had never crossed my mind that my sister was fatally ill until a week before I left for England. My sister-in-law Monica gave us the news over the phone. The words struck me like bolts of lightning. I was in a state of shock. The first person I contacted was Helene in Uganda. She would get in touch with the rest of the family. I also rang Mboni in London.

"Mboni, why didn't you ever mention about Sylvia's illness earlier?" I asked.

"Sylvia begged us not to tell you," she answered.

"I am beside myself with worry."

"Please Meggie, one of you has to come and help me. Sylvia is very sick."

My three children and I left for London on 31st July 1980. I was nervous about going to England and yet I thanked God I would be seeing my sister after a period of eight years. A good friend took us from the airport to Mboni's house, where my niece Jasmine was waiting for us. Jasmine rang Sylvia.

"Aunt Sylvia, I have a surprise for you, just hold on." Then she called me.

"Aunt Margaret, there is someone you'd love to hear from," handing me the phone.

When we both were on the phone we were short of words.

"Meggie, is that really you?" asked Sylvia suspiciously.

"Yes, my dear and I'm coming to see you right now," I answered.

"I can't believe I'm hearing your voice. I can't believe you're here . . . I'm so happy . . . Are you really in London? I don't believe it," sputtered Sylvia excitedly.

"You will when you see me, my dear. It's no joke," I answered.

"Give me time. I must make myself smart," answered Sylvia.

I was at the Harts' home in Ash Grove in a short while. As I rang the bell I crossed my fingers, my head bowed in prayer.

"God give me strength!" I prayed, "not to break down at the sight of my sister."

Sylvia opened the door, a smile lighting her face. I almost fainted when she appeared, but managed to control my emotions. The feeling of joy and tranquillity at seeing her was more vivid now than before, and yet I burst into tears. In front of me, stood a living skeleton — 5 feet 6 inches tall, 96 lbs, slightly hunched, her hair a rough, short afro, going a bit grey. Her fair skin had an indescribable pallor. Round her eyes the skin was pink and tender, her cheeks had dark brown patches, her neck very light blotches. Her face had grown wan, with sunken eyes. Sylvia was emaciated, thin as a rake. I looked at her and felt my soul die within me.

I gently embraced my sister, and wept unashamedly as we held each other as though we never wanted to be parted again. All the while the others just stood there quietly, a stillness settling over us.

"Excuse me for crying, I'm only too happy to see you," I said feeling rather embarrassed at crying in front of the children.

"I know . . . Oh look at little Harald. Doesn't he look like Daddy?" she said gently.

She kissed all the children, including Jasmine, and shook hands with our friend Ron. Sylvia went into the kitchen to make tea. She brought the children biscuits and other goodies. How they loved her at first sight. She put on music Elvis, 'I stopped, I stumbled, I fell', 'The Guitar Man', asking them to dance. I met Michael, for the first time. Sylvia's home was spick and span. One wouldn't have thought there was a very sick woman in the house. There were endless questions to be answered. My mind went back to when Sylvia was tall and slim, her skin soft as velvet. My thoughts ebbed suddenly and faded away.

"Don't worry, I have an ulcer but I should be all right. I feel really good. I am so happy," Sylvia at first said, her voice full of doubt.

I followed her into the kitchen to see what help I could give her. She knew I didn't believe her.

"Meggie, actually I've got cancer!" she whispered, her back towards me.

I pretended I had not known, smiled only because Sylvia was smiling. She seemed full of life and happiness. We talked non-stop about the old days, about home, about the family. Mboni had also been in hospital but we had a big family re-union at her house in Barnet. This gave me the chance to re-schedule some of my plans after seeing that Sylvia was even more seriously ill than I had expected. I resolved to ring Sylvia every day of my stay in England, no matter where I was.

Sylvia had only been home a week from hospital. Although she wanted us to stay with her I was against it. It would be too much work. I left the children in the care of Mboni's daughters and spent three days with Sylvia. Although all the rooms were empty, she asked me to sleep with her in the same bed.

"Mike is on night duty and I feel scared at times," she told me rather seriously.

Throughout the three nights Sylvia kept waking, rushing to the loo to be sick. I noticed that Sylvia did everything quietly, not wanting to disturb me. Next morning, looking for conversation, I asked her.

"Did you sleep well Sylvia?"

"Oh yes, I did," she looked skeptical. She probably guessed I knew about her restless night

"Actually I didn't," she then said jokingly. In all our lives we had never lied to each other.

"This stomach of mine keeps turning over. Hope I didn't disturb you."

"Of course you didn't, I didn't hear a thing . . . to be honest I heard you."

When the family back in Africa heard the news, they knew that Sylvia would need someone constantly there to help her out. I was almost afraid to tell mother, but Helene thought it best to tell her the truth. No-one in mother's family had ever died that young. I was afraid she might go into hysterics.

Apparently, she was very calm when given the news. But what went on deep inside her? We'll never know. Three weeks after my arrival, mother was in London. Michael met her and took her to Palmers Green to see Sylvia and attend to her needs.

After much thought I went with the children to Cornwall, about two hundred miles from London, to visit my working mate Mary Brincat, a Maltese, who was now married to an Englishman. Cornwall was very picturesque, hilly, cool and misty, something like Kabale. It had also been a mining centre. We recalled the exciting holiday Mary had spent in Uganda with us during our working years at Maryhill.

"I told my friends that an African Princess is visiting and they all want to see and meet you," she told me rather mischievously.

"You didn't!" I was rather alarmed.

"Practically the whole village will be here tomorrow. We are having a barbecue in your honour."

"Mary! I'm not a Princess, it's my Grandma, you know that," I told her vehemently.

All the same it was great fun meeting so many people. White people being so friendly was a new experience for me. They took the children out for picnics, swimming and expeditions. We did not want them to remember England only as a place of sickness and suffering.

Back in Barnet, my husband joined us and one day we called at Palmers Green where Sylvia had invited us to a lunch. Unfortunately we found her quite ill, lying on the couch, holding a small bible which she constantly read and studied every time she was tortured by pain. Sylvia tried to get up but I begged her not to. Mother was able to do all that was necessary.

Back in Kenya, in September 1980, I wrote Sylvia as many as three letters a week. She kept me informed with the latest news on how her health was progressing.

"I have to go every fortnight for my radiation treatment for one year, then the doctors will review my situation. My first treatment was terrible and I felt rather ill. I hate this treatment but I have no choice. It's take it or leave it."

"What can I do for Sylvia? What can anyone do?" I asked myself.

Again she fell very ill. A whole month passed before she wrote.

"I'm much better and stronger. There's a lot to do and it seems even more when one has no energy left. But when I get my strength back, things will not appear as difficult. I have to go to hospital every two or three weeks for my injections and check-ups. At the moment it's too early for me to say exactly how my health is or will be."

Helene was the next to visit London, accompanied by her father-in-law and her little daughter Alexandria, whom Sylvia had never seen. She wrote:

"Although Sylvia looks fine, I know she isn't well at all. All that weight isn't normal. We have fun dressing up. She makes me do her hair, just like the old days, then we go out, window shopping, visiting friends and relatives. She seems very happy. Sometimes I am quite frank with her and I ask her how long she thinks she'll live. Perhaps a year, perhaps five years, perhaps a hundred years! Sylvia is very diplomatic about everything. She wants so much to be back in Africa . . . so very much."

"Mike do you think I could go back home?" Sylvia asked Michael.

"Sure honey, we'll go next December," he said.

"Next December . . . Mike I won't make it till next December!" Sylvia protested, going red in the face.

"Of course you will," he assured her.

"Sure Mike honey, just wave your magic wand," she said genially.

They soon had a White Christmas, just a little snow. Alex was thrilled to see snow. Lucy and Alex became the best of friends and had great fun together. This helped Sylvia a great deal.

# WE THE UNGRATEFUL

In dreams I see Him,
A face so sad, so dim.
After all I've done for these,
My creatures are hard to please.
Yet I do love them dearly,
When my patience they try so fiercely.
I shall give them time to repent.
And then destruction I shall send,
Because of those who acknowledge me,
Are trying hard to make others see,
I'm a God of love and forgiveness,
I'm patient and just and send no illness,
That comes from mental and physical abuse.
Why not lean your head on me?
I cannot come down to teach you that,
When I came to teach you love.
You shut me out, you miserable creatures I made.
I should have given your mind to the animals instead.

## Sylvia, 1980

In January 1981, Helene was back in Uganda. She rang and gave me the latest news concerning Sylvia!

"She looks extremely well, and is getting the latest chemotherapy treatment, I am sure Sylvia will live a long time."

I doubted it. At school Josephine Martin died within months! I wrote to all my friends in England to either write to Sylvia, ring her up or visit her if they could and they did. February came. Sylvia wrote that her treatment was going on fine, that she felt much better. Then a long silence which made me very worried.

Finally, on 28th March 1981 I received her long-awaited letter. "At last I can sit down undisturbed and write to you. Please forgive me for the long delay but I've been meaning to write a long letter. The treatment I'm having has a drastic effect on me and I get rather depressed. But let me cheer up. The tablets they've been giving me for my skin have also helped to put my weight up. You will not believe it when I tell you I'm 8st 11 lbs! (123 lbs). How about that? I've been really feeding myself plus having a pint of Guinness a day and that, my dear, is a weight gainer."

184

However, now that I'm almost back to normal things are clearer. I can think clearly but I must admit I couldn't remember things that happened recently. Some of them I completely forgot until Mum reminded me. The doctor explained this was due to the illness and treatment. I may have periods of Amnesia. I go for treatment every fortnight and I REALLY hate it. They first take a blood sample for blood count analysis; if that is O. K., then they give me my injections. Sometimes they cannot find the veins and they jab me in quite a few places. It is painful and messy. I shall be glad to be free of it.

Since my little operation in January they released some adhesions of the scar, I have improved tremendously. How is the family back in Uganda? I'm praying very hard for them. Your friend Rama rang me and Gillian Brown wrote to me. It was very sweet of them. A neighbour of mine died of cancer recently. She was a very sweet lady and always helped me. I'm sure I'm going to miss her. You know Lucy remembers you and she says she is going to see Jacqueline and Aunty Mandy. She says Aunt Helene and Alex have gone to Africa."

A couple of weeks before her birthday, 31st March, I had asked as many friends as possible in Nairobi to send her birthday cards. She was thrilled to receive them but was unable to write back. Her fingers were extremely painful, she could hardly move them. After suffering from Amnesia for weeks on end, she finally replied on 24th April 1981:

"Thank you very much for your letter and money. It was very thoughtful of you. God bless you. I'm much better and I'm now 146 lbs! Everyone who sees me now remarks how well I look. Also I don't get too tired nowadays. I even stay up till after 10 p.m. which is something I couldn't do for a long time. I can go out for long walks with no ill effect. Things are looking up and my treatment doesn't affect me too much. Now and again I get rather irritable with everyone. I like to be alone at those moments but I'm very firm with myself. I've a lot to do and now life seems worthwhile, whereas before I just didn't know. Please tell Helene to let me know about how they are in Uganda.

I'll be finishing my treatment by August. Anyway, I really don't know whether they will allow me to come by August. How are the children? Do give them all a big kiss for me."

Soon after that Sylvia became quite ill, had a low blood count. The radiation treatment made her feel sick and she could not stomach anything. She wrote at the end of May.

"I'll be so happy when my treatment is over in August I'm putting on weight very fast. That seems to drain my energy. But my treatment is going on alright. I'm still trying to fix my Passport but these English are always on strike. Please forgive me for taking ages to reply but I've had a few things on my mind."

I wondered what was on Sylvia's mind. I had just about finished the manuscript I was working on and sent it to her by airmail. She was very happy when she received it.

"Thank you for sending the story you are writing about me, really Mandy, I feel embarrassed but pleased that you think so well about me. I'm not really as brave as you think. Sometimes, I feel frightened but God is with me. Things look better this end."

A month later Sylvia had a relapse and was at once hospitalized on 1st July 1981.

"I'm writing from hospital. I'm just waiting to be admitted for some investigations. I've been having abdominal pain and distension. So I've got to have some x-rays to check up what's going on inside. I've also had treatment for my liver which is enlarged. I haven't put on any more weight due to poor appetite.

God bless mother for all she's done for me. I wouldn't have made it without her help. I shall pray for the family that we may find peace and happiness in this world. We've been too long on the rough road and stormy sea. God will deliver us one day. Give my love to all my sisters, nieces and nephews, John Desta, Helen, the police woman and Trifosa."

My mind was in turmoil by now but was comforted that mother was there with her. Mother had been taking care of Sylvia for a year. Her ticket and stay in Britain had expired. But mother was not prepared to leave Sylvia, ill as she was. Sylvia could no longer cope with a child and a home. She asked the doctor at the Royal Free Hospital if there was a possibility of mother staying on a little longer. The doctors saw the necessity for help in her case. They wrote to the immigration and nationality section of the Home Office asking if they could extend Mother's stay as long as necessary. Permission was granted. Mother was very grateful to the British Immigration Department.

August came and I thought a holiday at the coast would do me good. I had just received a letter from Sylvia in which she mentioned she was to have a liver scan. The investigations took place at the Royal Free Hospital where she spent a night. The scanner is a device which records abnormalities in organs through reaction to nuclear medication injected into the body. The iodine injected into her veins left permanent bluish scars on both her feet. The scan revealed a liver studded with cancerous tumours. The tumours grew remarkably fast. Within two months she was unable to wear her clothes.

In spite of her illness, Sylvia remembered my birthday, "Happy Birthday Meggie." I was nervous but excited as I read her letter.

"I feel a lot better since the priest anointed me."

Momentarily I imagined a priest giving her extreme unction, the sacrament for the dying, and my heart sank.

"It is about eleven in the evening and my mind is restless until I write to you. Don't worry about me Meggie, God will see me through. I didn't want to tell you anything but you were worried about me getting into hospital and insisted on knowing how I am doing and I feel obligated to tell you. I am hoping to get my passport. I want to be with you. I am happy due to the love of God. I know you will have a share of it and we shall conquer. Many Happy Returns."

Going to Mombasa didn't stop me from constantly worrying about Sylvia. Every place I went reminded me of how she loved the coast. I carried a brave face so as not to spoil my children's holiday. September came and I was back home, in Nairobi. At least I'd be working. I'd have less time to think about my sister. Luckily she could still keep in touch.

"My liver is quite painful and very visible. I have lost a stone . . . I'm 123 lbs now. I feel better for losing all that weight I had. My skin has much improved and I can now move my fingers. I am not so anaemic as I'm taking a lot of tonics and vitamins. I'm on a new treatment for the liver which does not make me that ill."

A friend wrote to me from London on the 8th October saying that Sylvia was fine. At least she sounded great over the phone, the letter said.

Mboni wrote as well telling me that Sylvia was much better, that she was giving her a lot of vitamins . . . But she still felt very tired and irritable. Mboni begged me not to worry. Somehow, Mboni's letter did not put my mind at ease.

"I've got to talk to Sylvia myself," I decided.

"Oh, hi Meggie. I'm just fine don't worry about me . . . I was just giving Lucy a bath when I heard the phone . . ."

"How are you Sylvia? I want an honest answer," I pleaded.

"Well . . . it's only this tumour. I feel very tired and Lucy is quite a handful," she said casually.

A week later Sylvia's letter arrived.

"I am getting my passport fixed. I should be with you soon. Oh how happy I'll be to be back in Kenya."

My constant wish was to bring her back to Africa, I had so many "ifs" in my mind. Remembering part of Rudyard Kipling's poem:

## IF

If you can force your heart and nerve and sinew
To serve your turn long after they are gone.
And hold on when there is nothing in you
Except the will which says to them 'Hold on . . .

187

I'll just hold on, I shan't fall apart and go haywire. Yet again I forced myself to call London. Michael answered. I asked if I could speak to Sylvia.

"Mandy, I'm afraid Sylvia is not here," he answered.

There was a pause, I felt a heavy hammer hit me on the head and was tongue-tied.

"She's at Barnet with Mboni." What a relief it was hearing the last sentence.

"Is she all right?" I asked tentatively.

"Well Mandy, she looks a lot better. You probably won't believe me but I get down on my knees and pray for a miracle," said Michael.

Sending my love I hung up. I suspected that things weren't going on well.

Lucy started nursery school that October, and Sylvia was able to write as follows:

My Beloved Mother,

Do not worry about me dear. You sure had enough worries all your life. I'm in God's loving hands and He will not allow me to suffer more than I can bear.

I have come a long way since my illness and I'm going up, not down. I feel much better than I have for a long time. Do look after Lucy for me. I know she is troublesome sometimes but she has been through a rough patch. Mboni has been so good to me. May God Bless her always.

I love you all much too much, God knows. He will protect you all. For everything in life has a reason a time to laugh, a time to cry, a time to live and a time to die. I know the Lord is my Shepherd, I shall not want, fresh and green are the pastures where He leads me, near restful waters. He guides me to revive my drooping spirit.

My love always.
**Sylvia.**

My beloved Sis Meggie,

Thank you for all your letters and I do apologise for the delay, the reason being I was very poorly about two weeks ago. I had to go into hospital and receive three pints of blood. I feel much better now but I'm still low and today they have told me that my blood count is still low so I cannot receive my treatment. My stomach is very swollen and I have to wear maternity clothes. I find it difficult to move about. Anyway, I mustn't complain as there are people worse off who don't have any family to take care of them. Your letters are encouraging as lately I've been depressed; mainly the treatment makes me so.

The hospital has found a day nursery for Lucy where she will be all day. I hope the lady there still has a place. Today is sunny, cold and windy. I feel happier when the sun comes out. I'll write again soon.

Love to all.

**Your sister, Sylvia.**

These were the last letters Sylvia was to write. In fact she never even posted them. Sylvia had no courage to talk to anyone about her inner feelings, except her diary. Many entries refer to details of medication. Here are some of the more personal ones.

## 31ST MARCH 1981

How my friends love me. God bless them. I got cards and I got a letter from Esther and Shirley. Wish I could write to everyone. But I shall soon, God willing.

## 12TH APRIL 1981

I need to know my Lord, I pray, but do you hear me? Answer me Lord in the hour of my need.

## 6TH AUGUST 1981

Meggie's birthday — thinking of her. I wish I were with her. We could go to Mombasa together and go on the beach and talk about old times.

## 30TH AUGUST 1981

The pain is bad. I can't think Lord. I want to go home and walk on the sandy beaches of Mombasa and Malindi. I want to feel the hot sun on my back and run in the sea as it welcomes me again to its healthy waters.

## 3RD SEPTEMBER 1981

Peter was buried. They sang, 'Jesus wants me for a sunbeam'. I couldn't help crying thinking of young Peter dead. I prayed for his soul.

## 6TH SEPTEMBER 1981

I thought how the family is all ill. I wished my pain could take away theirs. I love them all very much.

## 7TH SEPTEMBER 1981

1 have a lot of pain and discomfort and I'm very depressed. I read Meggie's lovely letter — it made my day.

# TRIALS IN SICKNESS

From here on my sick bed and unto you,
Go on with your threats on us Christians,
You'll only strengthen the true Christians.
Only those who have doubts of their faith,
With your cunning tortures will make a date
Your threat to me has made my doubts flee.
I thank you dearly for now I see,
My faith from now shall be stronger!
No prisoner of my wicked thoughts any longer
I have also gathered that physical love does not last,
The Love our Saviour taught us, is Spiritual pure and just.

## Sylvia, 1981

A month later Sylvia's friends became rather alarmed at her loss of weight. She became easily tired and exhausted. Sympathetic neighbours offered Sylvia help with her over-active baby Lucy, an adorable, chubby, extremely healthy child, who was on the move for almost sixteen hours a day.

Sylvia's speech was increasingly slurring, she found her co-ordination of speech, movement and thought erratic and that was why she didn't often write. Her backaches continued unremittingly, although the orthopaedic surgeon who had performed the laminectomy had advised her to wear a special corset which supported her back, but this did not help much.

The cancer in the liver made this organ enormous, making movements very awkward and uncomfortable. However, she never complained. Her faith in God grew stronger by the day. She often walked down to St. Monica's Catholic Church, to light a candle and pray.

"If I ever become anxious or worried a church is where I'd go and I always come back feeling calm," she said.

Two priests kept in touch with her. The pains grew worse. Sylvia was re-admitted to the Royal Free Hospital. Here she stayed for a couple of days getting treatment. The doctors could do nothing more for her. At length Michael was told his wife had about three weeks to live. Sylvia too was prepared and was asked whether she'd like to stay at the hospital or go home.

"I'd like to go home," Sylvia said calmly.

Being in a home environment she felt a little better. Michael thought a holiday would do Sylvia some good. They took a fast train from Euston and went to Blackpool together with sixteen other holiday makers. Exhausted as she felt on arrival, Sylvia dressed elegantly in her black evening dress and joined the merry makers for dinner. Her strength, calmness and smiles were greatly admired by all. She then excused herself and went to bed. Michael stayed on, listening to pop-music and talking to friends until midnight.

The following day, they went to see the magnificent lights in Blackpool. Sylvia was fascinated; then they had a meal at a Chinese restaurant. Walking back to the hotel they listened to a Scotsman playing the bagpipes, 'Amazing Grace' was one tune she enjoyed.

On Sunday after breakfast Mike and Sylvia went window shopping. It was an exceptionally windy day. As they passed a music store they heard Shaking Stevens singing 'This Old House.' Later in the afternoon they decided on seeing a movie. Sylvia was completely exhausted by now. Next day they left for London. How she was able to sit in the train, two hundred miles, with that huge tumour left everyone mystified! She was incredible.

I regularly checked the post, hoping to get some news from Sylvia but to my dismay there was nothing. Being under great stress, I began having nightmares. Dreadful dreams of Sylvia dying. Sylvia's skeleton running after me and I, terrified, running away from her. I would suddenly wake up with palpitations, all nervous and sweaty. I told Helene about my fear and dreams.

"Come on Meggie you worry too much, you can't expect a letter from Sylvia every week."

I thought about Sylvia's courage during her illness, it was marvellous, something which dominated human suffering, something which could only be God-given.

Sylvia became progressively worse by the day. She held on to her Bible without fail. She knew that extreme pain can make people deny their home, their friends and, most important, their faith. Michael rang my husband.

"I'm afraid, Sylvia's pretty bad," he said.

For the next three days I received telegrams about my sister's condition:

"SYLVIA IN BAD CONDITION TRY AND COME OVER"
MICHAEL

"What can I do for Sylvia?" I constantly asked myself. I was almost going out of my mind.

"I'm sorry Mandy . . . But Sylvia is pretty bad, you must come at once," Mrs. Ella Hart confirmed on the phone. Both mother and mother-in-law were watching over Sylvia.

"Mandy, things don't seem too good with Sylvia. She keeps asking for you," Mother sounded calm, yet desperate for help. My mind was in a state of confusion.

"Will I make it on time. What if she dies when I am on my way?"

I went to church and placed myself in God's care. I had no passport, only a dependant's travelling document. I had no ticket, although I did ask my friend Sabrina of Swan-Air to keep me on the waiting list, just in case of an emergency. The people at the Immigration Department were very understanding and stamped my papers. Having completed all the necessary arrangements by five o'clock in the evening I left at eleven thirty at night.

I had said goodbye to Grandma and Aunt Nuru who were living in Nairobi. Grandma gave me a hand-written letter to take to Buckingham Palace to her friend "Elizabeth". She requested the Queen to give me a million pounds! Dear old Grandma. She also comforted me that people don't die these days especially abroad. Sylvia wasn't going to die . . . people were even getting heart transplants! My 84 years old Grandma was sharp!

# CHAPTER FOURTEEN:
## LET GO AND LET GOD

I was grateful to see Michael and Lucy at Heathrow Airport. I looked at little Lucy, her brown curls falling over her face.

"Do you remember me, Lucy?"

"Aunty Margaret," she answered.

Sylvia was lying in bed at home, not quite aware of what was going on around her. I gasped when I saw her cadaverous face. Her translucent skin showing every blue vein, a living skeleton, just like in my dream, was far worse than when I had seen her a year earlier. Her eyes were different, they were bulging out of their sockets. Her hair was very sparse. Her ears and forehead were of a very dark shade, her teeth unbelievably black.

Sylvia looked at me without any recognition.

"Sylvia, darling, it's me Meggie," I whispered, choking with tears. She didn't smile or move, just gave me a puzzled stare. I hurt.

"Sylvia, Sylvia do you remember Meggie." She closed her eyes attempting to gather her disordered memory, and then after a long stare she whispered.

"I'm so happy to see you I could fly," raising her weak bony hand, slowly but surely and pointing at the window.

"Sylvia don't soften up, the sister you've been crying for is here." Mother tried to bring back her memory. There was a pause.

"I know mother and I am very happy," she murmured.

I noticed Sylvia's liver was very swollen and she was quite bloated. The huge tumour had expanded her ribs. Being very anaemic, she felt pins and needles. She also developed hypercalcemia . . . the amount of calcium in her bloodstream was elevated. Sylvia began to hallucinate. The hallucinations were so frightening she actually saw hundreds of insects crawling all over her. She screamed, trembled and was terrified. She asked me to spray her bed and begged us to change her sheets which we did. Her temperature was high causing beads of sweat on her forehead. I got a cold compress to cool her. She felt a little better.

Mother often prayed in Arabic, "Oh Lord, take this illness and restore health to Sylvia. Amin."

From Tuesday to Friday I was up practically all night, as I heard the restlessness next door. Sylvia moaned and groaned and vomited non-stop. I admired mother's strength.

"Don't worry about me Meggie, go back to sleep. I'm sorry to disturb you," Sylvia apologised.

"Sylvia, I came because I want to help you. I am here for you."

"Thanks Meggie, isn't it wonderful to have a family that cares?"

How alone she must have been all these years, it really broke my heart to think about it. Every spoonful of food mother gave her was all brought up. Her temperature was high causing her to sweat profusely. I sat with Sylvia begging God to relieve her from the suffering she was experiencing. To take her mind off the tortures, I thought I'd read part of the manuscript I had written about her.

She smiled a little, and opened her eyes. I looked at her, knowing that she was beyond all hopes of recovery.

"Meggie, I am so glad you are here, we speak the same language," she said rather thoughtfully. I didn't quite get what she meant.

"Sylvia I hope you don't mind what I've written about you," I queried.

"Of course not; if I had my life again Meggie, I'd be the same old me," she guaranteed, and reminded me of some hilarious events.

When the pains tormented her, I heard her whisper a prayer.

"Meggie, could you massage my legs and feet." I noticed they were quite swollen, like elephantiasis.

"That feels good," she smiled, "Could you do me one more favour?"

"Sure, what is it?" I asked, glad to be of some service.

"Could you go downstairs, look in the record cabinet and play me 'One day at a Time' by Lena Martell please."

She was always apologetic every time I'd do something for her. Ill as she was, she'd struggle out of bed try to restore her equilibrium, using the wall as a support, to reach the lavatory.

"Sylvia, should I get you a bed-pan?" I asked.

"No Meggie, I'll manage," she assured me.

It was a painful five days as I watched her every move. On Friday, Michael took us to Barnet to spend a week with Mboni. Sylvia was terribly ill. Mike offered to carry her down the stairs but she refused.

"Don't worry Mike, I'll manage," she murmured.

She struggled down the stairs step by step, staring into space. I was sure she couldn't quite focus. We put cushions in the car to make her as comfortable as possible. She sat upright, still staring into space.

"How do you feel Sylvia?" I asked her.

"Fine. I'm fine. Thank you Meggie," she whispered, but she didn't seem happy about going to Mboni's house.

A room had been prepared for her. Brother Ramadhan was there and he prayed in Arabic over her.

The following week Sylvia's condition remained unchanged. The social worker visited, promising to collect her on Wednesday for her fortnightly examination at the Royal Free Hospital.

On Tuesday, Sylvia was gripped with an excruciating pain, she screamed a tortured scream with every bit of strength she had, saying the huge tumour was pushing her rectum out. I rushed over to her and held her. I never heard such a terrifying scream.

"Sylvia, just sit on my lap," I said tersely, tears pouring down my face. She sat.

"Am I not too heavy for you Meggie?" She sobbed, tears dripping down her cheeks as well. She was taller than me but that didn't matter.

"No my darling," I assured her.

"What about your back, Meggie?"

"I'm fine, put your head on my shoulder." How I prayed God would relieve her of the torture she was going through.

"Meggie, I don't want to die in Mboni's house, please get me to the hospital," she pleaded, whispering in my ear.

"I will for sure Sylvia, now don't worry," I answered.

She miraculously became very calm. I slowly settled her into bed. All the other members of the family were seated deep in prayers. Sylvia closed her eyes and fell asleep whilst I gently patted her forehead. When I went to bed that night thinking of nothingness; I tried to pray but I couldn't.

"Why, God, why?" I constantly asked. I had no right to question God.

On Wednesday, the social worker came and took us to the Royal Free Hospital. Sylvia was very calm as we were driven to the hospital. She sat in the front with the social worker. I sat in the back with mother, praying all the way. On arrival, at the huge hospital Sylvia was asked if she wanted a wheelchair.

"No thanks, I'll walk," she said.

I held her by one arm while the social worker held the other. It seemed like she was sleep-walking. We took her to the waiting room, helped her into the hospital gown and put her on the bed. It was the first time I had seen Sylvia during this visit with hardly any clothes on, and it was a great shock. She was an absolute skeleton.

"I'm sorry to tell you that your sister has only about three days to live," the doctor said to me.

Michael was in tears. Mother and I remained calm.

"Sylvia has asked to be taken to St. Joseph's Hospice in Hackney," she continued.

I couldn't bring myself to tell mother that Sylvia was dying, as she did not follow everything that was said in English. We had been taught never to be judges over life and death, that was God's decision. I did, though, explain to mother that Sylvia was to be admitted at a Catholic hospital. No way, she was not letting her daughter go alone to the hospital, she said. It was agreed upon that she'd be given a bed right next to her daughter. Off we went to Hackney.

It was a lovely, comfortable hospital. The staff smiled and seemed full of understanding. The hospital social worker, Ruth, explained that Sylvia had reached the last stage and that we should all make it a happy stay for her. The nuns and staff appreciated having mother to take care of Sylvia as she needed twenty-four hour attention. A priest came, gave Sylvia Extreme Unction, the last sacrament, and prayed over her. Every single day without fail I visited her, sometimes travelling for two and a half hours by bus, sometimes with sister Mboni or brother-in-law Henry. We walked in a cold deserted street. A lone bird twittered in a bare tree. Henry explained that the poor bird must have missed the "bird-meeting" at Trafalgar Square where thousands of birds meet every year, twitter and squabble before taking off for Africa.

Anyone who has watched over a patient in a terminal illness will remember the detached occasions when one has time to fill in between visits, the unreality of waiting in unfamiliar places. On one occasion I got lost in Hackney Shopping Centre and took a long time finding my way back to hospital carrying little Lucy. Another day Mboni and I left too late to get back to Barnet, so we stayed overnight with her friend Nuru. The weather was freezing cold; I felt like I was inhaling frozen pins that particular night! I wore a woollen scarf, leggings, used blankets and a hot water bottle, but I felt terribly cold and couldn't sleep. Next morning we woke up when the world was still black, cleaned the house, had breakfast and left for the hospital.

"We'll surprise mother and Sylvia," Mboni remarked happily.

We bought ginger soda and apples, two of Sylvia's favourites. When we got in so early the sisters and nurses were busy painting Christmas pictures on the windows and arranging flowers.

The next three days Sylvia lay quietly in bed, not talking much. I would visit her and spend the day in total silence.

"Life becomes priceless when there's so little of it left," I mused silently.

On the fourth day, she began to move about, talk and eat. Very soon Sylvia was smiling and joking. She comforted us rather than being comforted.

Now that I saw great improvement in my sister, I decided to go back home, but there are always difficulties about booking flights in December. Could I really have believed that the improvement would continue?

Sylvia was always happy to see Lucy. She seemed to be aware of everything Lucy was doing at school. I had made Lucy scribble some loving words on a picture she had drawn for her mother. Lucy had insisted on learning the sentence by heart as she was determined to read it for her Mum. It was quite a struggle but I helped her to do it.

"Meggie, I wish you could have Lucy, you've been so good with little children," said Sylvia.

"I wish I could with all my heart," I assured her.

Michael visited and collected us at around seven that evening. On Thursday, 3rd December, I went back to Piccadilly to the travel agency to confirm the date of my return to Kenya. I had just received a letter from my Aunt, informing me that Helene's son, who was staying with my children, had been hit by a car. I panicked and immediately decided to go back home. I asked for a letter from the hospital confirming that my sister was terminally ill, thinking I might need to produce it at my place of work, since I had left without any written notice whatsoever.

One of the nurses brought the letter saying, "Aren't you lucky going back to the sunshine!"

I hadn't told Sylvia or mother about my decision to return home, I knew it would hurt them terribly. Sylvia seemed sad.

"Yes Sylvia, I'm sorry but my children have no woman to care for them. You understand, don't you, my dear?"

"Mandy, why are you leaving your sister? Stay a little longer," said mother.

"Stay on until the end of the month," she pleaded.

In the evening when Michael came with Lucy everyone was as cheerful as ever. Sylvia tried to cuddle little Lucy as she talked to her, asking her about her new school. I sat and admired my young sister being so brave and cheerful. I knew that Sylvia was in pain only when I heard her whisper this prayer:

The Lord is my Shepherd I shall not want
He makes me lie down in the green pastures
He leads me besides the still waters
He restores my soul;
He leads me in the paths of righteousness for His name's sake.
Though I walk through the valley of the shadow of death,
I will fear no evil.

For you are with me,
And your rod and your staff will comfort me
In the presence of my enemies;
You anoint my head with oil
My cup runs over.
Surely goodness and mercy shall follow me
All the days of my life;
And I will dwell in the house of the Lord forever.


Again, it was time to leave. My sister-in-law Monica had invited Lucy and me for an early Christmas party on 6th December. Michael was to drive us to Newmarket for the weekend. We noticed that an altar had been prepared in the Macmillian's ward. Sylvia was the only Catholic patient in that ward but all the patients from the other wards were brought in to hear the Mass. Some were brought in their wheel-chairs. Others were slowly helped to walk. Sylvia was happy, very relaxed and seemed much at peace.

My brother-in-law and I couldn't stay for the Mass as we had about one hundred miles to drive to Suffolk.

"I wish you could stay for the Mass, Meggie. It's so comforting. I will take you to the Chapel one day, it's lovely," said Sylvia. "Meggie, you may not find me here, you heard what they said, I've only got three days to live." That hurt and frightened me.

"You'll make it Sylvia," deep inside I was very confident she wouldn't die within that period.

All the same I told Monica, "I doubt if she has very long to go now. You must see her soon if you can."

Although there was a lot of entertainment, people to meet, laughter ringing in my ears and great rejoicing, my thoughts were at Hackney, St. Joseph's Hospice. I was very tempted to ring the hospital and find out how Sylvia was doing but I didn't.

When Michael was late collecting us, my thoughts began to race like mad. What if something had happened to Sylvia? But it was not that. We visited others of his relations on the way. It was freezing cold and I could not get used to it. I was actually shivering, my teeth chattering. The Hart family told me what a wonderful person Sylvia had been and what a real shame it was that she had to suffer so much.

"Only a month ago she came to see us and in spite of being ill she was making the children laugh, riding their bike in the back garden," they told me.

The Hart parents' home at Walnut Cottage was similar to the houses in Muthaiga, Kenya. I felt quite at home, the warm fireplace with its blazing fire reminded me of Father's house at Kabale, except for the depression, a drizzle and dampness. I constantly kept thinking of getting back to London.

Back in Palmers Green, Lucy kept waking up, complaining of an ear-ache. Around six in the morning she fell asleep and so did I. Next morning I was in a deep sleep when Michael's loud knocking at the door woke me.

"Mandy, I'm sorry to wake you up but I have a surprise for you," he said with a smile.

For the first time in my life I was really mad! I hardly had a wink of sleep the previous night.

"Mandy I just want you to look outside," he said mischievously.

I lifted my eyelids as heavy as lead, and looked through the window. I was startled by a pristine whiteness outside that created a magical dreamland. The snow flakes, softly and gently falling, covered all of nature. Roads, pavements and cars were all white. Icicles hung on the bare trees. I noticed youngsters outside making snowballs and throwing them at each other. Some had even started building a snowman. I was never so overwhelmed!

"Snow, I don't believe it. I thought I'd go back to Africa without experiencing winter."

In no time at all I forgot about how tired I was, changed into Sylvia's warm jumper, scarf, boots, and woollen trousers. The world looked bright and frosty; the tree branches, laden with snow, looked as though they had been clad in a new outfit. It was a complete new world to me. I felt a gust of ice and cold wind blow against my warm face.

## APPRECIATING HEALTH

I am here awake and thoughtful,
Health quickly streaming from me.
It's like the days when back in school,
I feel like running, I feel so free.
It seems like years ago,
That pain gripping me making me insane.
New life is an open door,
I can plan and think clearly.
Take my time, not to rush,
Remember, dear friends to use health dearly.
And never ever make a fuss.

**Sylvia, 1981**

Sylvia and mother were at the window admiring the falling snow. When Sylvia saw us, she excitedly waved and I waved back. The feeling that she was alive was indescribable!

We talked a lot, I'd talk about our youth, my trip to England, about Father, times in Uganda, in Kenya, my children, Lucy. I am sure Sylvia had difficulty keeping up with me. I was apprehensive . . . so very distressed that I'd be losing her in a short while. I was afraid to be there with her and yet I wanted to be there. What could I do for someone I loved so much? I began going over questions concerning the meaning of life and death, which of late had come more and more frequently into my mind. How does one feel when one knows for certain that after a couple of weeks one would be gone forever? Was it worthwhile to live at all? What was our purpose to be alive?

I would then look at Sylvia, at her large hesitant eyes which were made more prominent by the emaciation ranging across her pale wan face. We would often just stare at each other, both short of words, both buried deep in thought.

"I wonder what she's thinking about."

I looked at those gentle, tranquil, honest eyes, and above all her smile, such an affectionate smile, which had radiated peace, joy and love.

"Oh, Meggie, I'm so happy to see you," she said joyfully. "I thought you were never coming back." She seemed suddenly sad.

"Why not Sylvia?" I asked, rather puzzled. There was a moment of silence.

"How long have you been gone? Three weeks?"

"No my dear just three days. I saw you Saturday morning, remember?" She was not lucid due to the high dosage of drugs.

"Did you? I thought you'd been gone for a long time. I was wondering why you hadn't said goodbye to me."

She was very confused about time. I suppose being in so much pain, even an hour never seems to end! But all the same she had a special radiance about her.

"I wish I were back in Africa, Meggie, I've really missed the warm sunshine," she said, almost like she was in a dream.

Shortly, Sylvia got into bed and dozed off. Her face muscles began to twitch, and I knew she was in pain. Mother called me over and told me that Sylvia had been very restless ever since I had left. She had been looking for me in every ward, asking the nurses if they had seen me. She kept seeing me and I kept disappearing.

"Don't ever leave your sister again. She was very upset and she missed you."

Mother spoke as if she was scolding me. I was hurt, terribly hurt, that I had caused Sylvia concern. Sylvia and Michael always seemed short of words when they met . . . they hardly said a word. He would sit for about fifteen to twenty minutes, excuse himself and leave. Perhaps he was afraid of facing his dying wife. She seemed to disintegrate before our very eyes by the day.

Although Sylvia hardly had any strength left, she held and cuddled her baby, questioned her, joked with her, answered her never-ending questions. I was nervous that Lucy, the over-active little girl, would jump on to her mother's tumour.

"Don't worry Meggie, let her enjoy herself," Sylvia would say as she gazed at us with solemn eyes.

She was relaxed and smiling, while some of the other patients seemed moody, always demanding attention.

I visited the Boston family at Shepherd's Bush. I decided to walk to the town there. I kept slipping on the ice with every step I took. Trucks passed by, salting the road to make it less slippery, but without much success.

"What if she passes away when I'm not around?" I wondered. I was really afraid so terrified, sleeping in a strange house, being in a foreign country, with just a little girl as my companion.

One of Sylvia's friends who lived nearly a hundred miles from London decided she must see Sylvia, come what may! Her husband drove her to the hospital.

"I was terribly worried I'd cry when I saw Sylvia, but to my amazement I didn't I felt peace," she wrote. "My friends had advised me not to visit a dying person, but something drove me to see your sister."

When she met her friends later she told them how she felt having seen Sylvia.

"After I saw Sylvia, I knew that people should never be afraid of death. Sylvia was a perfect example. She was clear, calm, comfortable and I believe free from pain, above all she was so dignified. I remember those big hazel eyes looking sleepily at me, she thanked me for coming to visit her."

"Did Sylvia ever cry or mourn about her illness?" she was asked.

"No, she would have put a lot of us people to shame," she said.

Michael worked practically eighteen hours a day throughout the five weeks Sylvia was in hospital. He spent very little time with either his wife or his little daughter. He was probably fighting what was going on within himself. He was irritable and very short-tempered. He would sometimes ring his mother crying over the telephone telling her that Sylvia didn't have long to live.

"Why me! Why couldn't it be some other man?" He asked himself aloud. I usually had no answer or comfort to give. He would abruptly leave for work.

One evening Lucy was rather restless, I just couldn't get her to sleep. I gave her an apple and made her sit on my lap while we watched television. I then decided to go upstairs and prepare her bed, just in case she fell asleep. Suddenly,

"Aunt Mandy, come down at once! An apple is up my nose!"

My mind went back to when Sylvia and I pushed beans up our noses! I was in a panic. I developed quite a few bumps slipping on the snow as we walked towards the clinic. Here, Lucy remained restless, noisy, and talkative. Finally, an old English lady told her off. I felt rather embarrassed until I met the doctor who told me how Sylvia suffered all those years and what a brave young woman she was. The piece of apple was removed with surgical tweezers in a few minutes. I had a much deserved peaceful night.

I was sure Sylvia was aware that not only was her body disintegrating, but her whole personality.

"I know that God will see me through my toughest hour. I just know that," she assured me.

A social worker came and played a game of draughts with Sylvia. She was amazed at how good Sylvia was. I watched my sister play the game under extreme pain, like a Spartan. She won the game and was thrilled. On the spur of the moment she left the game and decided we should talk to many old patients. Most of them were very pleased to have someone visit and talk to them. Perhaps she felt better off because she had us, other patients had no family.

"If only people knew how much a dying person wants people; people to talk to, to laugh with, for their company. Why not treat them as human beings instead of avoiding the dying, just because we are afraid we will break into tears? They need love," I thought to myself.

Sylvia's ward-mate showed me stacks of photographs taken when she was young. She had been amazingly good-looking. She too had cancer and seemed very disappointed with life and God, as she had had the illness for almost ten years. Sylvia comforted her, I tried, but nothing could touch her. She was eighty-four years old. Another jolly eighty-six year old told me she had to settle her insurance and house, showing me some papers. I asked her if she had any family. I had never seen anyone visiting her.

"My family have never kept in touch with me," her eyes misted over, her voice speculative.

Again Sylvia was completely spent and went to bed. She seemed exceptionally happy, looking at me and smiling. I thought I would take this opportunity to tell her something I always wanted her to know.

"Sylvia," I began.

"Yes, Meggie," she answered.

"You know Sylvia, when I was air-borne I thought to myself, if only I could give you my life . . ." I said desperately. "How I wish it were possible."

"Come on Meggie, don't worry about me . . . I'm okay," she smiled.

"Sylvia, I owe you my life, do you remember you saved me when I was drowning?" I reminded her.

"Oh Meggie, that was nothing," she assured me. "I do not believe in a capricious God. He knows why He has allowed me to suffer so. We cannot put God to question."

"If only a miracle could happen. If only I could pray for you for three solid days non-stop, maybe a miracle could happen, you could have my healthy body, not that I am very healthy . . . and I could have your illness," I said helplessly, unreasonable and unrealistic as it may sound, I was sincere.

"Look Meggie, I am happy, now stop worrying about me," she replied, her voice full of love and tenderness.

"Sylvia, what can I do for you?"

"Look after my baby."

"Oh sure, I've always asked you for Lucy haven't I ?"

I was supposed to be her elder sister, I felt what a mother feels for her sick child. It was torturous watching my once healthy sister suffer. As I sat looking at her, I realised that the most telling aspects of her past life must have prepared her for these agonies and the constricting pains in her gut as the cancer was finally taking grip on all her vital organs. She decided to take a walk and I accompanied her to the ladies.

Studying herself objectively in the mirror she said, "Meggie, I look at myself and don't see me; that's not my face. Look at my tumour, it's only three weeks I've been here and do you see how huge it has grown?" She asked me, amazingly, with a smile lifting her night dress and showing me the swollen stomach.

"Just feel how hard it is Meggie."

Oh Lord, how I wished she hadn't showed me this unproportional enormous tumour, hard as a rock. It was heart-breaking but I touched her. Only God knew what a state my thoughts were in. Give me strength Lord, I begged God. It was her philosophical acceptance of life's pains that amazed us all. How could I ever complain of a headache or other minor ailments!

In the evening when all was silent an old patient of ninety-two was dying. We all witnessed it.

"Why don't the doctors do something?" Mother kept saying.

The family around her wept softly, holding her hands. I could hear her struggling with each breath, long audible wheezes, her eyes and mouth open. I had never watched death before. Sylvia contemplated it calmly, deep in thought. I was sure she'd face death realistically. Mother was always with us, calm and smiling. One of mother's friends spoke to me as I was leaving.

"We've been waiting for you to come to London, since only you can persuade your sister to change her faith. If she dies a Catholic, she will go straight to hell." Emphasis was put on the latter word. I was shocked but somehow I found my tongue.

"I have no power to change anyone's religion. If Sylvia wants to die a Catholic, she will die a Catholic," I calmly said.

This friend of mother's had told mother she knew a doctor who could cure Sylvia if she denied her faith. She showed mother tiny white tablets that, she claimed, cured cancer. Sylvia continued praying saying the words of 'Amazing Grace.'

My eighty-five year old friend, Mrs. Young, opposite Sylvia, was in a coma the next day, but she seemed comfortable as if in a deep sleep.

Eighty-three year old, Mrs. Jefferson, on the left of Sylvia was almost a yellow colour by now. I couldn't believe it as only a couple of days ago she had looked well and healthy. She lay asleep, her false teeth almost out of her mouth. I thought to myself, surely she doesn't have to go too. Sylvia looked the strongest of the three patients.

"Meggie," said Sylvia, "you are leaving tomorrow?"

"Yes my dear, I'm sorry but I'd better go and see to the children; it's five weeks since I left them," I said helplessly, my voice choked with emotion.

"Mandy, how can you leave your sister?" Mother asked angrily.

"Come on mum, I'll be all right. The children need their mother," Sylvia assured mother.

That hurt me terribly, of course Lucy needs her mother too. Whatever can I do ? I was torn apart between being with Sylvia and my children.

"Meggie, do you have a pen and some paper?" Sylvia asked me in a very calm way.

"No, my dear. Do you want to write some letters?" I asked her gently.

"Yes, I want to write to my friends," she sounded rather speculative.

The old lady, Mrs. Jefferson, heard the conversation and handed me a pen and white pad. I watched as Sylvia carefully held the pen and pad and wrote:

## TO WHOM IT MAY CONCERN

"Meggie, I want to leave a letter giving you permission to have my little girl. Now how shall I put it?" She turned to me and asked. She was thinking out aloud.

"In the event of my death," she smiled and looked at me.

"Meggie is that all right?" she asked, breaking my heart. I did not answer.

"I leave my only daughter Lucy Amina, D. O. B, 15th February 1978, to my sister, Mrs. Mandy Louis of P. O. Box 61138 Nairobi, Kenya..." Signing the note, she handed it to me.

Michael had said he wasn't quite ready to part with his little girl. Sylvia seemed sad and unhappy. I was hurt that I'd be going away without Lucy. We had become very good friends.

"Don't worry Meggie, I shall pray for three days and Lucy will be brought to you," she assured me.

I totally believed her. I spent the whole afternoon with Sylvia. We talked, joked and laughed. The Salvation Army came and played Christmas hymns outside the hospital for the patients. The nuns and sisters had artistically painted all the windows with events of the birth of Christ. Each ward had a big colour television which the patients could watch. It was such a happy atmosphere, everyone who visited their loved ones always left with radiant faces.

The cold weather was agonizing, I just couldn't get warm. Dinner time came and Sylvia ate a little. Mother asked me to go and buy some fish and chips, preferably something from an *halal,* shop run by some Turkish Muslims. Although I was used to Hackney, I was reluctant to go out into the freezing cold which had now turned in a blizzard. When I brought the food my appetite was gone. Mother coaxed me to eat a little as I had lost a considerable amount of weight. Sylvia was sitting on her bed watching us eat.

"Meggie, the fish smells good, can I have a little, please?"

I was afraid to give it to her. Anyway, I gave her a little piece. Five minutes later Sylvia brought it all up. She messed up all her sheets and the floor. Oh, no not again, I remembered doing that to Helene when we were only children. I quickly ran and called the sister. Two nurses came running. Sylvia was apologetic. She didn't want to be humiliated by needing a helping hand. The sheets were changed and the floor cleaned. We all left our food and sat buried in thought.

I could see that Sylvia's ability to function was wearing out rapidly and she was becoming alarmingly frail. But her faith in Christ was unshaken, and she prayed without fail.

I was up early on 11th December. At about a quarter to eight, sombre as it was, I made breakfast, dressed Lucy for school, cleaned the house, checked my bags and tickets, confused about whether or not I wanted to leave.

Michael said we would go to the hospital early, for me to spend the day with Sylvia. Unfortunately, the car wouldn't move. I was in a panic, I tried to call the hospital only to find the telephone was out of order. Deep inside I felt an emptiness. I couldn't understand this strange feeling I had. The journey seemed endless when at last the repairs were done. There were traffic jams everywhere due to the heavy snow. Cars were sliding all over the roads. I prayed and prayed that we'd reach the hospital.

We arrived at a quarter to five in the evening. It was piercing cold and very dark that particular day. I had palpitations and cold sweat as I went up the stairs to the ward. On arrival I saw Sister Catherine and other members of the staff around Sylvia. I stopped in the doorway, gazed at my helpless sister, my heart pounding against my ribs. Her lips were pallid and her skin a grey shade. She must have had a slight heart attack, I thought. I seemed glued at the entrance, just gaping. I could see nothing but stark misery and confusion upon poor mother's face. I was shocked, and wished to just vanish.

"Mike please take me to the airport," I sobbed.

I wanted solitude, I didn't want to see or talk to anyone. I couldn't face my dying sister. A nun and a sister came over and held me, Sylvia lifted her head, looked my way and smiled.

"Mandy, you are not going, your sister will die! Don't you want to bury her?" asked mother. She sounded hard, perhaps bitter.

"Come on Mandy, your sister has been asking for you all this time. Don't go back to Kenya. Stay with her. She needs you . . . wipe your tears and talk to her," I heard voices of mother, Sister Catherine, the nurses, all at the same time echoing, drumming in my head.

"Come on Mandy pull yourself together, and come to your sister," continued mother; she seemed composed and dignified.

"I can't face her mum, just feel my heart."

My heart was racing like mad. I was a nervous wreck. All this while Sylvia watched, her eyes pleading. Miraculously the pain, fear and palpitations disappeared. I wiped my tears and a force drew me to my sister. Her look hypnotised and calmed me, slowly I walked towards her. I scrutinised her. Sylvia's features were pinched and drawn, her lips were extremely pale and parched, her eyes sunken, her face blanched, her long fingers a deathly white, thin as a wand. Sylvia smiled and offered her cold pale hand and took a good grip of my hand with every last bit of strength she had left.

"You can't leave tonight, no airline is taking off because of the bad weather. Oh, Meggie, I'm so happy to see you," she whispered, staring at me.

I tried to understand that look in her eyes —was it love, pity, bewilderment or understanding? I shall never know. I looked at that hollow-eyed face with disbelief.

"I'm not going anywhere Sylvia, don't worry. I'm staying right here with you. O. K.? I'll just go for a little while, cancel my bookings and bring Mboni," I assured her, choking in the throat.

"O.K. Meggie," said Sylvia with an encouraging smile

She seemed in comfort and peace. I sincerely felt Sylvia needed the comfort of our presence in her last stage, and I was grateful to St. Joseph's Hospice for allowing us to stay with her. It is said solitude is one of the worst of all human experiences.

I asked Michael to ring the Airline and cancel my flight. I had explained to them previously that I might need to cancel the flight booking. They agreed and booked me for the 1st January 1982. When I got a satisfactory answer, we went to Barnet to collect Mboni. I could hardly speak.

Mboni couldn't believe she was seeing me after I had just said farewell. She thought I was already airborne. Mboni and my niece, Farida, immediately rushed to the hospital. Sylvia stretched out both her arms and offered them to Mboni and me. We each held a hand in ours, rubbing them gently to get them warm. Sylvia talked a little, asking me to make her look pretty — to comb her hair, and tidy her up. She tried to sit up, the nurse put more pillows for her. I didn't want to brush the wispy hair since it was falling out with each stroke of the brush.

"Hurry up Meggie, I'm in a lot of pain," she moaned.

I helped her to lie down. This time she asked for a pain-killer injection which she had refused all the three weeks she was there. A sister came and gave her an injection. All the while, she talked quietly and sparingly, trying to conserve her strength. Her breathing was quite normal.

"My head is going round and round," she opened her eyes and murmured.

I noticed her eyes turning in opposite directions. It was most frightening. She shut them and whispered softly.

"Meggie, please massage my head and my back especially downwards, along my spine, it hurts."

"Sure, Sylvia," I said hopelessly.

"I hope I'm not disturbing you. I know you have a bad back yourself," she said.

I told her I was fine and not to worry. I massaged the skeleton very gently, feeling the hardness of a swollen disc. Two days before her kidneys had failed and she had developed jaundice. The whites of her eyes were yellow. Her legs had swelled tremendously like elephantiasis, in spite of the special tights. Her liver was enormous and as hard as a rock, her ribs expanded incredibly.

"Sylvia talk to us, do you have anything you want to tell us?" coaxed Mboni.

"I don't know what to say. You talk to me and I'll listen," whispered Sylvia.

I began confronting death. What lay ahead for me, suffering, death and eternal oblivion?

"Lord make my death fast," I prayed.

Sylvia went through all the stages of a slow, painful death. Isolation, fatigue, depression, loneliness and finally, acceptance.

"Yes, my Lord," I heard her whisper.

I wondered if some supernatural being was questioning her. It made me think, as I sat beside my sister in absolute quietness, that prolonged illness is more destructive to the dying and those near them left alive than the most brutal sudden death. So much strain, stress and heart-breaking agony. Just yesterday, we had sat staring at each other, both buried deep in thought. Now I stared at her helpless body; the body that I had once held, hugged, had helped to go on in life, to pray, to get up and walk again; in pain and despair, joy and hope, even when our faith was tried and tested. She had been part of me. Everything was now ending, the flesh dissolving, or was it already dissolved?

After a couple of hours, Farida went to sleep. Mother too got into her bed . . . The nuns had brought blankets, an extra bed, pillows, and tried to make everyone comfortable. I had that swimming feeling in my head and my feet were leaden. The nuns covered me, brought me an extra chair to put my feet up. I could not move out of my chair. I stayed right beside Sylvia holding the cold, icy, hand which she kept offering me, I felt the weak pulse, listened to Sylvia's peaceful breathing and the soft tick of the cardiac monitor.

"Oh how I wish I could get you warm."

I rubbed her hand, held it in mine, covered it, but it was like holding a piece of ice. Mboni placed Sylvia's hand under the blanket and she too went to sleep, as it was midnight. Then I heard Sylvia say something I didn't quite understand. It sounded like an answer to a question. Everything was quiet and peaceful.

"Yes, yes." Sylvia stretched forth both her arms and muttered.

My thoughts were racing. Is she being questioned? I was extremely exhausted when I dropped off to sleep. Suddenly, I woke up when my face touched Sylvia's frozen face. The hymn 'May the Good Lord Bless and keep you . . whether near or far away' crossed my mind. She had loved that hymn.

I could hear the wind blowing and blustering, outside. I thought about the many times I had taken deep breaths of snowy, frosty air. Sylvia's breathing was gentle. Or was there any breath? God, dear God, help me. She didn't struggle like the many dying people I heard of. She had peace until the end. I knew that her past experience had prepared her to take death calmly, gracefully, and yet, death is not easy to the living. It's like the glorious African sun going down behind the horizon; within no time at all all the beauty and warmth is gone, and a cold darkness comes. This was a time I really wanted the sun to shine, but it didn't. My memory reflected how at one time I loved and longed for darkness so no-one could see us and abuse us.

I listened to a few snores from an old patient, apart from this there was absolute stillness, you could have heard a pin drop. What could I do aside from holding Sylvia's cold unsubstantial hand and dropping to sleep close to her chilled face. I took the Holy Water which Sylvia had on her side cupboard and blessed her, the very Holy Water she had blessed me with, a day before her death.

"Sylvia, wherever you are, please pray for me."

I felt completely shattered and utterly alone. How could two people I loved more than life itself just leave me? First Father, now Sylvia. These two episodes were entrenched in my mind. Will I ever get over them? I wondered. Although I believed in God, I became angry. I felt cheated. Life wasn't worth living any more. This feeling of aloneness can be very frightening and threatening. I thought of my young sister who set an example none of us could ever equal. She showed us love, understanding, patience, endurance and forgiveness. She smiled until the end. At around four forty five in the morning, mother woke up.

"You are still sitting, holding your sister's hand. Give her something to drink," she said harshly.

She was gone but I had no heart to tell mother. I felt a hard lump in my throat when I tried to talk. Mother touched Sylvia's clammy face and put her frozen lifeless arm under the blanket. I just held on to the other hand Sylvia had given to me. Mother offered her juice with a spoon. I heard a gurgling sound.

"Why me?" I asked myself.

I gulped down sobs that rose within me and brushing away the tears that filled my eyes. I was sorry for myself. Sylvia was my other self, part of me had gone. Will anyone ever understand this? How could they? I continued sobbing, silently.

"What about poor mother and the rest of the family?" I thought.

Mother did not quite understand what had just happened. Maybe she was fighting against the truth. Poor mother.

"Mandy, the juice I gave Sylvia did not go into her mouth. It just dribbled out," mother said.

Mother then put her hand next to Sylvia's nose, there was no breath.

"All praise is due to God - *Al-Hamdu Lil lahi*. Oh God, grant forgiveness to our living and to our dead - *Allhumma ghfir li hayyuna wasmayyi tina . . .*," she prayed. She roused Mboni and whispered, "Sylvia is not breathing, Mboni "

Mboni at once woke up and touched Sylvia. She did not believe Sylvia was no more. Mboni too prayed. Farida quietly got out of bed where she had been lying next to her mother. I could still hear the sound, a monotonous *beep,*

*beep, beep*, on the electrical device.

My life seemed to have also ended. I felt threatened by the superficial relationships and cruelties in this insensitive, uncaring world. I had to accept the hard fact that true happiness cannot be found in the transitory pleasures of this world; there must be something more to life. Wealth, fame, health, relationships, even with people you have shared your life with, will slip away and be forgotten. I had a feeling of absolute aloneness as if I were left stranded on a strange shore. We sat there in utter silence. Tears flowed down our cheeks.

"She's now closer to us in her new life than she has ever been on earth," I comforted myself.

Mother instructed us not to trouble the sister in charge as everyone around was sound asleep. A nun and night duty nurses came over and found Sylvia dead.

"May the souls of the faithful departed in God's mercy rest in peace," they prayed.

They then said a little of the rosary, tidied the bed and placed a big black rosary in Sylvia's hands. I had seen such a rosary on dead nuns when at Maryhill years back. At six forty five, mother, Mboni, Farida and I went to sit in the hospital parlour. Mother and I were drained. The nuns gave us their deepest sympathy and brought us cups of tea. I appreciated that, as the weather was extremely cold. There was another bout of snow. The dark gloomy sky only added to our misery and the sun didn't shine at all. Where could the sun be? Sylvia had so often cried for the African sun, but she didn't get to see it. I didn't think I would ever see it again either.

I asked the sisters if they could kindly give me something to relax me and help me sleep. After feeling my pulse the sister gave me five milligrams of valium. Members of the nursing staff came and expressed their sympathy.

The hospital called Michael and he was at the hospital sooner than expected. He went to the Macmillian ward to see the body of his dead wife. He cried and we all gave our sympathy. Afterwards, he dropped us at Barnet, all quiet and dumbfounded. The Boston family came to sympathise. Mrs. Khadija Boston stayed on to keep mother company. Mboni kept making hot tea for us.

I had severe migraine the whole of 12th December and felt quite ill. By the end of the day we had a house full of guests. Michael brought Lucy, who stood in her winter coat and boots, locks of curls falling around her face.

"Mummy has died, hasn't she?" she demanded, shaking her little forefinger.

No-one answered. We all stared at her, the wounds being pierced with every word she said. I've got to say something, Lord help me. I prayed.

"Yes, my darling, Mum has gone to heaven," I said softly.

"Has she gone to the angels? Will she get better? Will she come back? She's coming back when she gets better isn't she?" she blurted out without waiting for an answer, fighting back tears.

Michael said he felt complete emptiness, and asked me if I could keep Lucy for a while. Lucy seemed the only person who kept talking non-stop. I thought it would do her good if she let out anything that was within her.

Michael had arrangements to make for the funeral and the weather wasn't very much help. The deputy High Commissioner for Uganda, Mr. R. Ibreck, came over to see us and he kindly offered to make calls for us to our friends and relatives all over England informing them about Sylvia's death and the funeral arrangements. He also volunteered to put a death announcement in the London evening papers. I had to telephone the news and change of travel plans to my husband and my sister Berit, who passed the message to all the members of my family in Uganda and Nairobi.

The funeral was held on 21st December at Southgate Catholic Chapel. Michael's family, the staff of St. Joseph's Hospice and many friends joined us. There were splendid wreaths, including one from the Ugandan Embassy and one from Prince Ronnie Mutebi. The priest asked if we would mind if he took a few for the church.

"I am sure Sylvia would have loved that." I said.

The requiem mass is a special occasion celebrating the passover of a member of the Catholic community through death to the Kingdom of God's Mercy. We prayed and commended Sylvia to the forgiveness of God our Father and prayed that she might be united with Christ in death and share his resurrection to eternal joy. The priest gave a short account of Sylvia, how she remained faithful to Christ's gospel to the hour of death. We prayed, 'The Lord is my shepherd' and sang, 'Nearer my God to Thee'; 'Take my Hand Precious Lord'; 'One Day at a Time'; must have been sung but my mind was distant. It was very cold. All the tombs, graveyard, trees, were crystal white. Sylvia's grave was partially covered with snow. I saw no mud. As the coffin was lowered gently, I saw the lone red rose I had placed nearest to my sister's heart. My prayer was only "Pray for us wherever you are."

Christmas day, we went for the midnight mass with my friend Wendy, at Hounshow. The singing was uplifting. 'Hark the Herald angels sing,' 'The Holly and the Ivy,' 'Oh come all Ye Faithful,' which brought me a lot of peace. Lucy lay fast asleep in my arms throughout the mass.

Friends were hospitable and understanding during this time of sorrow. The world had changed, or perhaps it was just my understanding of the world. Now I knew I had excellent Sikh, Bohora, Hindu, Ismaili and Goan friends.

My last few days were with mother, Mboni and her family at Barnet. I

211

was to leave for Kenya on 1st January 1982. Michael collected me and we left Lucy with the Greaves children as we were sure she would make a scene at the airport if I left her behind. Being free from strife, I slept well right through the journey.

What a great change it was to be back at home amidst all the warmth and brightness of Kenya. My husband and Prince Henry were at Nairobi Airport to meet me. I felt as though I had come from a deep freeze into a blazing fire. My eyes had to adjust to the brightness. In the plane I had removed all the warm clothing, a jumper, scarf, gloves, thick stockings. I had no choice but to keep my boots on and a big coat which I held in one arm. I learnt that Henry's sister had died only two weeks before. Other people also lost their loved ones. A week later my children came from Mombasa where they had been staying with their grandma. It was a joy seeing them after eight weeks. Members of the family visited us and asked endless questions about Sylvia, mother, Mboni and her family. I was amazed at myself. I didn't cry or feel hurt any more. I was able to talk of Sylvia with some kind of comfort. The weight had been laid aside like the heavy clothing. I was happy, I had seen her through.

Every member of the family seemed very concerned about what would happen to Lucy.

"She is coming to stay with me," I said confidently.

"How can you be sure, Meggie? You know her father won't part with her," they said.

"Sylvia said so and I believed her," I assured them.

And sure enough in February 1982, Michael wrote that he was bringing Lucy to stay with me. She stayed for six months. I took her to the nursery school where I was employed and she seemed happy and loved by everyone who met her. We had a lot of fun with Lucy. There was not a day that she didn't talk of her mother.

In September 1982, Michael flew down to Kenya and collected his daughter. She was very much a part of the family and we were sad to lose her. She seemed happy to go back to England.

I was to visit seven year old Lucy in 1986, in England. Michael took me out to dinner with her. She had grown into a beautiful, very mature, intelligent girl.

"Aunt Margaret, did Sylvia die of old age?" she asked doubtfully.

"Well she looked terribly old but she was young," I answered her.

"Do I look like Sylvia?"

"You sure do."

I wondered why she didn't call her mum as she did when she was three years old. The innocence of a child is a source of both strength and inspiration.

# POST-SCRIPT

I was in a lovely, green park, full of flowers, plants and trees. Looking up at the sunlight, as it spilled its brightness across rolling fields, I smiled. The light, its clarity slanting horizontally through the unravelling clouds, made me experience a moment of beauty and perceptual glow. In the distance was mother, unpacking a picnic basket.

"Mandy, Mandy. . ." Grandma appeared in the distance.

"Grandma, Nana," we enfolded each other.

I looked at her, full of joy. She had put on weight, grown taller, just as she looked to me when I was a little girl. I noticed she was wearing my harem suit, which changed into a straight long dress, gran's style. Running like a young girl with out-stretched arms, Nana was trying to catch me. I felt a child's simple wonder.

"Where are you Mandy. . . Mandy. . ."

I woke up smiling. . . wondering about the strange dream I had had. It was Wednesday 12th April 1989 and my thoughts were suddenly fixed on Grandma. I wondered how she was. I hadn't seen her in over a year.

Next morning, I woke up early in anticipation of just relaxing in a bubble bath, something I don't find time to do during working days. I sank lower until the water was level with my chin and stretched out my legs, my feet bouncing against the end of the tub, relaxing my gnarled joints, easing the muscles along my back. I worked assiduously up each arm. *Tring, tring.* . . I could hear the phone, ringing over the blaring radio 'saying I love you' by Billy Ocean.

"Jacqui. . . Harald. . . somebody get that phone," I was surprised to hear myself yell. A few moments later, a knock at the door.

"Mum, you're wanted immediately by Aunt Berit."

This is it . . . instantly, I put on my maroon night gown, wet as I was and rushed to the sitting room. Stay calm . . . I told myself.

"Hi Berit," I said cheerfully.

"Are you seated?' I was asked. Hem! She doesn't sound too happy.

"Yes I am."

"Well, Grandma was ill, I rushed her to hospital but she died two hours after admission."

"Did she suffer?" My arms were suddenly covered with goose flesh.

"No, not that much. She had a bad chest and difficullty in breathing, but was cheerful and very independent. She didn't even want us to help her into the car. She refused to be carried but after trying to take a few steps she laughed and said 'this time I'm defeated'. . . You are sure you're O. K.?"

I was breathing hard. She must have been able to hear it over the phone. My palpitations started.

"I'm O. K. I'll probably be hit later."

"Do you think you could make it to the funeral? You know she's a Muslim. I expect she'll be buried tomorrow at the latest. . . You could come by air."

"I'll see what I can do."

Twisting a strand of hair around my little finger, I felt my insides knotted up. Yet Grandma had died at the age of ninety in full possession of her faculties. That should not be sad. I hurriedly dressed and rushed to town. It was four thirty that evening when I finally completed the necessary arrangements for my departure.

I left the next day, Friday, at eleven. As the plane ascended we were enveloped in silvery clouds, the outlines like a thread of light blue. Above us was a clear almost deep blue sky with a brilliant morning sun casting a soft pinkish sheen over a variety of clouds; cumulus and stratus in the far distance, cirrus-cumulus and nimbus just below us, some already causing rain in patches. As we ascended further up, we were above the alto-cumulus clouds. I was glad I had this opportunity to fly this very moment, this very day, to be enveloped in this bliss, reflecting my childhood dream of flying. The rain had given the landscape a sleek, washed look, with spots of deepening greens.

After cruising for an hour in what seemed like haze and mist we landed at Entebbe Airport. I was filled with apprehension, not having been home for eighteen years. Many of them had been hard years for Uganda. Thoughts of the Israeli hostages and Idi Amin crossed my mind momentarily. I had seen the movie *Entebbe Raid* years back. I wondered whether there would be someone to meet me. I was a total stranger. It took almost an hour before I was through all the airport formalities.

The forty-five minutes taxi ride to Mengo cost me ten thousand Uganda shillings. It was hard to realise how little the currency was now worth. On arrival, some members of my family looked puzzled, wondering who I was, and when they came to, they were over-whelmed. I went into mother's opened arms, and we both wept. I hadn't seen mother for over two years. She seemed exhausted and aged. Berit was there, busy organising lunch for the many sympathisers. Grandma's body had just been taken to Kasubi by members of Kabaka Mwanga's family. The Muslims had hoped to bury her at Kawempe where Prince Badru was to pray the *Hitma*. Aunt Nuru wanted her buried on our burial land at Bombo. The royal family prevailed. Our home was filled to capacity with friends and relatives, faces I remembered from the time I was a child. It seemed as though I had gone back thirty years. I recognised the childless lady who had loved fussing over baby Sylvia.

"It was sad she had to die: part of me died too," she told me

Aunt Nuru, Helene and the family had accompanied Grandma's remains to Kasubi, for the Baganda royal burial ceremonies. My Cypriot-Greek brother-in-law, George Epaminondas, his sons and my Japanese nephew, Michael Ohguchi, took me to view the body. The edifice was packed with the populace of Buganda.

"Hi Muzungu," some giggly youngsters addressed me. I answered in perfect Luganda, shocking them.

"She speaks our language," they exclaimed.

"I do, and you are coming to bury my grandmother."

"We are so sorry," whispers followed, "we thought you were a Muzungu not a Muganda."

On arrival in the hut, there was a murmur, a muted buzz. Helene was surprised to see me. She introduced me to more friends and relatives. The hut was quite dark, as there was no electricity that day, kerosene lamps were used instead. Unfortunately, I couldn't quite see Grandma's body, just her narrow ashen face. Slowly, politely and sympathetically, people came to give me their condolences. They were rather suspicious and unsure I was really a Muganda Princess's grandchild.  —

*"Nga kitalo nyo"*    how very sad.

*"Kitalo"*    sad, I answered, as was the custom.

I noted Helene looked quite worn out. "I haven't slept for the last twenty hours," she said.

"Why don't you go home and have a couple of hours rest?" I suggested. I knew how she felt, remembering the time Sylvia died.

"We have to be here, being the immediate family," she explained.

We went out for a breath of fresh air. Meeting Aunt Nuru, I gave my sympathy. She was not as distraught as I imagined she might be.

At four thirty Nana's body was prepared; bathed, wrapped in twenty metres of white strips of material like a mummy, by Aunt Nuru and some Muslim women. Prayers were said in the big compound alongside the open coffin. There were hundreds of Muslim men, women, and children, all deep in prayer. Brother John had made most of the arrangements. He looked better than when I last saw him, nearly two years before. I was thrilled to meet Kapere, who I last saw selling water when I was just five years old! Amazingly he was still handsome, had that same smiling face and seemed as energetic. His straight black hair was now silver, and he was shrunken, much smaller than me. Did he remember me? Yes indeed.

"You've grown old and thin," he said, giving me a loving smile revealing a perfect set of ivory teeth.

I greeted him although this was against the Baganda customs at burials. I followed the procession to the outer side of the edifice, where the female members of the royal family are buried. The Kings are buried inside.

The Haji Muslim priest who said the *Hitma* promised that a mosque would be built over the grave in commemoration of Kajja-Obunaku. A brief history was given by Prince Badru emphasising the kindness and generosity grandmother had shown towards the needy and orphans.

"She was the most unprejudiced woman I have ever known. As you can see, the family have married into all races and religions."

The tall majestic looking Prince Bulwada paid his respects as well. By early evening, dark clouds began to build up in the west. As the sun went down, the women began cooking. Dozens of goats were slaughtered, piles of steamed matoke and pilau were made. The brilliant full moon let out a sliver of light from behind the black clouds, casting shadows in the huge compound, where silhouetted figures scattered here and there.

After dinner we all gathered into the hut lit with kerosene lamps. We were to spend the whole night awake, singing about historical myths, dancing, and celebrating. Helene and I were honoured to uncover the sacred, ceremonial drums as we were the only *Kiwewesi*, grandchildren, present. Kabaka Mutesa's son, Prince Walugembe, was to play the drums all night through. Berit did not attend the night celebrations as she was spent. John went home to recuperate and joined us late in the night.

At about eleven o'clock that evening amid the singing, drumming, shuffling and swaying of hips, the *Mukongozi,* a man chosen by the spirit of Kabaka Mwanga, was brought by respresentatives. This belief is highly respected by all Baganda. Mother, Aunt Nuru, Helene and I were introduced and he gave his condolences and blessings. Those who had any problems came forward and were given advice. I was completely exhausted and had developed terrible migraine. By four o'clock in the morning, my head whacked with every drum beat. Although the music was uplifting, the singing interesting and the dancing fascinating, my headache felt like a hammer *slam, bam, boom, boom.* I kept dropping off to sleep. Wonderful sleep always cured my misery and pains. Amazingly, Helene was awake throughout.

When night turned to dawn we were requested to leave the hut. It was unbelievably cold as the clouds were almost touching the ground. The air was fresh, but felt damp. After a short break we again congregated in the hut and were presented with Grandma's *Mulongo* twin wrapped in bark material. We were to hold it and make a wish or say a prayer. Money was given and wrapped in different layers of bark material. Other donations were contributed, in *Ebbibo* baskets, to Kabaka Mutesa II, Kabaka Mwanga II, Kabaka Daudi Chwa II and Mutesa I. The chosen heir was announced. Our niece, Princess Jasmine, was Grandma's own choice. When I got home at nine o'clock that morning, I dropped off to sleep like a light. At two o'clock, mother gently woke me up for lunch.

The few days I had left, I decided to visit as many of my childhood places as I could. Kisubi Convent School was my priority. It was only ten miles from home, not a hundred as I thought when I was a child. Helene volunteered to accompany me with her husband. Sister Jijelle, who had known us for many years in Mangu, gave us a warm welcome. We were met in the very room father had met us in when he visited in 1953.

We saw the boarding block, it seemed to have shrunk, the statue of the Blessed Mother in the compound, which once seemed to touch the sky, was only about five foot tall. The church, which had seemed miles away, took a couple of minutes to reach. I got goose flesh and my heart throbbed when I saw the open cubicles from a distance, re-living my childhood for a split second. After nearly thirty-five years, neither Helene nor I had enough courage to actually go inside them. The forest had been cut down and a new school block built, the water-tank Sylvia used to climb seemed pretty old. Just around the corner, was the place where our foreheads were shaved.

Later in the week, I visited Rubaga Cathedral, Namirembe Cathedral Kibuli mosque; even Mulago Hospital brought back happy memories. Some spots almost broke my heart, especially Kololo Hill, and the centre of Kampala, where I found the roads were very much in need of repair. But most of the main roads had been made up, the new government had done a fantastic job on them. Riding a motor-bike with my nephew Constantine was quite an experience for me. We passed the house of the late Nalinya, Kabaka Mutesa's sister. Gran had taken me to visit her when I was barely five years old.

Memories flooded back. A friendly pup came sniffling me all over. Dogs terrified me, no matter how loving they tried to be. I saw myself running like a fanatic, with the pup, thoroughly enjoying himself, barking with happiness. I was filled with trepidation, screaming, tears flooding down my hot red face. Everyone seemed, to be trying to save me. Grandma ran towards me with open arms and literally scooped me up, holding me against her warm bosom, my most treasured comfort. We then visited Nakulyabe.

"See that house over there, that's where Nana visited me when she took me from mother, after she spanked me," I told my nephew.

Visiting the city later, I didn't see Christos, our favourite cafe-restaurant. The movie theatres were run down. The Odeon Cinema was now a Christian Centre, a Pentecostal Church. How thrilled I was to meet Mr. Ruzindaro, Father's faithful worker.

"People complain about the white man, but your father treated me like a brother. We ate from the same plate, slept in the same room. Your father nursed me, cleansed my sores, my own brother could not have done that. Your father gave me his old car when he bought a new one. Now, you my daughter, you are welcome to my house any time, everything that I own was due to your father." The dear old man held my hand for minutes on end. "You've got hair like your father, locks used to fall over his face and he'd swing his head back like so," he said, showing me how father threw his head back.

I was invited for lunch at Ruzindaro's house, where I met his whole family. On leaving, I was presented with a live very healthy-looking chicken.

When going back to the airport, it suddenly struck me that it was new, not the one I remembered. Looking out of the window, at the waiting room, I noticed a vast variety of birds, storks, hawks, a few robins and other species. I supposed Lake Victoria was the main attraction. I heard their incipient screams, gurgling and hawking. I felt peace, and was glad I had helped to bury Grandma, though now I was looking forward to being with my family. Since then Kapere, Prince Badru, Prince Henry and Prince Walugembe, Mutesa II's son and Rebecca Nava have died, but we have come to terms with death.

And so life goes on.

Made in the USA
Middletown, DE
11 June 2020